T0334652

Eva Illouz, one of sociology's most innovative thinkers, brings together an engaging group of scholars to explore the complex relations between our consumption practices and the world of emotion. Framed by Illouz' theoretical vision, *Emotions as Commodities* takes us into a varied tour that includes Club Med resorts, Israeli sex cards, greeting cards, psychotherapy and more. The book contributes to the sociology of consumption markets but its insights will also appeal to a general audience.—**Viviana A. Zelizer**, Lloyd Cotsen '50 Professor of Sociology at Princeton University and author of *Economic Lives: How Culture Shapes the Economy*

Through intriguing theoretical discussions and fascinating empirical case studies, this book throws new light on the paradox of contemporary capitalism furthering both increased rationalization *and* an unprecedented intensification of emotional life. A must read for sociologists, marketing scholars and anyone interested in contemporary consumer capitalism, a culture ever more centered on emotional commodities or 'emodities'.—**Adam Arvidsson**, Associate Professor, Department of Social and Political Sciences, University of Milano, Italy

Emotions as Commodities

Capitalism has made rationality into a pervasive feature of human action and yet, far from heralding a loss of emotionality, capitalist culture has been accompanied with an unprecedented intensification of emotional life. This raises the question: how could we have become increasingly rationalized and more intensely emotional?

Emotions as Commodities offers a simple hypothesis: that consumer acts and emotional life have become closely and inseparably intertwined with each other, each one defining and enabling the other. Commodities facilitate the experience of emotions, and so emotions are converted into commodities. The contributors of this volume present the co-production of emotions and commodities as a new type of commodity that has gone unseen and unanalysed by theories of consumption – emodity. Indeed, this innovative book explores how emodity includes atmospherical or mood-producing commodities, relation-marking commodities and mental commodities, all of which the purpose it is to change and improve the self.

Analysing a variety of modern day situations such as emotional management through music, creation of urban sexual atmospheres and emotional transformation through psychotherapy, *Emotions as Commodities* will appeal to scholars, postgraduate students and postdoctoral researchers interested in fields such as Sociology, Cultural Studies, Marketing, Anthropology and Consumer Studies.

Eva Illouz is Rose Isaacs Professor of Sociology at the Hebrew University of Jerusalem, Israel and Directrice d'Etudes at the EHESS, Paris.

Routledge Studies in the Sociology of Emotions

Further information on the series is available at: www.routledge.com/sociology/series/RSSE

Emotions as Commodities

Capitalism, Consumption and Authenticity

Edited by Eva Illouz

Routledge
Taylor & Francis Group

LONDON AND NEW YORK

First published 2018 by Routledge

2 Park Square, Milton Park, Abingdon, Oxfordshire OX14 4RN
52 anderbilt Avenue, New York, NY 10017

Routledge is an imprint of the Taylor & Francis Group, an informa business

First issued in paperback 2019

Copyright © 2018 selection and editorial matter, Eva Illouz; individual chapters, the contributors

The right of Eva Illouz to be identified as the author of the editorial material, and of the authors for their individual chapters, has been asserted in accordance with sections 77 and 78 of the Copyright, Designs and Patents Act 1988.

All rights reserved. No part of this book may be reprinted or reproduced or utilised in any form or by any electronic, mechanical, or other means, now known or hereafter invented, including photocopying and recording, or in any information storage or retrieval system, without permission in writing from the publishers.

Notice:
Product or corporate names may be trademarks or registered trademarks, and are used only for identification and explanation without intent to infringe.

British Library Cataloguing in Publication Data
A catalogue record for this book is available from the British Library

Library of Congress Cataloging in Publication Data
A catalog record for this book has been requested

ISBN: 978-1-138-62823-6 (hbk)
ISBN: 978-0-367-35498-5 (pbk)

Typeset in Times New Roman
by Swales & Willis Ltd, Exeter, Devon, UK

Contents

PART III
The ideal of mental health and self-improvement:
emotional self-monitoring as commodity

Contributors

Yaara Benger Alaluf is a PhD candidate at the Department of History of The Free University of Berlin and a member of the International Max Planck Research School for Moral Economies of Modern Societies at the Research Center "History of Emotions" at the Max Planck Institute for Human Development in Berlin. Her research explores the entanglement of emotional and economic discourses from the nineteenth century onward and its moral implications. Her work examines the history and sociology of emotions in the tourism industry; the construction spatiotemporal characteristics of emotional experience; and the impact of psychological repertoires on the conceptualization of work and leisure. She has published on the evolution of the consumer as an emotional agent, the phenomenology of consumption, and the relation between therapeutic culture and economic rationalization.

Edgar Cabanas has a PhD in Psychology from the Universidad Autónoma de Madrid. He is currently Associate Professor at the Universidad Camilo José Cela and Adjunct Researcher at the Center for the History of Emotions (Max Planck Institute for Human Development), in Berlin, where he held a Postdoctoral Research position for two years. His main field of research focuses on the political, economic, and social uses of the contemporary psychological notion of happiness. He has published several papers and book chapters on this topic, such as *Rekindling Individualism, Consuming Emotions: The Construction of Psytizens in the Age of Happiness*; *Inverting the Pyramid of Needs: Positive Psychology's New Order for Labor Success*; and *The Making of a 'Happy Worker': Positive Psychology in Neoliberal Organizations*. He has been a visiting scholar in the Center for the Study of Rationality at The Hebrew University of Jerusalem in 2011 and 2013, and he is a team member of several R&D International Projects.

Daniel Gilon is a PhD candidate in the Department of Sociology and Anthropology at the Hebrew University of Jerusalem and a Clinical Psychologist. His main research interests are the sociology and cultural history of emotions, as well as psychological theories and practices and their development. His PhD dissertation traces the co-modification of fear, through the study of the development of the American cinematic Horror genre. He has published a chapter dealing with emotions and cultural theory, and an article regarding training in psychotherapy.

Eva Illouz is Professor of Sociology at the Hebrew University of Jerusalem and a Directeur d'Etudes at the EHESS in Paris. Illouz is the author of 80 articles and book chapters and 10 books that have been translated into 15 languages.

Dana Kaplan is a cultural sociologist, specializing in critical heterosexualities, middle class culture and neoliberal subjectification. She has earned her PhD from the Department of Sociology and Anthropology at the Hebrew University. Her current research projects include commercial sex and urban branding; Israeli beauty: how class, gender and ethnicity co-constitute under neoliberalism; and the construction of new religious categories of identity. She has published in various journals, including *Sociology* and *Food Culture and Society*, as well as several book chapters.

Ori Schwarz is a cultural sociologist and a senior lecturer of sociology at Bar-Ilan University. His studies explore the ethic of authenticity (its contribution to ethno-racial inequality, its contribution to the emergence of new cultural evaluation dynamics, and its ideological role in online self-presentation); the sociology of art consumption (art tasting techniques); the sociology of boundary work (the role of sonic styles and sensitivities in national and ethno-class boundary work); and the sociology of digital technologies and the internet (governance of social network sites, political unfriending and homophily, digital memory, digital subjectivities, and digital photography). His studies were published in journals such as the *American Journal of Sociology*, *Cultural Sociology*, *American Journal of Cultural Sociology*, *Theory Culture & Society*, and *Ethnic and Racial Studies*.

Mattan Shachak is a PhD candidate in the Department of Sociology and Anthropology, and the Federman Center for the Study of Rationality, in the Hebrew University of Jerusalem. His main research interests are the sociology and cultural history of rationality and emotions in expert knowledge systems and professional practices, and their role in shaping modern individualistic morality. He studies the impact of the "cognitive revolution" on conceptions and practices of selfhood, rationality and emotionality in psychology and economics; and the role of psychologists and economists in producing and disseminating repertoires and practices of self-interest and personal choice into different social spheres. He has authored and co-authored several articles and book chapters.

Emily West is Associate Professor of Communication at the University of Massachusetts, Amherst, USA. Her research and teaching arc in the areas of consumer culture, audience research, cultural studies, and health. She is the co-editor of *The Routledge Companion to Advertising and Promotional Culture* (2013), and the author of several journal articles on greeting cards as an emotional commodity. Her current research focuses on consumer subjectivity and digital culture, consumerism in representations of US healthcare, and media discourses about the end of life.

Acknowledgements

Unlike Freud's cigar which was only what it seemed to be, this is not an edited book. This is the result of intense collaborative work with students at various degrees and stages of their career. During the endless meetings, readings, discussions that enabled the formation of the ideas that form the main architecture of this book, it became clear that the hierarchy between teacher and students was meaningless, and that everybody became alternatively everybody else's teacher and student. This book is a keen example of a collective intellect.

Anonymous reviewers for Routledge should be thanked for their enthusiastic remarks and critical comments. Elena Chiu at Routledge has offered the most professional and incisive editorial help.

This research was made possible by two institutions: The Humboldt Foundation and especially the Annaliese Maier Award for Excellence in Research without which discussions, reading, workshops, writing, editing and translation would not have been possible; and the Chair of Excellence of Paris Sciences Lettres at the EHESS, which helped me bring this project to its completion.

In face of a human world destroyed by the commodification of everything, Foundations as the Humboldt or PSL Chair of Excellence are reminders of a world where money is used for the gratuitous advancement of thinking and critique. It is to this "wasteful" use of money this book is dedicated.

Introduction

Emodities or the making of emotional commodities

Eva Illouz

Catherine Townsend, the sex columnist for the *Independent*, has abundantly documented the dilemmas of modern sexuality through her weekly autobiographical stories. In one of her columns, she recounts her lengthy preparations for a much-anticipated date with a man, thus providing us, sociologists, with a crisp opportunity to understand the conjunction of sentiments, sexuality, and consumer practices.[1]

A week before

For my second date with my new crush, I start mentally sketching out my outfit a full seven days before Date-Day. Because I am going for the "take-me-home tonight" vibe, I head to Topshop and choose a short black bubble skirt. Sadly, I realise I have no suitable first-time underwear. I find it hilarious when male friends complain about dropping three-figure sums taking women out to dinner, because women take the hit when it comes to pre-date preparation. All the boys have to do is show up and smile sweetly in the same suit they wear to work, having showered and perhaps applied a daub of aftershave. The cost for women is far higher, in time and cold, hard cash.

Five days before

I'm heading to Selfridges desperately seeking suspenders, plus killer heels. I bring a male friend, Jonathan, for second opinions. My eye is immediately drawn to the Gina stilettos with rhinestone buckle, dominatrix-chic. "Do I look hot or scary?" I ask John, modelling them. "This is scary," he says, pointing to the £365 price tag, "Jesus Christ! That's half your rent."

Slightly hyperventilating, I ask if he thinks that splashing out on lingerie would be a better investment. Can I justify spending £80 on a bra? "Are you kidding? If you play your cards right he won't even think about looking at your feet. Definitely go for the underwear." So I focus on a pink satin and black lace Agent Provocateur bra and underwear set, complete with fishnet stockings and stilettos. Palms sweating, I hand over my credit card and feel my knees turn to jelly when I spot the total: £203. "It's going to be worth it," Jonathan says. "He is going to have a heart attack."

Having just added to my spiralling debt, I know the feeling. Still, I justify the expenditure by telling myself that had I bought the Gina shoes, I would have spent twice as much. So, really, I saved £162. In Selfridges' sex toy emporium, I pick a mini bottle of Edible Mint Lube for £4.99. Being prudent, I also grab a three-pack of condoms for £3.55.

Visibly sweating, Jonathan bales out. But I'm in a full-on shopping frenzy, and since I had decided to go for the smoky-eyed temptress look, I buy a Benefit Bad Girls black eyeliner and shimmery body powder from Boots to pat on my push-up bra-enhanced cleavage. Total cost: £32.

Two days before

I make the trip to the salon to have the obligatory Brazilian wax (£30), since previous DIY at-home attempts in my nether regions have led to blood, sweat and many tears. There's also the matter of my feet, which due to my heel habit during the summer seem to have morphed into something befitting a Lord of the Rings character. So I opt for a pedicure (£28), but do my nails myself, thus "saving" another £15. I'm so nervous about seeing him that I've been biting them all off, anyway.

Four hours before

The big day has arrived and all that's left to do is frantically change my outfits a total of six times, do my hair and make-up and pull out the right pair of shoes, which takes more than three hours.

Half an hour before

I shell out £15 for a taxi because my shoes simply can't do public transport – and an umbrella because I forgot mine, and kissing in the rain only works when a couple is already in love. I'm not risking anything ruining my efforts tonight. In the end, I decide that the massive expenditure was worth it – because I really do feel beautiful – no matter what the date's outcome. And the taxi is my final expenditure, since it's my rule never to pay for anything on a second date, whereas he ends up spending close to £300 on dinner and drinks. So was it worth it? Well, we had a fantastic time and he's already called for a third date. I just hope that I can afford it."

COST
Topshop skirt: £29
Agent Provocateur bra, knickers, suspender and fishnet stockings: £203
Make-up: £32
Bedroom accessories: £8.54

Pedicure/Brazilian bikini wax: £58
Taxi: £15
Emergency umbrella/breath mints: £6
Total: £351.54

TIME
Shopping at Topshop: one hour
Shopping at Selfridges: three hours
Buying make-up: one hour
Waxing and pedicure: one hour
Hair, make-up and dressing: two hours
Total: eight hours.

The article then moves to a man's description of the preparation for a date who similarly recounts the time and money expenses for it.

The man's story by *Martin Deeson*

Thirty-six hours before

As I get dressed in the morning, I idly wonder what to wear tomorrow night. But it is no more than a passing thought. "Probably my best suit," I think. I like wearing suits on a date – it looks like you've made an effort, and it's kind of sexy (as long as you look more brat pack than bank pack). And besides, I've got five of them and I never get to wear them for work.

7pm the day before

Back from work, I give my outfit a bit more thought. Perhaps a suit will look too smart. Perhaps I'll wear jeans. But that'll look too casual. I chastise myself for my complete lack of understanding of the words "smart casual." I don't really do smart casual. Unless I wear my best jeans and a suit jacket. Then I worry that this will make me look like a City boy trying to dress down. The phone rings and I start thinking about something else.

Two hours later

While cooking dinner I decide that I definitely don't want to look like I've made too much effort. Perhaps I'll wear my jeans with the ripped knee and a really old T-shirt and that way I'll look scruffy, but interesting. The microwave pings and I stop worrying and eat my dinner. I decide not to drink tonight to minimise any facial "bloat."

11pm

While brushing my teeth, I look at my hair in the bathroom mirror. I decide it needs washing. But my hair looks rubbish straight after I wash it, kind of like blond straw. And if I wash it now it'll be wet when I go to bed and then I'll wake up looking even more rubbish. I decide to leave it. After brushing my teeth I decide to brush them again with the whitening toothpaste I picked up for $12 on my last trip to New York.

1am

As I go to bed, I think: "No, I'll definitely wear my best blue suit. But will I wear a shirt and shoes? Or a T-shirt and trainers with it? Hmm. dunno." I go to sleep.

8am

I wake up and take one look in the mirror and decide I must wash my hair immediately and to hell with the consequences. I decide not to use conditioner as it makes my hair go flat and dead. I will live with the dry straw effect instead. I also use the whitening toothpaste again and wish I'd got my teeth professionally whitened and fixed years ago. I trim any pesky nose hair and cut my toenails in anticipation of the date being a success.

8.30am

After breakfast I decide to go back into the bathroom and exfoliate my face with some face scrub that must be three years old. I think I got it free in a goody bag after a magazine party.

8.40am

As I get dressed I decide I can't possibly wear jeans. I will wear my nice suit. Suddenly in a panic I wonder if my suit needs cleaning. I pull it down from the rail and give it a once-over. Not bad apart from something nasty stuck to the collar. It looks like wasabi. Luckily it comes off when I scrape it with a fingernail. Now, what shirt will I wear? The nice white one. I look in the wardrobe. It's not there. I look in the dirty linen basket. It is there. There's nothing for it, I'm going to have to buy a new shirt in my lunch hour. I cycle to work in the optimistic belief that this will lead to last-minute weight loss.

1pm lunchtime

I am not a natural shopper. I could go to Selfridge's menswear department but there is too much choice and time is short. I decide to go to Kilgour's on Savile Row and buy a white shirt. Hang the expense, it's a beautiful shirt which will last for years and it's worth the extra money for the experience of buying it in 20 minutes on Savile Row rather than going to Selfridge's and being overwhelmed with choice for an hour. It costs £130.

6.30pm

Get home from work, have a shower and my second shave of the day – to avoid the chance of giving my date razor burn. Faff around with my hair for five minutes. Get dressed. Call a cab.

COST
Whitening toothpaste: $12 (£7)
New shirt: £130
Total: £137

TIME
Buying shirt: 20 minutes
Faffing with hair: five minutes
Total: 25 minutes.

However facetiously written, this article contains many important insights into the ways in which private emotions find their way into consumer culture.

Both Catherine and Martin seem to operate at once as rational and emotional actors. They each calculate the cost of the date and the amount of time they invested preparing for it, and when the date is over, they make an overall assessment of its worth, where worth implies an implicit comparison of its monetary to its emotional value and the ratio of their effort against its emotional return. This is consistent with the view that capitalism has made rationality into a pervasive feature of human action, as modern individuals have become increasingly goal-oriented, act upon their self-interests legitimately, use abstract knowledge to make decisions, and refine the cognitive means to reach their goals (Carruthers and Espeland 1991; Illouz 2007, 2008; Illouz and Finkelman 2009; Simmel, 2004 [1900]; Weber 2010 [1904–1905]; Wood 2002). Yet Catherine Townsend and Martin Deeson are equally oriented to their own pleasure, and to their sensual, sexual, and emotional experiences. Far from heralding a loss of emotionality, capitalist culture has on the contrary been accompanied with an unprecedented intensification of emotional life, with actors self-consciously pursuing and shaping emotional experiences for their own sake (Ahmed 2010; Hardt and Negri 2005; Hochschild 1983; Illouz 2007). Such intensification of emotional life is manifest in many ways: The fact that personal life has become oriented to the realization of emotional projects (e.g., "romantic love," "overcoming depression," "finding inner peace," "becoming compassionate"), the increasing legitimation of actions based on pure emotions (e.g., leaving careers or marriages because of insufficient emotional enjoyment), and the pursuit of emotional projects such as emotional intensity, emotional clarity, or inner balance for their own sake (Belk et al. 2003; Campbell 1987; Dittmar 2007; Giddens 1992; Gill and Pratt 2008; Hesmondhalgh and Baker 2008; Holmes 2010; Honneth 2004; Hughes 2010; Hunt 2012; Lasch 1979; McRobbie 1998, 2002; Seidler 2007; Sennett 1977; Von Osten 2007). Even casual observers can take note of the fact that in the second half of the twentieth century, personal life and emotional fulfilment have become central pursuits and preoccupations of the self. Emotional life-projects are central to identity, while individuals increasingly have recourse to rational economic modes of thinking and decision-making in a wide variety of domains. This seamless marriage of opposites structuring selfhood requires close scrutiny: How should we understand that emotions have become smoothly imbricated in rational modes of conduct promoted by ever-deepening grip of economistic forms of thinking in various realms of life?

Another observation follows: In the vignette above objects serve as meeting points for both the man and the woman in their plan to live a sexual, sensual, and emotional encounter. The vignette describes an ongoing network of relationships between objects and emotions in at least three ways: Objects have an emotional-sensorial meaning constructed by a complex network of image-making industries (*this* bra *is* more sexy than others because of *this* shape, color, and texture); objects are consumed in the framework of emotional motivations and intentions that are themselves framed by consumer culture (I want the "take-me-home date," because I define myself as a sexy human being); finally, at the moment of consumption, these objects help create an emotional atmosphere between two or more people and mediate between their different desires (this lingerie creates a sexy, romantic atmosphere between us, it will generate his sexual desire). In other words, objects here are seamlessly intertwined with the short-term and long-term emotional projects of actors. They are meeting and transaction points in emotional interactions. If that is indeed the case, this demands a new epistemology to explain how commodities produce emotions and how emotions are turned into commodities: that is, how emotions and objects co-produce each other.

A third and more familiar observation derives from this one: Consumption directly taps into the core elements of social identity – sex, gender, desire. In their attempt to be sexually attractive to their partner, Catherine and Martin have recourse to gender scripts, to models of masculinity and femininity, inscribed and displayed in the very process of consumption.[2] Clearly, consumption works from within the very core of the cultural scripts of selfhood, shaping the man's and the woman's sexual identities as daily strategies of interactions, producing and reproducing gender through the experience of seduction and sexuality. Rather than being a false layer superimposed on selfhood, consumption works from within the core of social relationships, identity, and emotions. More exactly, consumer culture has organized sexual identities around a panoply of experiences and objects, which mark at once one's sexuality and one's sexual attractiveness. One cannot say and repeat enough that consumer culture has recruited subjectivity through sexuality and that it is through the performance of sexual meanings that emotional, gendered, and consumer identities are co-produced all at once.

These remarks in turn raise the problem of the possibility of authenticity when identity is shot through consumer objects. This question is all the more acute that, as we show in this book, economic practices of consumption feel "natural" and authentic because they are steeped in emotional practices. Such emotionality, built-in the very cultural and economic practices of consumption, brings us to the question of what is the meaning of authenticity from a normative standpoint: How should we criticize at all the texture and nature of authentic or inauthentic experiences? Can we still articulate a horizon for authenticity in contemporary culture?

To make things even more complex, consider this: This autobiographical vignette, documenting and reporting on the various emotions involved in the preparation for a date, is itself an object to be consumed; the private thoughts and fleeting feelings of the protagonists are made explicit for the consumption of the newspaper's readership. In that respect, we may speak about a broader consumer unit which starts with Townsend's emotions of anticipation excitement-anxiety to produce for a "take-me-home date" and end with the *Independent*'s reader of the made-for-the-newspapers emotional accounts. In other words, we have a chain of autobiographical, emotional, and consumer acts, organized in a complex unit of consumption, which consists of a series of purchases, each expressing or creating emotional states, then converted into a newspaper article for the purpose of the evoking the reader's emotions. In this seamless chain, emotions and consumption are inseparable. They form a seamless system expressing a subjectivity busy performing her emotions and desires.

This example highlights this book's central claim: consumer acts and emotional life have become closely and inseparably intertwined with each other, each one defining and enabling the other; commodities facilitate the expression and experience of emotions; emotions are converted into commodities. I dub this process the *co-production of emotions and commodities* and the many nodes in which emotions and consumer acts coincide an *emodity*. This process accounts for the fact that consumer capitalism has become an intrinsic aspect of modern identity. More than that, because consumer culture has systematically turned emotions into commodities, what we modern people call emotional "authenticity" is both the psychological-cultural motivating structure of a great deal of consumption and the performance itself of consumption.

This book ultimately offers an ethnography of authenticity, an ethnography of the cultural strategies modern individuals draw on to construct and establish their sense of self, anchored in an ontology of emotions. In this sense, authenticity is taken to be one of the most powerful performances of the self through objects. Authenticity is the experience generated by the co-production of emotions and consumer practices.

Rationality, objects, and emotions in consumer culture

If rationality and emotionality have been equally powerfully institutionalized in the cultural organization of capitalism, we need to explain how capitalist culture has integrated and imbricated these conflicting features in the cultural structure of the modern consumer (Horkheimer and Adorno 1979 [1944]; Habermas 1985; Simmel 2004 [1903]; Smelser 1998; Weber 1978; Welcomer *et al.* 2000). Rationality is a feature of cognitive thinking, which usually demands an orientation to long-term planning, approaches the world systematically, and evaluates objects in the world by comparing them to each other and/or according to their suitability to one's self-interest (Boudon 2009; Parsons 1937; Scott 2000; Weber 1947); the pursuit of pleasure and emotionality is in general oriented to the present, wants immediate gratification, and is based in the senses (Mitchell 1910; O'Shaughnessy and O'Shaughnessy 2002; Scott 2000: 126–128). If we assume that cultures have coherent institutional cores, this raises the question: How can action be simultaneously increasingly rationalized and more intensely emotional? A number of paradigms account for the fact that in capitalist culture, both rational and emotional forms of individualism have intensified.

One is the *cultural contradiction thesis*, shared by neo-Marxists as well as by sociologists of post-industrial societies such as Daniel Bell, who postulate that capitalist mode of production and culture are rife with contradictions, i.e., that conflicting values are institutionalized in different spheres and thus create split cultural personalities (Bauman 1988, 1992; Bell 1976; Firat and Dholakia 1998). While the sphere of capitalist production stresses discipline and renunciation, the sphere of consumption stresses ideals of self-liberation, authenticity, and emotional fulfilment. Some sociologists view contradictions as a structural weakness of capitalist societies, with aspirations to personal fulfilment undermining the work ethos; others view these contradictions as the basis for the strength of capitalist cultural control, with contradictions creating confusion and thus increasing the need to rely on experts.

This line of work has been fruitful in highlighting the ways in which modern capitalist cultures became dominated by a hedonist ethos, central to the legitimation and appeal of consumer culture. But the hypothesis of cultural contradictions has the main flaw of not having forecasted the triumph of a hedonist ethic and the demise of the work ethic; it thus failed to predict the simultaneous growth of working hours and the strengthening of personal life characteristic of the last few decades (Schor, 1992), which would suggest that there is no structural internal contradiction between economic rationality and personal, hedonist, pursuits. Moreover, the cultural contradictions thesis does not account for the fact that actors use both cultural repertoires – restraint and liberation, economic calculus and emotional self-realization – *without* experiencing contradictory pulls. There is thus a gap, a lacuna between macro structure and the ordinary experience of actors. An adequate explanation should be able to offer a simple mechanism explaining how rational and emotional forms of individualism are intertwined in the experience of ordinary people rather than simply reflecting separate spheres; and this mechanism should also explain how macro cultural structures translate into micro structures of experience. More precisely: "hedonism" is not a more natural aspect of the self than rationality; in fact, it has become increasingly institutionalized through consumer culture in such key motives as sexuality and excitement, obtained in a variety of arenas such as tourism or the consumption of cultural cinematic genres.

A second hypothesis can be found in the view that the capitalist workplace, wishing to accommodate and defuse workers' grievances, has accommodated or encouraged *moral claims* to personal life, autonomy, and emotional fulfilment (Deranty 2008; Houston 2008). This is the view offered by Axel Honneth (1995, 2004) who argues that by the second half of the twentieth century individual self-realization had become an institutional demand, a part of what he calls the "ideology of de-institutionalization." This was a consequence of the intertwining of wide institutional and cultural changes in post-industrial societies: the growing variation of lifestyles, the instability of work-markets, the expansion of consumption activities as a means of identity formation, and the ideal of authenticity.

A variation of this view can be found in Boltanski and Chiapello (2005), who argue that managerial capitalism has co-opted its critiques, that is that capitalist theories of management have acknowledged and integrated claims to personal life (Alvesson 1994; Alvesson and Willmott 2002; Fleming and Sturdy 2009; Hatch 1993; Kunda, 2006; Polter and Land, 2008; Swedberg 2005). Acknowledging workers' feelings is thus a part of a more general strategy of capitalism to increase its legitimacy. In this view, the encouragement to personal life is a reluctant concession of capitalist control to claims which are fundamentally inimical to its interests.

These views are very useful in their claim that the pursuit of emotional fulfilment has become a part of our moral discourse and fabric; claims to personal fulfilment and emotional life now have a moral force "somehow" intertwined with the fabric of the capitalist workplace. But they make too many assumptions about the nature of capitalist control, assuming a very high level of sophistication and adaptability on the part of capitalists to intangible claims to emotional life. More crucially, they do not inquire into the *very conditions* which make possible claims to emotional and personal self-fulfilment, and simply assume that these claims are always there for the capitalist owners to respect or dismiss, as if they were natural demands of modern actors. In contrast, I suggest that the very fact that emotional and personal life have become the object of moral claims needs itself to be explained, and that this must be explained in a way which is consistent with our general understanding of the logic of capitalism. Thus, for example, there has been an emotionalization of the workplace, a transformation of criteria of evaluation of work in terms of emotional satisfaction, emotional management, and emotional expressiveness, which itself is a part of the centrality of emotions to the general economic process (Cabanas and Illouz 2016; Illouz 2008). The development of personal life is no less a part of the history and sociology of capitalism than the fact that emotions have become a part of the production process, of private life, of the public sphere. This three-fold presence of emotions in social life suggests that emotions have become the major social form which transforms the moral repertoires present in the work sphere, in private life, and in the public sphere.

A third possible explanation comes from the ranks of cultural sociologists and *anthropologists of money*, for whom interpersonal relations are always closely, regularly, and routinely intertwined with economic exchange (Hasday 2005; Parry and Bloch 1989; Polanyi 1944). In her path-breaking work, Viviana Zelizer (1994, 1996, 2005) has argued that economic calculus and intimate relations are far from being antithetical, that monetary transactions and intimate relationships are co-produced and mutually sustaining, and that there is no opposition between intimate relationships and so-called impersonal exchange, between rational and so-called irrational action. This perspective is essential to grasping the cultural underpinnings of economic exchange and the ways in which they are organized to sustain interpersonal relations, a view I myself adopt. However, this approach rejects the view that modernity rationalizes economic exchange in an unprecedented way and thus lacks historical force, that is, it cannot conceive – and even less explain – the fact that the relationship between intimate emotions and money has been profoundly transformed in and by highly monetized economies. Neither can it account for the intensification of emotional life observed in the twentieth century. How the moral economy of social relations variously organizes economic exchanges should itself be an object of inquiry. Starting from the assumption that economic exchanges are embedded in moral and social frameworks, this book wants to examine the historical transformations of such embedded-ness: Why has the normative force of personal life and projects increased, and how has this occurred when commodification processes have also increased?

This book offers a historically simpler and sociologically more robust hypothesis that can be used to analyze and explain the process at hand. It accounts both for the historical dynamic of the expansion of capitalist production *and* for the fact that emotional life has come to acquire a considerable importance for modern individuals: *Consumer capitalism has increasingly transformed emotions into commodities and it is this historical process which explains the intensification of emotional life.* This explains the intensification of emotional life in "Western" capitalist societies since the late nineteenth century and more clearly in the second half of the twentieth century. This is a simpler hypothesis because it is more parsimonious in the sense that it makes fewer assumptions about capitalist control, and it can account for the ways in which capitalist culture generates simultaneously economic and emotional forms of individualism. According to Mayer (1995), parsimony should be a crucial feature of cultural analysis, because parsimonious explanatory models of culture are based on a greater economy of assumptions, thus offering more powerful explanatory models of culture production. Moreover, this explanation is more robust because it identifies a macro mechanism by which emotions are produced as economic products as well as for the micro processes that make them lived as emotions and emotional pursuits. Robust models of cultural analysis reveal the mechanisms by which macro structures translate into the micro self-understandings of ordinary actors. The elucidation of the micro-macro link remains one of the main tasks of cultural analysis (Alexander 1987; Diprete and Forristal 1994; Jensen 2007).

In offering this hypothesis – that emotions have become commodities – the group of authors in this volume aims to recast the very conceptual frame with which the history of capitalism has been conceived, and to claim that from World War Two, and most decisively after the 1960s, there has been a stable expansion of emotional commodities which, once properly conceptualized, discloses a different dimension of the history of capitalism. This investigation is broadly inscribed in the program of critical theory as it was relaunched by Axel Honneth in his *Paradoxes of Capitalism* at the Institut für Sozialforschung.[3] Within the program of the Frankfurt School, I aim to add here the category of the emotional commodity.

Emotional commodities, emodities

Since the 1970s and most decisively since the 1990s, capitalism has been increasingly defined in non-materialist terms. "Cognitive capitalism" designates new modes of accumulation centered on knowledge and technology, with more flexible work, more horizontal structures of labor, which uses collective intelligence systems, and virtual rather than physical objects. Cognitive capitalism then redescribes the entire capitalist process initially accounted for by Marx: it redescribes what the worker is selling (her cognitive attention and processing rather than her body and sheer strength); the process of production (signs and knowledge rather than commodities); labor relations (horizontal rather than vertical). Cognitive capitalism redescribes by and large the very activity of production, and to a lesser extent, consumption (De Angelis and Harvie 2009; Morini 2007; Moulier-Boutang 2012; Vercellone 2008).

More recently yet, capitalism has been redescribed as aesthetic capitalism, with a more resolute emphasis on consumption. This is a form of capitalism which, while being no less aggressive or cynical than financial capitalism, targets the emotional capacities of actors. This is why in hyper-modern capitalism, as Lipovetsky rightly observes, the economic and aesthetic spheres overlap, creative and commercial activities overlap, and the emotional capacities of consumers and workers are tapped (Lipovetsky and Serroy 2013). Both approaches to capitalism represent a considerable refinement of our understanding of the cultural transformations of capitalism, but have not adequately conceived of what is the central topic of this book: the emotional commodity or emodity.

The emotional commodity has gone under the radar of theories of consumption but, as we try to show throughout, is one of the strongest threads accounting for the development of capitalism from the mid twentieth century onward. The purpose of this book is to draw a typology of *emodities* (emotional commodities), and to analyze the process by which emotions are not only an ingredient in the process of packaging commodities, but more importantly, *created as commodities*. Because the production of emotions occupies major sectors of contemporary economy and because such production is cardinal to an understanding of contemporary emotional individualism, this project may have a significant impact on our understanding of the cultural dynamic of contemporary capitalism, which intensifies economic rationality (in its ever-expanding commodification of the person) and emotional life-projects (which are solicited by and achieved through the market and consumer culture).

Rethinking the commodity

In *Capital* Marx (1977 [1887]) defined commodities as objects *outside us* (a material object in space with clear boundaries), which are both tradable (have exchange value) and useful (have use value: "a thing that by its properties satisfies human wants of some sort or another"). While Marx conceded that this use value may be as abstract as aesthetic pleasure, he claimed that a commodity's exchange value is roughly determined by the abstract labor necessary to produce it. In this frame, the producer and consumer are neatly separate entities; the commodity is an object, endowed either with subjective meaning and value (the use value), or with a monetary one (its exchange value), which takes a definite amount of labor to be produced.

As early as the 1920s, the commodity took on characteristics which Marx had not anticipated. The formation of the consumer sphere was also accompanied by a new conceptualization of the consumer, which was no less the product of consumer culture; the consumer was not simply a person who now consumed: s/he was conceptualized by an entire cultural system which produced the consumer as much as the good s/he was consuming. In other words, the story of consumer culture is not that the market simply tried to adapt itself to a consumer whose needs and desires were pre-existent, only waiting to be discovered; rather, it shaped the consumer in the image of the goods it was producing. For example, Freudian views of the psyche exerted an important influence in the formation of marketing science, and served as a justification for the idea that commodities had to appeal to emotions. People working in advertising and marketing deliberately opted for strategies which increased the emotional and symbolic value of goods (Bennett 2005; Caru and Cova 2007; Holbrook and Hirschman 1982; Lury 2004; Mazzarella 2003; Vargo and Lusch 2004), a practice which became known as "branding." Defined as the deliberate association of products and trademarked names with ideas, concepts, feelings, and relationships, brands self-consciously use cultural icons and myths to forge their identity and tap into emotional meanings activated by collective symbols (Holt 2004). "Emotional branding" has become a common marketing tool, and illustrates the role that emotions have played in the conceptualization of the consumer and consumption process by people working in marketing and advertising professions (Illouz and Benger 2015). The main emotions used in branding are positive emotions such as love, romance, lust, optimism, cheerfulness, coolness, and self-confidence. The point here is that it is *not* the case that advertising and marketing tapped into a reservoir of "real" emotions; rather, in bestowing upon goods an emotional meaning, marketers contributed to the construction of the consumer as an emotional entity, thus making consumption into an emotional act and legitimizing the identity of the consumer as driven by emotions.

Culturalist views of commodities expanded the materialist Marxist view of commodities (as tradable useful 'objects') to include 'information' and 'knowledge,' and emphasized the semiotic dimension of commodities. Scholars as different as Jean Baudrillard (1998), Mary Douglas and C. Baron Isherwood (1979), Arjun Appadurai (1986), and Pierre Bourdieu (1984) have all claimed that we purchase commodities not only for what they *do*, but also for what they *mean* and what they *say* about us, such that identity is constructed through a semiotic work of marking. The next generation of sociologists of consumption went one step further in describing the dematerialization processes which the commodity has gone through (e.g., Featherstone 2007; Jansson 2002; Lash and Urry 1993; Slater 1997; Wernick 1991). Such dematerialization includes the shift from goods economy to service economy; the emergence of informational/cognitive commodities like software code; and the fact that even in traditional material commodities, most added value derives from the non-material (aesthetic/symbolic) components, i.e., the R&D, design, and branding/advertisement stages, rather than the manufacturing stage. Commodities there became promotional, taking advertising as a paradigm for the whole economy. Value became far removed from either scarcity or congealed labor time, with branding possibly increasing one hundredfold the monetary value of a commodity. In this view, the sign has taken over and has become an autonomous aspect of the very production of the commodity. In the process of manufacturing commodities, advertising loads products with emotions through various rhetorical and semiotic devices, a claim which is bolstered by psychologists (e.g., Zajonc and Markus 1982) who demonstrate the importance of affect in decision-making and in the process of constructing preferences in general, consumer preferences in particular. Reflecting this knowledge, 'emotional branding' was the next step in the panoply of marketing tools (Gobé 2001; Roberts 2005; Rossiter and Bellman 2012) and attempts to harness more directly consumers' subjectivity to the market. Here, emotions explain what is commonly viewed as *irrational* consumption with consumers being enticed to consume against their interest by the manipulations of advertising (Brown and Woodruffe-Burton 2015; Falk 1994; Gill 2009; Vakratsas and Ambler 1999. cf. Campbell 1987 on *manipulationism*). Emotions are thus viewed as what motivates us to buy and consume, regardless of cost-benefit value.

Such historical and sociological analyses have contributed much to our understanding of consumption as a social and semiotic act, yet they have omitted a crucial aspect of the historical dynamic of capitalism: its capacity to create *emotions as commodities*. While the critical purchase of the emotions as enticement paradigm is obvious, it does not however account for the fact that the emotional promises of consumer items are not *always* deceitful; rather than being contained in a structural cycle and circuit of disappointment, some consumer objects actually deliver the emotional effects they promise (Campbell 1987; Hirschman 2013 [1977]; Scitovsky 2013 [1952]). This is also the reason why such consumption feels authentic: it produces a real emotion, it is part and parcel of practices of authenticity, ways of engaging with a concrete world of objects in order to achieve authenticity. The sociology of commodities which developed in the 1970s overlooked the emotionally performative dimension of commodities.

Ann Friedberg (1993) moved toward this approach in her important notion of *commodity-experiences*, which includes commodities like tourism or entertainment shows. These are *intangible* commodities that turn the consumer into an object upon which they act. Taking Friedberg's argument one step further, it may be suggested that a crucial dynamic of the expansion of capitalism has been to extend commodity-experiences.[4] Emotions motivate consumption, are a part of the meaning of the commodity, but more crucially *are* the very commodity at once purchased and manufactured. Marketing experts like Pine and Gilmore (1999) agree. For them, economy turns into an "experience economy" in which consumers become "guests," producers into "stagers of events," and commodities into experiences. What we buy is no longer "outside us," and no longer uniform: different consumers have different experiences, and become *co-producers* of the product. The production of these late-modern commodities (and their value) does not end at the factory gate, but rather is completed only during their consumption by an interaction with the consumer (Baudrillard 1975; Friedberg 1993), endowing the act of consumption with performativity. This also implies a new relationship between labor time and commodity; either it becomes irrelevant in defining the emotional commodity; or it is no longer the time put into the production of the commodity, but rather the time that accompanies the progressive production of the emotional commodity (as when one is consuming an exciting vacation). Furthermore, as we show in the book, consumer objects are, increasingly, parts of networks which produce complex chains of emotions and management of emotions.

Closest to the approach of this book is the relatively recent notion of affective capitalism. Affective capitalism is based on Negri's (1999) claim that affect is reintegrated within the "fold" of capitalism itself. Meaning, affect and affection are extensively organized, produced, and maintained for the needs of capitalism (Karppi *et al.* 2014). Although there are recent attempts to capture affect in different fields of contemporary culture, labor, and social networks, the notion is still vague (Dowling 2007; Dowling *et al.* 2007; Massumi 2005; Peters *et al.* 2009). Both affect and affective capitalism operates in different areas of sense and experience (Karppi *et al.* 2014) and refer to a diffuse emotionality pervading commodities, thus sometimes becoming indistinguishable from the activity of "branding."

The notion of emodity clarifies the central process of affective capitalism since it connects performatively emotional experience and commodity designed for the production of this experience.

The commodity-emotion chain

Emotions are conventionally viewed as a dyadic relation between two points: subject X feels something toward person/object Y. Within this common model, the only legitimate object for emotions are people, with emotions toward objects/goods being viewed as artificial vicarious fetishes (Latour 1999; Miller 1987; Olsen 2003) despite the increasing orientation toward objects as sources of relational intimacy, as both *mediators* of intimacy and *partners* for relatedness and emotional attachment (Knorr Cetina 1997; Knorr Cetina and Bruegger 2002). This representation of emotions as being an attribute of persons is dominant among laypersons, but also among sociologists (e.g., in social network analysis, where each person is represented by a single node and emotions are conceptualized as lines that connect them and determine the strength of each dyadic tie). However, if what we call the internal experience of emotions is actually shaped by objects that create a certain atmosphere (Illouz 1997), or medications (Crossley 2000), and if emotions follow cultural scripts (Hochschild 1983), then we must jettison both the equation of emotions with interiority and the dyadic model (Bericat 2016; Illouz *et al.* 2014). Instead, we view the inner life as organized by social and linguistic acts, by organizations and by objects, by what Foucault called a *dispositif*, that is, a heterogeneous ensemble consisting of discourses, institutions, practices, architectural settings, etc. (Foucault 1980: 194). In other words, we offer to go beyond a culturalist or discursive approach to emotions, and instead we propose to view them as existing, empirically, within a network of organizations, objects, images, and discourses. Emotions are a way for actors to transact with people and objects, to introject such people and objects inside the self. A romantic atmosphere, for example, is somewhere at the threshold of the private self and the public realm of consumer objects: a romantic restaurant and its props (lighting, candles, music, elegant silverware, refined food and wine) generate and organize feelings of mutual attraction into an atmosphere that exists both objectively (in the restaurant set up) and subjectively (in the feelings such a set up creates). An "atmosphere" is in fact typically the result of a network of objects and persons, where emotions express the ways in which objects and subjects coalesce.

This leads us to an alternative model of emotions as the products of socio-technical assemblages, mediated by cultural ideals. The economic process of production of emotions which started in the nineteenth century was at once cultural and economic, with what many have viewed as the creation of a private psychological self and identity intensely preoccupied with its emotions. As numerous historians and sociologists of the US have claimed, the rise and triumph of industrial capitalism was strongly correlated with, if not the actual cause of, the emergence of ideals of authenticity, emotional sincerity and expressiveness, and intimacy, through transformations of the public sphere and of the role of the family (Cavanaugh and Shankar 2014; Demos 1995; Dittmar 2007; Lears 1994; Pfister and Schnog 1997; Sennett 1977). Such ideals postulated that the innermost psychological and emotional core of a person defined her/his identity, who s/he truly was. In this sense then, a model of selfhood based on privacy increasingly made people in Western Europe and the US experience their self as an emotional one and such a self, conceived as endowed with an emotional interiority, was in need of expression, management, and achievement (Taylor 1989). Cultural ideals of emotional authenticity and self-realization, offered by the consumer market, channeled this new perception of the emotional self and its authenticity as something to be achieved (Lears 1994). The rise of clinical psychology, which was to sweep over the cultural landscape of Western countries, bolstered and even institutionalized the ideology that emotions were entities which could be managed and manipulated, that they needed to be expertly managed for healthy and authentic selfhood to be achieved (Brunner 1995; Cushman 1996; Herman 1995; Illouz 2007, 2008). Parallel developments in the psycho-medical sector (i.e., psychiatric and pharmaceutical industry) (Abraham 1995; Moynihan and Cassels 2005) enhanced the objectification of emotions as (medicalized) objects. These cultural and institutional processes made emotions into "objective" categories to be known and transformed. This inscription of emotional life into the classifications of psychology became accentuated by other changes in the sphere of production as well.

After World War Two, but more clearly after the 1960s, labor became increasingly "immaterial." The notion of "immaterial labor" posits that since the 1960s, in the information and knowledge-based economy, laborers have brought into their labor not just their bodies but also their intellectual and emotional capacities, in order to create "immaterial products, such as knowledge, information, communication, a relationship, or an emotional response" (Hardt and Negri 2005: 108).[5] In her seminal study *The Managed Heart*, Arlie Hochschild (1983) had called our attention to the feeling rules an increasing amount of workers needed to use to manage their emotions inside the corporation. But Hart and Negri went one step further and viewed the production of informational, cultural, symbolic, and emotional commodities as mobilizing workers' true emotional capacities and inclinations. Typically self-employed, project-oriented, and autonomous, these immaterial laborers invest their own and real subjectivities into the production process, which is no longer solely confined to the factory floor or the corporate board room. In this new labor environment, the laborers are required to be authentic; the ethics of "just be yourself" takes precedence over that of the calculated and self-controlled laborer of early industrial capitalism (Fleming and Sturdy 2009; Gill and Pratt 2008; Hardt and Negri 1994, 2001, 2005; McRobbie 2002). These transformations – the intensification of private life, the definition of selfhood in terms of emotional authenticity, the increasing emphasis on emotional labor in economic environments, the objectification of emotions through knowledge systems, all of these form the background of the process of the production of emotional commodities.

The conceptual shift put forward in this book is the claim that emotions are not just mere components of the motivational structure of the consumer or a set of adjunct meanings "loaded into" other goods, but also and more significantly *actual commodities* in themselves. By this, we do not mean the private emotional meanings and attachments which commodities accumulate after being purchased (Ilmonen 2004), but rather that *commodities are designed in order to create emotions and affects, be they deep or shallow, with a transient or long-term impact, and that they are consumed as such*. That is, emotions are not only *marketed* and commodified, they are also shaped and created in the context of specific acts of consumption.

Emodities do not emerge full-blown, but rather only after a process that is heavily mediated by cultural and moral ideals, such as those of happiness, intimacy, self-realization, and mental health. In that sense, emodities point to the economic performativity of cultural categories (transforming categories as "mental well-being," "emotional balance," or "relaxation" into commodities). An emotion – connected to these ideals – needs to be culturally identified and named before it is commodified. For example, as Yaara Benger Alaluf or Daniel Gilon show, "relaxation" or "horror" as an aesthetic emotion, are named and identified by doctors or cinema entrepreneurs and then rechanneled in the production process. Emotions are thus culturally produced by the juncture of cultural ideals of selfhood and commodification processes. The market produces emotions by using the three most important cultural templates for ideals of selfhood: a) emotional authenticity and liberation; b) intimacy, friendship, collegiality, and emotional expressivity; and c) emotional self-knowledge, self-control, and self-improvement conducive to mental health. This three-fold articulation of the market, culture, and emotions leads to the following typology of emotional goods: emotional experiences and moods, relational emotions, and emotional self- transformation.

Liberating the self: emotional experiences and moods

The ideal of authenticity and emotional liberation started dominating the USA and Western Europe from the middle of the nineteenth century. These ideals used Rousseauian ideals of Nature untouched by corrupt civilization, and were channeled in a culture of "experiences" and "moods." Emotional experiences and moods are offered by a variety of industries, predominantly related to the sphere of leisure. These consumer products present themselves as experiences which provide moods, sensations, to be later captured as memories and stories to tell.

Historically, two significant sites of consumer practices which have channeled and created authenticity through *experiences* and *moods* are tourism and music (Berger and Del Negro 2004; DeNora 2000; Friedberg 1993; Grazian 2003; Page and Connell 2006). The tourist industry has observed one of its largest expansions since World War Two. After World War Two, tourist experiences started to be shaped by tourist resorts which took the dimensions of global corporations. Tourist resorts are defined by the fact that the commodity consumed is actually an experience, organized within a well-defined time slice and alternative spatial frame, by the fact that the commodity purchased can be encapsulated as a "slice of life," or biographical event ("my vacation in the Seychelles"); and by the fact that the experience is highly aestheticized: that is, organized in and induced by spatial layout, music, food, objects, and architectural design which correspond to highly aestheticized icons or vignettes (Coleman and Crang 2002; Urry 1990, 1995).

These experiences produce emotional moods, before, during, and after their experience (e.g., anticipatory excitement, relaxation, happiness, flirtatiousness, friendliness, and nostalgia). An emotional mood differs from an emotion proper because it is often aroused by *sensory* stimuli, and is more diffuse, that is, it is less clearly valenced toward a specific and circumscribed object than an emotion, and by the fact that it may contain a variety of affects (e.g., relaxation, sexual arousal, self-confidence can coexist in an emotional mood). Yaara Benger Alaluf's chapter on the production of relaxation in Club Med resorts shows how this multi-national resort industry emerged precisely as an attempt to control and manipulate the emotional moods of tourism, and turned tourism into an emotional experience.

A second example of *emotional mood* can be found in the realm of music provided by the chapter of Ori Schwarz. A case study is "mood music compilations," a phenomenon which started in the 1950s following the invention of the LP record (Lanza 2004). Since then, these compilations have become explicitly marketed and consumed as "legal mood-manipulators" (DeNora 2000). These compilations organize music around emotional themes such as "relaxation," "romance," "nostalgia," and "melancholy." Unlike most classical pieces and rock albums, there is no shift in tempo, mood, or emotion within any single album. Music compilations are also different from mood music used in the film industry or played as muzak in shops and restaurants, as individual subjects *consciously choose* to consume them in order to both express and manipulate the emotions of themselves and others. They are usually free of any pretension to cultural/artistic inner value, and are used not for social distinction, positioning, or identity-work (i.e., as a sign-commodity), but rather for their predictable, desired emotional effect (i.e., as an emotion-commodity), to set the mood of the listeners and/or their activities (lovemaking, yoga practicing, nostalgia). People don't only buy mood-compilations, but also compile them while organizing musical digital files according to emotional categories such as "sad," "I hate men," or "feel good" (Bentley *et al.* 2006; cf. Kim and Belkin 2002), and thus use normal performers' albums for mood manipulation (see DeNora 2000). Ori Schwarz's chapter on "Emotional ear drops" documents the rise of emotional listening in music, thus providing an important way of understanding the transformation of music into an emotional-cultural commodity.

The consumption of emotional moods is both sensory and activated through imagination as Colin Campbell (1987) argued in a seminal book. For example, Daniel Gilon's analysis of the packaging of a cinematic genre of the horror movie into a formula packed with emotional intensity is a powerful empirical example of the ways consumer imagination was shaped and managed by an emotional formula. The horror movie is both produced and consumed as an emotional commodity by tapping into the imaginary emotions of suspense and horror.

As mentioned above, commodities which produce emotional moods are strongly anchored in imaginary anticipation and in bodily sensations during their experience (Campbell 1987). Emotional moods are thus induced by sensory events, and point us to the organization of the senses in and by consumer culture. The point here is not only that one experiences one's individuality in a hedonic mode, i.e., with hedonic meanings, but also that the actual experience is increasingly structured through the manipulation of sensorial stimuli. We can take as an example of this process the new profession of "restaurant and cafe design" which puts great emphasis on "atmosphere." An atmosphere, however, is not only the attempt to structure the sensorial stimuli of an environment, and to use objects and cultural codes of objects to deliberately engineer emotional moods. Atmospheres are produced by the creation of emotional moods mediated by objects. It is also the outcome of less directed, ephemeral processes entailed by symbolic and material qualities, in which actors are immersed and call for their attention. Dana Kaplan captures the fuzziness of urban "sexual atmosphere" by examining the affective labor attached to the diffusion of sexual cards in Tel-Aviv streets. An "atmosphere" seems intangible but is actually the result of the spatial configuration of objects and circulation of narrative genres.

Ideal of intimacy: relational emotions

The second cultural ideal organizing consumption for identity purposes is that of intimacy (Beck *et al.* 1995; Giddens 1992; Honneth 1995; Illouz 2007, 2012). Another category of emodities play an active role in both signaling and creating emotions in caring social relationships, most conspicuously in friendship, romance, and the family. These commodities emerged in the context of the withdrawal of the family into the private sphere, its redefinition as an emotional unit, and the increasing emphasis on emotions and intimacy for the formation of self and identity at large. Emotional individualism – that is, an individualism in which emotions are valued and cultivated for the ways in which they give expression to an individual's singularity – is a *relational individualism*, geared to the achievement of intimate relationships of various kinds, such as friendship, love, sexuality, and intimacy.

In the context of an ideal of personal life, emotions were made into commodities through the spectacular growth of gift-giving practices, viewed by anthropologists as crucial to the maintenance of interpersonal bonds. Many have documented how in many non-modern and non-Western societies, the gift has an economic status and is exchanged so as to affirm one's social status (Bauman 1993; Parry 1986), and to maintain social obligations (Mauss 1954). In contrast, the "West" has developed a unique ideology of the "pure gift," according to which the ideal gift has a strictly emotional value, presumably disconnected from its monetary or social value (Carrier 1995). Yet many analyses have missed the fact that Western gift-giving practices have been institutionalized simultaneously as consumer and emotional practices. For example, such holidays as Mothers' Day and Valentine's Day (Schmidt 1991, 1993, 1997) are at one and the same time consumer and loving rituals. Valentine's Day became popular in the US as a consumer holiday as long ago as the 1850s, while Mothers' Day arose around the 1910s. These two days were from the outset simultaneously consumer and emotional practices, oriented toward gift-giving, affirming one's membership both to the market and to a *caring unit*. They do not create emotions so much as demand their ritual renewal, and thus illustrate the ways in which consumer culture is organized in a dense web of social relationships and obligations, which it intensifies by foregrounding a moral economy of emotional expressivity.

An example of such emotional labeling of gift-giving practices can be found in the practice of sending greeting cards, a product category dominated by the Hallmark Cards company (West 2004, 2007, 2008, 2009, 2010). Hallmark has become the largest manufacturer of greeting cards worldwide. Greeting cards have become an ordinary token of exchange among people of various degrees of acquaintance and closeness. As the chapter by Emily West suggests, greeting cards are exchanged as a way to establish, maintain, and affirm emotional bonds, by naming and objectifying specific emotions exchanged in these relations. Hallmark and other card companies have increasingly used niche marketing, targeting a product to specific groups of people according to race, ethnicity, and gender. But beyond targeting cards to specific demographics, the industry creates cards that carry specific names of emotions and sending situations such as gratitude, nostalgia, regretful apology, admiration, respect, romantic love, from friend to friend, from boss to employee, or from step-daughter to step-mother. The high level of specificity available in greeting cards invites a performativity of emotion, via the market place, so characteristic of emodities.

The ideal of mental health and self-improvement: emotional self-monitoring as commodity

The third ideal shaping selfhood is that of self-knowledge and self-improvement through psychological models of mental health. This cultural ideal is related to the rise of two related industries: the psy-industries (psychological counselling of all persuasions, workshops, self-help books, coaching) and the psycho-medical industries (including psychiatric and GP services, and the pharmaceutical industry). These industries, based on knowledge formation, deal almost exclusively with the creation and/or regulation and management of emotions. These industries are pivotal to our understanding of the medicalization of emotions in general, produced by the pathologization of some emotions such as anxiety or sadness. Throughout the twentieth century, the psy-industries and psycho-medical industry have considerably expanded the scope of their activities, as they have progressively moved from the "insane" to the general population (Porter 1987), enlarging the market of consumption by offering a panoply of emotional commodities. The most obvious such commodity is emotional medicine (antidepressants or medicine against social anxiety), but the inventory also includes workshops, self-help literature, psychologist consultations, and television and radio programs all based on verbal and physical techniques for transforming one's psychological-emotional make-up.

One of the most original and distinctive aspects of the twentieth-century economy is the fact that the person and her emotions have become the target of an industry which sells mental health, self-realization, well-being, and an ideal emotional make-up (Illouz 2008). What psychologists, new age therapies, workshops, self-help books, coaching, and psychiatric medications have in common is their use of expert knowledge (psychological, pharmaceutical, genetic) to effect emotional change, such as reduce stress, reduce anger, provide well-being, increase a couple's intimacy, provide self-confidence, reduce feelings of worthlessness and powerlessness, and increase self-esteem. It should also be noted that these experts operate within the state system, and it has been suggested that the expansion of psychiatric services during the post-war period is closely associated both with financial logic and with the emergence of the modern welfare state (Busfield 1986; Lewontin *et al.* 1984; Nolan 1998). It is in this sense that the psy-sector has been regarded by some as a key player in the structuring of the capitalist social and moral order. Consumer society and knowledge systems produced by the "psy" sciences have made trading in insanity and pathologized emotions feasible. This kind of commodity is produced by knowledge systems, takes the person as its object, and can, in theory, be endlessly recycled and re-consumed: one can consult a psychologist after a post-partum depression, after a divorce, after retirement, go to inspirational workshops, occasionally meet a life coach, etc. The "psy" industry is geared at increasing the experience of positive emotions and moods, which explains why negative emotions are commodified on the mode of self-control (as in, for example, attending anger control workshops). The two chapters by Mattan Shachack and Edgar Cabanas each exemplify the commodification of the person, of emotional self-control, and of positive emotions through coaching and positive psychology, which each aim at creating an emotional surplus-value, so that the self erases or controls negative emotions and produces more positive emotions than it normally would in order to be highly adapted in an emotional economy.

The process described in this book is then fundamental to the formation of consumer capitalism in which the consumer has been socialized to produce and to consume his/her emotionality. The Internet and new social media have been excluded from the scope of this book as they would have required a direct focus on "technology" rather than, as we do here, on objects or knowledge systems. In the cultural and economic process described in this book, ideals and models of emotional authenticity, intimacy, and emotional health are co-produced with and objectified through the market in the form of emotional commodities, *emodities*.

This co-production is both processual and performative, that is, culture and economy produce each other only after a cultural process in which emotions are objectified, labeled, and integrated into ideals of personhood and pursued in the forms of moods, emotional/relational acts, and self-improvement. The economic production of emotions is thus co-produced along with cultural ideals of selfhood and knowledge systems to manage selfhood. This process ultimately explains why it is virtually impossible to separate emotional "authenticity," emotional fulfilment, emotional expression, and emotional health from the market.

This study hopes to revise both the history of capitalism and its sociology by establishing that consumer culture plays an important role in constituting emotions, social transactions, and sociability; and more crucially, that economy is performative in that it generates and creates emotional and moral worlds. If, as Bruno Latour (1999: 214) suggests, "objectivity and subjectivity are not opposed, they grow together and they do so irreversibly," then one of the greatest challenges is to understand precisely how such "irreversible" co-production of emotional and economic worlds through the mediation of moral and cultural ideals of selfhood and knowledge systems takes place (Jasanoff 2004). Contemporary society is indeed characterized by greater intimacy between the technological and the social, tied in ever more intricate networks (Knorr Cetina 1999; Latour 1999), and emotions are obvious components of these intricate networks. The formation of capitalism must be understood as a result of mutually constituted interactions between humans and non-humans, material and non-material actants, emotional and rational components of action. The framework that we propose offers a clear theory and methodology to reveal the mechanisms that tie heterogeneous elements together, such as commodities and persons, emotions and rationality, consumption and knowledge systems, from the perspective of institutional analysis and sociology of consumer practices. By offering the new concept of "emodity," our proposed framework helps to resolve the question of how emotional authenticity and commodification occur simultaneously, and how contemporary individualism seamlessly interweaves rationality and emotionality. The last chapter by Eva Illouz discusses how the concept of emotional commodity changes the meaning of authenticity, and the critique of authenticity itself. Ultimately, this book tries to reformulate a critical theory of capitalism and subjectivity which reckons with the fact that there is no subjectivity outside the compass of capitalism.

This book then hopes to shed new light on the ways in which the moral economy of social relations organizes economic exchange through emotions. It also helps us understand how economy shapes the fabric of our emotional worlds in a way which shows how the dichotomies between rationality and emotion, and authenticity and commodification, are actually seamlessly and effortlessly translated into consumer practices.

Notes

1 Catherine Townsend. 2005. "Gender vs spender: The cost of being single." *The Independent – This Britain*, September 30. Available at: www.independent.co.uk/news/uk/this-britain/gender-vs-spender-the-cost-of-being-single-316367.html.
2 For a general discussion on reflexive embodiment and its relation to social relations in late modernity, see Crossley (2006).
3 www.ifs.uni-frankfurt.de/forschung/abgeschlossene-projekte/paradoxien-der-kapitalistischen-modernisierung-zur-begrundung-eines-ubergreifenden-forschungsthemas-des-instituts-fur-sozialforschung/paradoxes-of-capitalist-modernization-the-foundations-of-a-comprehensive-research-project-of-the-institute-for-social-research/. See also Hartman and Honneth's article (2006).
4 This resonates with the evolution from *Goods Purveyors* to *Sensation Gatherers*: Bauman 1995.
5 Hardt and Negri use the notion of affective labor to describe one type of immaterial labor. They view affective labor as focuses on human contact and interaction and on the creation and manipulation of affect; its products are "intangible, a feeling of ease, well-being, satisfaction, excitement, or passion" (Hardt and Negri 2000: 292–293). Hardt (1999: 95) added that "health services, for example, rely centrally on caring and affective labor, and the entertainment industry and the various culture industries are likewise focused on the creation and manipulation of affects." However, besides mentioning it they do not expands on this notion further.

Bibliography

Abraham, John. 1995. *Science, Politics, and the Pharmaceutical Industry*. New York: St. Martin's Press.

Ahmed, Sara. 2010. *The Promise of Happiness*. Durham, NC: Duke University Press.

Alexander, Jeffrey C. 1987. *The Micro-Macro Link*. Berkeley, CA: University of California Press.

Alvesson, Mats. 1994. "Talking in organizations: Managing identity and impressions in an advertising agency." *Organization Studies* 15(4):535–563.

Alvesson, Mats and Hugh Willmott. 2002. "Identity regulation as organizational control: Producing the appropriate individual." *Journal of Management Studies* 39(5):619–644.

Appadurai, Arjun. 1986. *The Social Life of Things: Commodities in Cultural Perspective*. New York: Cambridge University Press.

Baudrillard, Jean. 1975. *The Mirror of Production* (trans. Mark Poster). Candor, NY: Telos Press Publishing.

Baudrillard, Jean. 1998. *The Consumer Society: Myths and Structures*. London: SAGE Publications.

Bauman, Zygmunt. 1988. *Freedom*. Minneapolis, MN: University of Minnesota Press.

Bauman, Zygmunt. 1992. *Intimations of Postmodernity*. London: Routledge.

Bauman, Zygmunt. 1993. *Postmodern Ethics*. Oxford, UK: Blackwell.

Bauman, Zygmunt. 1995. "Making and unmaking of strangers." *Thesis Eleven* 43(1):1–16.

Beck, Ulrich, Elisabeth Beck-Gernsheim, Mark Ritter and Jane Wiebel. 1995. *The Normal Chaos of Love*. Cambridge, MA: Polity Press.

Belk, Russell W., Güliz Ger and Søren Askegaard. 2003. "The fire of desire: A multisited inquiry into consumer passion." *Journal of Consumer Research* 30(3):326–351.

Bell, Daniel. 1976. *The Cultural Contradictions of Capitalism*. New York: Basic Books.

Bennett, David. 2005. "Getting the Id to go shopping: Psychoanalysis, advertising, Barbie Dolls, and the invention of the consumer unconscious." *Public Culture* 17(1):1–26.

Bentley, Frank, Crysta Metcalf and Gunnar Harboe. 2006. "Personal vs. commercial content: The similarities between consumer use of photos and music." In *Proceedings of the SIGCHI Conference on Human Factors in Computing Systems*, 667–676. Montreal, Canada.

Berger, Harris M. and Giovanna P. Del Negro. 2004. *Identity and Everyday Life: Essays in the Study of Folklore, Music and Popular Culture*. Middletown, CT: Wesleyan University Press.

Bericat, Eduardo. 2016. "The sociology of emotions: Four decades of progress." *Current Sociology* 64(3):491–513.

Boltanski, Luc and Eve Chiapello. 2005. *The New Spirit of Capitalism*. London: Verso.

Boudon, Raymond. 2009. "Rational choice theory." *The New Blackwell Companion to Social Theory*, pp. 179–195.

Bourdieu Pierre. 1984. *Distinction: A Social Critique of the Judgment of Taste* (trans. Richard Nice). Cambridge, MA: Harvard University Press.

Brown, Jane and Helen Woodruffe-Burton. 2015. "Exploring emotions and irrationality in attitudes towards consumer indebtedness: Individual perspectives of UK payday loan consumption." *Journal of Financial Services Marketing* 20(2):107–121.

Brunner, José. 1995. *Freud and the Politics of Psychoanalysis*. Oxford, UK; Cambridge, MA: Blackwell.

Busfield, Joan. 1986. *Managing Madness: Changing Ideas and Practice*. Cambridge, UK: Polity Press

Cabanas, Edgar and Eva Illouz. 2016. "The making of a 'happy worker': Positive psychology in neoliberal organizations." In *Beyond the Cubicle: Insecurity Culture and the Flexible Self*, edited by Allison Pugh. New York: Oxford University Press.

Campbell, Colin. 1987. *The Romantic Ethic and the Spirit of Modern Consumerism*. New York: Blackwell.

Carrier, James. 1995. *Gifts and Commodities: Exchange and Western Capitalism since 1700*. London and New York: Routledge.

Carruthers, Bruce G. and Wendy Nelson Espeland. 1991. "Accounting for rationality: Double-entry bookkeeping and the rhetoric of economic rationality." *American Journal of Sociology* 97(1):31–69.

Caru, Antonella and Cova Bernard. 2007. "Consuming experiences: An introduction." In *Consuming Experience*, edited by Antonella Caru and Cova Bernard, 3–16. New York: Routledge.

Cavanaugh, Jillian R., and Shalini Shankar. 2014. "Producing authenticity in global capitalism: Language, Materiality, and value." *American Anthropologist* 116(1):51–64.

Coleman, Simon, and Mike Crang. 2002. *Tourism: Between Place and Performance*. New York: Berghahn Books.

Crossley, Nick. 2000. "Emotions, psychiatry and social order." In *Health, Medicine and Society: Key Theories, Future Agendas*, edited by Williams Simon J, Jonathan Gabe, and Michael Calnan, 277–295. Basingstoke, UK: Taylor & Francis.

Crossley, Nick. 2006. *Reflexive Embodiment in Contemporary Society: The Body in Late Modern Society*. London: McGraw Hill.

Cushman, Philip. 1996. *Constructing the Self, Constructing America: A Cultural History of Psychotherapy*. Boston, MA: Da Capo Press.

De Angelis, Massimo and David Harvie. 2009. "'Cognitive capitalism' and the rat-race: How capital measures immaterial labour in British universities." *Historical Materialism* 17(3):3–30.

Demos, John Putnam. 1995. *The Unredeemed Captive: A Family Story from Early America*. New York: Knopf Doubleday Publishing Group.

DeNora, Tia. 2000. *Music in Everyday Life*. Cambridge, UK: Cambridge University Press.

Deranty, Jean-Philippe. 2008. "Work and the precarisation of existence." *European Journal of Social Theory* 11(4):443–463.

DiPrete, Thomas. A. and Jerry D. Forristal. 1994. "Multilevel models: Methods and substance." *Annual Review of Sociology* 20(1):331–357.

Dittmar, Helga. 2007. *Consumer Culture, Identity and Well-Being: The Search for the "Good Life" and the "Body Perfect"*. Hove, UK: Psychology Press.

Douglas, Mary and Baron Isherwood C. 1979. *The World of Goods*. London: Allen Lane.

Dowling, Emma. 2007. "Producing the dining experience: Measure, subjectivity and the affective worker." *Ephemera* 7(1):117–132.

Dowling, Emma, Rodrigo Nunes and Ben, Trott. 2007. "Immaterial and affective labor-explored." *Ephemera* 7(1):1–7.

Falk, Pasi. 1994. *The Consuming Body*. Vol. 30. London: SAGE.

Featherstone, Mike. 2007. *Consumer Culture and Postmodernism*. London: SAGE.

Fırat, Fuat A. and Nikhilesh Dholakia. 1998. *Consuming People: From Political Economy to Theaters of Consumption*. New York: Routledge.

Fleming, Peter and Andrew Sturdy. 2009. "Just be yourself!" *Employee Relations* 31(6):569–583.

Foucault, Michel. 1980. *Power/Knowledge: Selected Interviews and Other Writings, 1972–1977.* (trans. Colin Gordon *et al.*). New York: Pantheon Books.

Friedberg, Anne. 1993. *Window Shopping: Cinema and the Postmodern.* Berkeley, CA: University of California Press.

Giddens, Anthony. 1992. *The Transformation of Intimacy: Sexuality, Love, and Eroticism in Modern Societies.* Stanford, CA: Stanford University Press.

Gill, Rosalind. 2009. "Beyond the 'sexualization of culture' thesis: An intersectional analysis of 'sixpacks,' 'midriffs' and 'hot lesbians' in advertising." *Sexualities* 12(2):137–160.

Gill, Rosalind and Andy, Pratt. 2008. "In the social factory? Immaterial labour, Precariousness and cultural work." *Theory, Culture & Society* 25(7–8):1–30.

Gobé, Marc. 2001. *Emotional Branding: The New Paradigm for Connecting Brands to People.* Oxford, UK: Windsor Books International.

Grazian, David. 2003. *Blue Chicago: The Search for Authenticity in Urban Blues Clubs.* Chicago, IL: The University of Chicago Press.

Habermas, Jürgen. 1985. *The Theory of Communicative Action. Volume Two: Lifeworld and System: A Critique of Functionalist Reason* (trans. Thomas McCarthy). Boston, MA: Beacon Press.

Hardt, Michael. 1995. "Affective labor." *Boundary 2,* 26(2):89–100.

Hardt, Michael and Antonio Negri. 1994. *The Labour of Dionysus: A Critique of the State Form.* Minneapolis, MN: University of Minneapolis Press.

Hardt, Michael and Antonio Negri. 2001. *Empire.* Cambridge, MA: Harvard University Press.

Hardt, Michael and Antonio Negri. 2005. *Multitude: War and Democracy in the Age of Empire.* London: Hamish Hamilton.

Hartmann, Martin and Axel Honneth. 2006. "Paradoxes of capitalism." *Constellations* 13(1):41–58.

Hasday, Jill Elaine. 2005. "Intimacy and economic exchange." *Harvard Law Review,* 119(2):491–530.

Hatch, Mary Jo. 1993. "The dynamics of organizational culture." *Academy of Management Review* 18(4):657–693.

Herman, Ellen. 1995. *The Romance of American Psychology: Political Culture in the Age of Experts.* Berkeley, CA: University of California Press.

Hesmondhalgh, David and Sarah Baker. 2008. "Creative work and emotional labour in the television industry." *Theory, Culture & Society* 25(7–8):97–118.

Hirschman, Albert Otto. (2013 [1977]). *The Passions and the Interests: Political Arguments for Capitalism before its Triumph.* Princeton, NJ: Princeton University Press.

Hochschild, Arlie Russell. 1983. *The Managed Heart: Commercialization of Human Feeling.* Berkeley, CA: University of California Press.

Holbrook, Morris B. and Elizabeth C. Hirschman. 1982. "The experiential aspects of consumption: Consumer fantasies, feelings, and fun." *Journal of Consumer Research* 9(2):132–140.

Holmes, Mary. 2010. "The emotionalization of reflexivity." *Sociology* 44(1):139–154.

Holt, Douglas. B. 2004. *How Brands Become Icons: The Principles of Cultural Branding.* Boston, MA: Harvard Business School Press.

Honneth, Axel. 1995. *The Struggle for Recognition: The Moral Grammar of Social Conflicts* (trans. Joel Anderson). Cambridge, MA: Polity Press.

Honneth, Axel. 2004. "Organized self-realization: Some paradoxes of individualization." *European Journal of Social Theory* 7(4):463–478.

Horkheimer, Max and Adorno Theodor W. 1979 [1944]. *Dialectic of Enlightenment* (trans. John Cumming). London: Verso Editions.

Hughes, Jason. 2010. "Emotional intelligence: Elias, Foucault, and the reflexive emotional self". *Foucault Studies* 8:28–52.

Hunt, Alan. 2012. "The civilizing process and emotional life: The intensification and hollowing out of contemporary emotions." In *Emotions Matter: A Relational Approach to Emotions*, edited by Alan Hunt, Kevin Walby and Dale Spencer, 137–160. Toronto, ON: University of Toronto Press.

Houston, Stan. 2008. "Beyond homo economicus: Recognition, self-realization and social work." *British Journal of Social Work* 40(3):841–857.

Illouz, Eva 1997. *Consuming the Romantic Utopia: Love and the Cultural Contradictions of Capitalism*. Berkeley, CA: University of California Press.

Illouz, Eva. 2007. *Cold Intimacies: The Making of Emotional Capitalism*. Cambridge, UK: Polity Press.

Illouz, Eva. 2008. *Saving the Modern Soul. Therapy, Emotions, and the Culture of Self-Help*. Berkeley, CA: University of California Press.

Illouz, Eva. 2012. *Why Love Hurts: A Sociological Explanation*. Cambridge, UK: Polity Press.

Illouz, Eva and Yaara Benger. 2015. "Emotions and consumption." In *The Wiley Blackwell Encyclopedia of Consumption and Consumer Studies*, edited by Daniel Cook and J. Michael Ryan, 263–268. London: John Wiley & Sons.

Illouz, Eva and Shoshannah Finkelman. 2009. "An odd and inseparable couple: Emotion and rationality in partner selection." *Theory and Society* 38(4):401–422.

Illouz, Eva, Daniel Gilon and Mattan Shachak. 2014. "Emotions and cultural theory." In *Handbook of the Sociology of Emotions: Volume II*, edited by Jan E. Stets and Jonathan H. Turner, 221–244. Dordrecht, The Netherlands: Springer.

Ilmonen, Kaj. 2004. "The use of and commitment to goods." *Journal of Consumer Culture* 4(1):27–50.

Jansson, André. 2002. "The mediatization of consumption: Towards an analytical framework of image culture." *Journal of Consumer Culture* 2(1):5–31.

Jasanoff, Sheila. 2004. "The idiom of co-production." In *States of Knowledge: The Co-Production of Science and the Social Order*, edited by Jasanoff, Sheila, 1–12. London: Taylor & Francis.

Jensen, Casper B. 2007. "Infrastructural fractals: Revisiting the micro – macro distinction in social theory." *Environment and Planning D: Society and Space* 25(5):832–850.

Karppi, Tero, Anu Laukkanen, Mona Mannevuo, Mari Pajala and Tanja Sihvonen. 2014. "Affective capitalism (call for papers), ephemera: Theory and politics in organization." Retrieved September 1, 2016 (www.ephemerajournal.org/content/affective-capitalism).

Kim, Ja-Young and Nicholas J. Belkin. 2002. "Categories of music description and search terms and phrases used by non-music experts." In Proceedings of the 3rd International Conference on Music Information Retrieval, Paris, France, 209–214.

Knorr Cetina, Karin. 1997. "Sociality with objects: Social relations in postsocial knowledge societies." *Theory, Culture & Society* 14(4):1–30.

Knorr Cetina, Karin. 1999. *Epistemic Cultures: How the Sciences Make Knowledge*. Cambridge, MA: Harvard University Press.

Knorr Cetina, Karin and Urs Bruegger. 2002. "Traders' engagement with markets: A postsocial relationship." *Theory, Culture & Society* 19(5–6):161–185.

Kunda, Gideon. 2006. *Engineering Culture: Control and Commitment in a High-Tech Corporation*. Philadelphia, PA: Temple University Press.

Lanza, Joseph. 2004. *Elevator Music: A Surreal History of Muzak Easy-Listening and Other Moodsong*. Ann Arbor, MI: University of Michigan Press.

Lasch, Christopher. 1979. *Haven in a Heartless World: The Family Besieged.* New York: Basic Books.

Lash, Scott M. and John Ury. 1993. *Economies of Signs and Space.* Thousand Oaks, CA: SAGE Publications.

Latour, Bruno. 1999. *Pandora's Hope: An Essay on the Reality of Science Studies.* Cambridge, MA: Harvard University Press.

Lears, T. J. Jackson. 1994. *No Place of Grace: Antimodernism and the Transformation of American Culture, 1880–1920.* Chicago, IL: University of Chicago Press.

Lewontin, R. C., Steven Rose, Leon J Kamin and Rose L. Kamin. 1984. *Not in Our Genes: Biology, Ideology, and Human Nature.* London: Pelican Books.

Lipovetsky, Gilles and Jean Serroy. 2013. *L'esthétisation du monde. Vivre à l'âge du capitalisme artiste.* Paris: Editions Gallimard.

Lury, Celia. 2004. *Brands: The Logos of the Global Economy.* New York: Taylor & Francis.

Marx, Karl. 1977 [1887]. *Capital*, vol. 1 (trans. Ben Fowkes). New York: Vintage Books.

Massumi, Brian. 2005. "Congress CATH 2005: The future birth of the affective fact." Conference Proceedings: Genealogies of Biopolitics, 2. Retrieved May 29, 2016 (www.leeds.ac.uk/cath/ahrc/congress/2005/programme/abs/164.shtml).

Mauss, Marcel. 1954. *The Gift* (trans. I. G. Cunnison). London: Cohen and West.

Mayer, Thomas. 1995. *Doing Economic Research: Essays on the Applied Methodology of Economics (Economists of the Twentieth Century).* Cheltenham, UK: Edward Elgar Publishing.

Mazzarella, William. 2003. *Shoveling Smoke: Advertising and Globalization in Contemporary India.* Durham, NC: Duke University Press.

McRobbie, Angela. 1998. *British Fashion Design: Rag Trade or Image Industry?* New York: Routledge.

McRobbie, Angela. 2002. "From Holloway to Hollywood: Happiness at work in the new cultural economy." In *Cultural Economy: Cultural Analysis and Commercial Life*, edited by Paul Du Gay, and Michael Pryke, 97–114. London: SAGE Publications.

Miller, Daniel. 1987. *Material Culture and Mass Consumption.* Oxford, UK: Blackwell Publishers.

Mitchell, Wesley C. 1910. "The rationality of economic activity." *The Journal of Political Economy* 18(3):197–216.

Morini, Cristina. 2007. "The feminization of labour in cognitive capitalism." *Feminist Review* 87(1):40–59.

Moulier-Boutang, Yann. 2012. *Cognitive Capitalism.* Cambridge, UK: Polity.

Moynihan, Ray and Alan Cassels. 2005. *Selling Sickness: How the World's Biggest Pharmaceutical Companies Are Turning Us All into Patients.* New York: Avalon Publishing Group.

Negri, Antonio. 1999. "Value and affect." *Boundary 2* 26(2):77–88.

Nolan, James. L. Jr. 1998. *The Therapeutic State. Justifying Government at Century's End.* New York: New York University Press.

Olsen, Bjørnar. 2003. "Material culture after text: Re-membering things." *Norwegian Archeological Review* 36(2):87–104.

O'Shaughnessy, John and Nicholas Jackson O'Shaughnessy. 2002. "Marketing, the consumer society and hedonism." *European Journal of Marketing* 36(5/6):524–547.

Page, Stephen J. and Joanne Connell. 2006. *Tourism: A Modern Synthesis.* London: Cengage Learning EMEA.

Parry, Jonathan. 1986. "The gift, the Indian gift and the 'Indian gift'." *Man* 21(3):453–473.

Parry, Jonathan and Maurice Bloch. 1989. *Money and the Morality of Exchange.* Cambridge, UK: Cambridge University Press.

Parsons, Talcott. 1937. *The Structure of Social Action.* New York: McGraw-Hill.

Peters, Michael A., Rodrigo Britez and Ergin Bulut. 2009. "Cybernetic capitalism, informationalism and cognitive labor." *Geopolitics, History and International Relations* 1(2):11–40.

Pfister, Joel and Nancy Schnog. 1997. *Inventing the Psychological: Toward a Cultural History of Emotional Life in America.* New Haven, CT: Yale University Press.

Pine, B. Joseph and James H Gilmore. 1999. *The Experience Economy: Work Is Theater & Every Business a Stage.* Boston, MA: Harvard Business Press.

Polanyi, Karl. 1944. *The Great Transformation: The Political and Economic Origins of Our Time.* Boston, MA: Beacon Press.

Polter, David and Chris Land. 2008. "Preparing to work: Dramaturgy, cynicism and normative 'remote' control in the socialization of graduate recruits in management consulting." *Culture and Organization* 14(1):65–78.

Porter, Roy. 1987. *Mind Forg'd Manacles: A History of Madness in England from the Restoration to the Regency.* Harmondsworth, UK: Penguin

Roberts, Kevin. 2005. *Lovemarks: The Future Beyond Brands.* Brooklyn, NY: Power House Books.

Rossiter, John and Steve Bellman. 2012. "Emotional branding pays off." *Journal of Advertising Research* 52(3):291–296.

Schmidt, Leigh Eric. 1991. "The commercialization of the calendar: American holidays and the culture of consumption, 1870–1930." *The Journal of American History* 78(3):887–916.

Schmidt, Leigh Eric. 1993. "The fashioning of a modern holiday: St. Valentine's day, 1840–1870." *Winterthur Portfolio* 28(4):209–245.

Schmidt, Leigh Eric. 1997. *Consumer Rites: The Buying and Selling of American Holidays.* Princeton, NJ: Princeton University Press.

Schor, Juliet B. 1992. *The Overworked American: The Unexpected Decline of Leisure.* New York: Basic Books.

Scitovsky, Tibor. 2013 [1952]. *Welfare & Competition.* London: Routledge.

Scott, John. 2000. "Rational choice theory." In *Understanding Contemporary Society: Theories of the Present,* edited by Gary, Browning, Abigail Halcli and Frank Webster, 126–138. Thousand Oaks, CA: SAGE Publications.

Seidler, Victor, Jeleniewski. 2007. "Masculinities, bodies, and emotional life." *Men and Masculinities* 10(1):9–21.

Sennett, Richard. 1977. *The Fall of Public Man.* Cambridge, UK: Cambridge University Press.

Simmel, Georg. 2004 [1900]. *The Philosophy of Money* (trans. Tom Bottomore and David Frisby). New York: Routledge.

Simmel, Georg. 2004 [1903]. "The metropolis and mental life." In *The City Cultures Reader,* edited by Miles Malcolm *et al.,* 12–19. London: Routledge.

Slater, Don. 1997. *Consumer Culture and Modernity.* Cambridge, UK: Polity Press.

Smelser, Neil J. 1998. "The rational and the ambivalent in the social sciences: 1997 presidential address." *American Sociological Review* 63(1):1–16.

Swedberg, Richard. 2005. "The Economic Sociology of Capitalism: An Introduction and Agenda." In *The Economic Sociology of Capitalism,* edited by Victor Nee and Richard Swedberg, 3–40. Princeton, NJ: Princeton University Press.

Taylor, Charles. 1989. *Sources of the Self: The Making of the Modern Identity.* Cambridge, MA: Harvard University Press.

Urry, John. 1990. *The Tourist Gaze: Leisure and Travel in Contemporary Societies.* London: SAGE Publications.

Urry, John. 1995. *Consuming Places.* New York: Taylor & Francis.

Vakratsas, Demetrios and Tim Ambler. 1999. "How advertising works: What do we really know?" *Journal of Marketing* 63(1):26–43.

Vargo, Stephen L. and Robert F. Lusch. 2004. "Evolving to a new dominant logic for marketing." *Journal of Marketing* 68(1):1–17.

Vercellone, Carlo. 2008. "The new articulation of wages, rent and profit in cognitive capitalism." Paper presented at The Art of Rent, a seminar held at School of Business and Management, Queen Mary, University of London. Translated by A. Bove. Retrieved, June 11, 2016 (www.generation-online.org/c/fc_rent2.htm).

Von Osten, Marion. 2007 "Unpredictable outcomes: A reflection after some years of debates on creativity and creative industries." In *My Creativity Reader: A Critique of the Creative Industries*, edited by Greet Lovink and Ned Rossiter, 49–58. Amsterdam: Institute of Network Cultures.

Weber, Max. 1947. *The Theory of Social and Economic Organization* (trans. Talkott Parsons). New York: Oxford University Press.

Weber, Max. 1978. *Economy and Society: An Outline of Interpretive Sociology* (trans. Guenther Roth *et al.*). Berkeley, CA: University of California Press.

Weber, Max. 2010 [1904–1905]. *The Protestant Ethic and the Spirit of Capitalism* (trans. Stephen Kalberg). New York: Oxford University Press.

Welcomer, Stephanie A., Dennis A. Gioia and Martin Kilduff. 2000. "Resisting the discourse of modernity: Rationality versus emotion in hazardous waste siting." *Human Relations* 53(9):1175–1205.

Wernick, Andrew. 1991. *Promotional Culture: Advertising, Ideology and Symbolic Expression.* London: SAGE Publications.

West Emily. 2004. "Greeting cards: Individuality and authenticity in mass culture." Retrieved January 1, 2004). Dissertations available from ProQuest. Paper AAI3152125. (http://repository.upenn.edu/dissertations/AAI3152125).

West, Emily. 2007. "When you care enough to defend the very best: How the greeting card industry manages cultural criticism." *Media, Culture & Society* 29(2):241–261.

West, Emily. 2008. "Mass producing the personal: The greeting card industry's approach to commercial sentiment." *Popular Communication* 6(4):231–247.

West, Emily. 2009. "Doing gender difference through greeting cards: The construction of a communication gap in marketing and everyday practice." *Feminist Media Studies* 9(3):285–299.

West, Emily. 2010. "Expressing the self through sentiment: Working theories of authentic communication in a commercial form." *International Journal of Cultural Studies* 13(5):451–469.

Wood, Ellen Meiksins. 2002. *The Origin of Capitalism: A Longer View.* London: Verso Books.

Zajonc, Robert B. and Hazel Markus. 1982. "Affective and cognitive factors in preferences." *Journal of Consumer Research* 9(2):117–123.

Zelizer, Viviana. 1994. *Pricing the Priceless Child: The Changing Social Value of Children.* Princeton, NJ: Princeton University Press.

Zelizer, Viviana. 1996. *The Social Meaning of Money.* Princeton, NJ: Princeton University Press.

Zelizer, Viviana. 2005. *The Purchase of Intimacy.* Princeton, NJ: Princeton University Press.

Part I

Liberating the self

Emotional experiences and moods

Chapter I

"It is all included – without the stress"

Exploring the production of relaxation in Club Med seaside resorts

Yaara Benger Alaluf

Tripadvisor reviewer *MariaM99* describes the Club Med resort where she spent her holiday as "the ideal place to relax and let your troubles & stress melt away," a place where she was "able to easily escape the stress of life." Similarly, *JeanPaulLanfranchi* writes that Club Med was exactly the resort he needed to regenerate himself "after a tough period of stress at work."[1] To the casual reader, there is nothing remarkable in these reviews. After all, seaside resorts are supposed to be relaxing. But this assumption has a history which explains why relaxation is widely taken for granted as part of contemporary holiday-making. Some might say that the sea is relaxing. Yet, even if we accept this claim as given, seaside resorts, including those run by Club Med, are much more than a beach: they are a whole industry. My aim in this chapter is to explore how this industry produces the experience of relaxation which we so naturally attach to it. Through the example of relaxation in Club Med resorts, I want to demonstrate the process of the commodification of emotions in tourism and to illustrate how a specific touristic site leads to a defined emotional experience – in the case of Club Med seaside resorts: the Emodity of relaxation.

The chapter consists of two main parts. After a theoretical introduction, I will highlight three historical processes which enabled the construction of tourism as an emotional industry: (a) the emotional idealization of nature; (b) the emotional consequences of the differentiation between work and leisure; and (c) the standardization of tourism, which I argue has expanded tourism's emotional dimension. Following the exploration of these cultural conditions, I will trace the emergence of relaxation as a tourist demand, which contemporary vacation resorts address. The second part of the chapter is dedicated to the task of uncovering the production and supply of relaxation in Club Med resorts. Through the analysis of 55 online reviews written by vacationers, I examine the influence of the resort experience on the emotional state of its customers according to my inference of three main characteristics of a Club Med vacation: spatial differentiation, blurring of economic exchange, and focus on the individual. Through each of these sections I will analyze the contribution of the specific characteristic to the production of relaxation in light of the subjective descriptions of the reviewers.

Tourism as an emotional industry

The tourist industry is a good case for the study of the commodification of emotions. It is one of the world's largest economic sectors and integrates economic and emotional aspects on a global scale.[2] Indeed, much has been written about tourism as a commodity (e.g., Burkart and Medlik 1974; Cohen 2004; Urry 1990, 1995; Watson and Kopachevsky 1994).[3] This literature includes some discussion on the intangible products of this industry: Bell and Lyall (2002) emphasize that tourism's value is mainly aesthetic; Coleman and Crang (2002) relate to tourism as a market of experiences; for Friedberg (1993) tourism is "the experience of 'foreign' spaces" (Ibid.: 3) as well as a commodified traveling experience (Ibid.: 59); Watson and Kopachevsky (1994) stress that the tourist experience includes the consumption of "signs, symbols, cultural experiences" (Ibid.: 649–650).

The experiential quality of tourism is certainly acknowledged in these accounts, i.e., it necessarily includes a cognitive or sensual engagement – but what exactly characterizes this experience, and how is it commodified? This question has been addressed by two sociologists of tourism, John Urry and Ning Wang, who perceive the tourist experience as basically constructed vis á vis our experience of daily modern life (Urry 1990: 1–2; Wang 2000: 92). What forms the tourist experience is therefore difference: the experience and its anticipatory expectations are constituted in the light of, and in contrast to, certain non-tourist experiences. That is what makes the tourist experience both multiple and contingent.

However, Urry and Wang differ in their answer to the second question, concerning how this experience is commodified. For Urry, tourism is the visual consumption of sights and places through what he calls "the tourist gaze," implying that the antithetical experience emerges as an effect of aesthetic signs which are out of the ordinary (Urry 1990: 3). Following Cohen's analytical distinction between sightseers, who seek novelty, and vacationers, who seek change (Cohen 2004), Wang claims that the holiday tourist's need for change is etched into "the temporal structure of modernity" (Wang 2000: 91). From his point of view, what is commodified is "free time" (Ibid.: 109–110).

Although I accept Urry and Wang's conception of tourism – and especially holiday-making – as an antithetical experience, my argument differs from theirs in two key ways. First, I focus on emotion as the cardinal object consumed in twentieth-century recreational tourism, and its commodification as the source of the contrasted experience. Indeed, emotional aspects of the tourist experience are present in Urry and Wang's studies as well as in other works on tourism.[4] However, neither of these consists of a clear argumentation of emotion as a commodity which is produced and consumed through tourist activity. Second, via the example of relaxation as an Emodity fabricated in Club Med resorts, I aim to explain how specific sites and activities are deliberately designed to manipulate emotional experiences. In this sense, those spatial and temporal qualities which were interpreted by Urry and Wang correspondingly as the essence of the antithetical tourist experience, are reconceptualized here as components of a set of mechanisms by which the resort shapes the emotional experience. By highlighting the emotional essence of tourism, I wish to unravel the reciprocal relation between emotional experience and economic industry. From this perspective, "leisure" is seen as a realm of production increasingly focused on creating and inducing intense emotional experiences, be they exciting or relaxing.

What makes tourism an ideal realm for the commodification of emotions? Whereas it is a truism that any experience has an emotional dimension, the key question here is whether this experience is framed and labeled as emotional. This labeling is a necessary condition since the commodification of emotions presupposes their constitution as objects. The objectification of emotions is achieved only once "emotional experience is organized, labeled, classified, and interpreted" (Illouz 1997: 3) within a specific cultural frame. As a matter of fact, emotion has not always been considered a clear object of the tourism experience, but has emerged more recently as a core aspect of tourism; for this reason alone, this claim demands careful examination. My goal here is not to tell the story of contemporary tourism, therefore I will concentrate only on the components of the history of tourism which have turned this industry into a potential field for the commodification of emotions.

Travel, and even organized travel, existed in pre-modern societies. However, it is widely accepted that tourism is a modern phenomenon (Cohen 2004; MacCannell 1976; Urry 1990; Wang 2000). The word "tour" was first used – in the sense we use it today in the term "tourism" – in the early eighteenth century (Wang 2000: 3). The "Grand Tour," a journey taken by young aristocrats around canonical sites in Europe, with the aim of developing their education, is usually given as the birth of tourism as a modern phenomenon, and it became firmly established at this time (Berghoff 2002). The aristocratic practice of "taking the waters," that is, bathing in and drinking mineral waters in search of medical cure, also emerged around this time. These two practices laid the foundation for holiday-making. Although until the nineteenth century tourism was clearly limited to the upper classes, by the second half of the century the commercialization of tourism allowed growing sectors of society access to the tourist experience, thus "democratizing" tourism (Urry 1990, 1995). Over the course of its development, three major processes have tightened the link between tourism and emotions: the emotionalization of nature, the distinction between work and leisure, and the standardization of tourism.

The emotionalization of nature

For hundreds of years, the increasingly secularized western tradition saw nature not as a space of divine revelation or for individual recreation, but as a dangerous and alien place. By the end of the seventeenth century, travelers (themselves a privileged few) still described nature as sublime, powerful, and terrifying (Bell and Lyall 2002: 4–6; Corbin 1994). The colonization of the New World and the spreading domestication of lands in Europe started to change people's attitude towards nature: "mythological explanations of nature faded; unproductive land was seen as ugly; and domesticated, inhabited landscape was seen as beautiful, and how it should be" (Bell and Lyall 2002: 7). Although nature was less frightening and subordinated to human needs to an unprecedented extent, these needs were essentially material. Nature was not a focus of tourism yet.

By the end of the seventeenth century, some philosophers and theological scholars in France and Britain marked the beginning of a transition in the perception of nature. Natural theologians and Enlightenment naturalists ceased to see nature as an analogy between human and universe or between the physical and the spiritual and started to interpret nature as an expression of God – a meaningful spectacle (Corbin 1994: 22–26; Daston 2004: 101–102). However, travel for non-commercial purposes still focused on art and classic culture, as demonstrated in the case of the "Grand Tour." Raw nature did not have a "secular" emotional appeal yet. Only with the rise of Romanticism did uncivilized nature become a point of interest and curiosity. Romantic thought led both to the aesthetic appreciation of nature's authenticity and to a new intellectual and reflective interest in the emotional authenticity of the self.[5] Increasingly, nature was attached to concepts of authenticity, harmony, and sensitivity, and the emphasis was put on the individual experience, pleasure, senses, and emotion (Bell and Lyall 2002: 7–8; Urry 1990: 20).

The distinction between work and leisure

The distinction between the work sphere and the leisure sphere became clearer during the second half of the nineteenth century as an effect of the regularization of industrial time. This distinction is usually discussed in the context of the emergence of consumerism, simply because the combination of defined free time and stable wages led to the swift expansion of "consumerist leisure" (Illouz 1997: 27; Stearns 2001: 49–50). However, this distinction designates not only specific space, time, and activity for each of the states – work and leisure – but also distinct emotional repertoires.

The wish to "buy" a different emotional experience during leisure time is expressed in Stearn's words regarding the first decades of industrial capitalism:

> [t]he unpleasantness of much industrial work had long been recognized. Gradually, some of the workers involved decided that, while the unpleasantness could not be reversed directly, it could be mitigated if labor could bid for a better life off the job.
>
> (Stearns 2001: 56)

The reduction of working time and the democratization of holiday-making starting from the last decades of the nineteenth century converted leisure into an affordable mechanism for emotional alternation. Holidays away from the city offered release from the monotonous work, the harsh discipline in the factories, the crowded urban space, and a general liberation "from boredom and frustration" (Cross and Walton 2005: 63).

The standardization of tourism as leisure

Gradually, and markedly after the Second World War, tourism transformed from a luxury into a commodity: standardized, rationally produced, and accessible to the masses (Berghoff 2002; Watson and Kopachevsky 1994). This development was supported by managers and theoreticians who believed that the organization and rationalization of leisure time would contribute to workers' morality and health, and consequently lead to industrial efficiency (Bailey 1978: 57–60; Meller 2013: 11). Although many scholars, following the "Frankfurt School" spirit, have criticized the rationalization of tourism as turning it into a staged and patterned practice (MacCannell 1976; Watson and Kopachevsky 1994), it does not follow that the rationalization of tourism is incompatible with its emotionalization. In typical neo-Marxist style, Watson and Kopachevsky stress that in consumer society, leisure time "becomes another routinized, packaged, commodity, thereby failing to be anything like a carefree, relaxed, alternative to work" (Watson and Kopachevsky 1994: 645). However, apart from ignoring the phenomenological fact that many people do find relief in their free time, as will be shown later, a central flaw of the "staged consumption" argument derives from its simplistic interpretation of the commodification process.

In a post-Fordist reality, standardized and rationalized production does not necessarily result in a homogeneous product and an alienated experience of consumption. On the contrary, many products have become a platform for endless possibilities of individual consumer experiences (Lash and Lury 2007). One of the main outcomes of the standardization of tourism is that, being standardized, the vacation becomes predictable: it requires less planning and less active and conscious involvement of the tourist (cooking, searching for attractions, etc.), hence opening up more space for individual emotional experience.

Demanding relaxation

The constitution of relaxation as a central emotional experience to be achieved in holiday-making can be seen as the outcome of the intersection of three processes: the rise of the spa and seaside resort industry, the democratization of leisure time and the creation of mass tourism, and the emergence of the psychological concept of "stress" (Benger Alaluf 2016). From the late eighteenth century onwards, Western Europe witnessed the widespread growth of spas and seaside resorts. Although the use of nature for human purposes was not new, by this time the instrumentalization of nature in search of a (secular) personal transformation was restricted to physical alternation (health, cure) and modified facilities (baths, pools) (Adams 2015; Beckerson and Walton 2005). Going out to wild nature without human accommodation in search of physical cure was not common before the late eighteenth century (Corbin 1994). This change should be seen as a widening of the instrumentalization of nature: the focus is still on its physical curative virtues, but these are attached to the sea, sun, and air, and not only to a specific bathing ritual. Hence, more locations were marketed under the "health" label (sunny beaches, mountain air, etc.). The shift from physical health to emotional alternation as the central objective of holiday-making at watering places took place only once its effectiveness had been put into question and after a new objective had emerged.

One of the main reasons for the prevalence of health resorts in nineteenth-century Europe was the confidence in the curative properties of water. This was a result of the scientific study of hydrotherapy as a field of medicine since the eighteenth century (Adams 2015; Larrinaga 2005). However, this confidence faded through the first half of the twentieth century, both because of the growing scientific criticism of hydrotherapy, and because developments in medical science had provided more reliable and effective alternative therapies (Weisz 2001, 2011). This process harmed the health travel industry, and a way to overcome this challenge was, in Weisz's words, "to move into the 'wellness' business and provide essentially healthy people with services that make them feel good or better" (Weisz 2011: 142). Indeed, as Beckerson and Walton note, "the association of health with pleasure, even as the latter came to dominate the image of . . . resorts, was a successful and enduring strategy used at all levels of the holiday industry" (Beckerson and Walton 2005: 63). However, the feasibility of this "strategy" was based at least in part on the characteristics of a new consumer audience – namely working people, as well as on the rise of modern psychology, which created a new justification for holiday-making.

The emergence of mass holiday-making and of leisure consumption in general depended primarily on people with free time. Therefore, it is not surprising that mass holiday-making appeared in Western Europe hand in hand with the process of reduction of working time and holiday legislation. Interestingly, starting from the 1870s, one of the central justifications for workers' holidays was the increasing concern about the physical, mental, and emotional consequences of work, such as neurasthenia, overwork, and fatigue – the ancestors of "stress" (Pietikainen 2007; Rabinbach 1992).[6] Indeed, although stressful conditions and threatening events have existed since the dawn of human history, "the general idea that life places difficult demands on individuals, who then succumb under the strain to psychological or biological disease," was a by-product of the nineteenth-century critique of modernity (Abbott 1990: 437). As a consequence, from a diagnosis formerly common for the upper classes, neurasthenia was becoming, in the late nineteenth century, less of an elite disease and rather a cross-class syndrome (Gijswijt-Hofstra 2001; Pietikainen 2007).

A systematic pathological theory of stress began to emerge in the interwar period, and the interest in stress grew after the Second World War (Abbott 1990: 437; Cooper and Dewe 2008; Weber 2010: 2–3). At this point, stress was not merely perceived as one of modernity's malaises, but as a psychological problem that affects mostly working people and requires a solution. In this sense, the popular argument that twentieth-century seaside holiday-making is an outcome of a process through which the former medicinal uses of watering places gave place to a new objective of "mere" recreation, fun, and amusement (e.g., Beckerson and Walton 2005; Cross and Walton 2005; Urry 1990; Weisz 2011), is inaccurate. Once we link the history of tourism to that of psychology it is easy to see that, in fact, the perception of watering places as therapeutic did not vanish. Rather, it was the pathology that changed. As a new pathology emerged – one related to the stressful implications of modernity – a new kind of cure was needed – one concerned with creating a "relaxing" emotional experience.

As tourism was becoming a mass culture practice, this same mass was increasingly exposed to the therapeutic discourse, becoming more and more aware of and preoccupied with emotions. The psychotherapeutic discourse, by simultaneously pathologizing everyday life and offering a supposedly accessible solution, resulted in the democratization of illness and the responsibilization of the individual (Illouz 2008: 38–42; see also Cabanas, this volume). The democratization of both holiday-making and stress, together with the psychotherapeutic message that we all can and should individually regulate our emotions in order to cope with our difficulties, were the strong catalysts for the reinvention of the "therapeutic vacation," now focused on the objective of emotional alternation from stress to relaxation. Nowadays, the emotional significance of tourism is widely acknowledged, as is the place of relaxation as a central motivation for holiday-making: "the most traditional motive for tourism is to take a break from the stress and pressures of everyday life" (World Tourism Organization 2002a: 11; see also Chen 2007; Ibrahim and Gill 2005).

Club Med: relaxation for sale

In 1945, the Belgian government asked businessman Gerald Blitz to administer a rehabilitation center for concentration camp survivors. At that time, Blitz's family was operating a sports club which offered people a short break from their war trauma. Influenced by this concept, and based on "the recuperative power of relaxation, play, and the sun" (Furlough 1993: 66), Blitz established the first *Club Mediterranee* resort in Mallorca, Spain, in the summer of 1950. Following the Mallorca prototype, the Club Med resorts were conceptualized as a closed complex where vacationers were provided with lodging, dinning, and recreational activities with the main characteristic that all of these services were included in a fixed price.

Club Med was founded as a non-profit association, but in 1957 it was reconstituted as a commercial organization. During the 1960s, as its resorts spread through the globe, Club Med became a multinational corporation and a central player in the tourism industry (Furlough 1998). Today, Club Med is described as "an international leisure empire with two billion dollars in annual revenues and has become a template for much of the global North-South tourist industry"

(Lagerquist 2006: 43). Blitz's initiative focused explicitly on the fulfillment of passions, physical pleasure, and escape from routine life. Evidently, from its outset the project had the clear intention of influencing vacationers' emotional state. More than half a century later, this intention is still clearly declared in the company's official website (2015):

> Happiness Maker Since 1950 ... The aim of life is to be happy. The place to be happy is here. The time to be happy is now ... each Gentil Membre (G.M) could find replenishment in contact with nature, sport and others, ensured of the kindness of the Gentils Organisateurs (G.O) and Gentils Employés (G.E).[7] This pioneering idea generated a profoundly human and warm story, an unrivalled territory of values in the tourist industry: conviviality, freedom, creativity, sharing, opening to others, happiness...
>
> (Club Med, n.d.)

Recent reviews by Club Med vacationers reveal that relaxation is one of their major desires, and that in many cases it was achieved. In other words, many customers are supplied with the product of "relaxation":

> "After a Very stressfull year, i have been relaxing And enjoying every minute" (*Liesbeth80*); "We chose the concept because we wanted a completely relaxed holiday, and it did not disappoint" (*DE1966*); "Excellent choice for a relaxing vacation!" (*ivandk*); "I am a stay at home Mom and he is an executive who works very hard so we both needed a break. If you want a place to relax and enjoy while your children are being looked after, this place is great" (*ShaShaShelby*); "We would definately return as we had a fantastic, relaxing and fun holiday there" (*Sarah M*); "It was without a doubt the most relaxing vacation I have ever had" (*Caymus59*).

But what is relaxation, and how it is achieved? In Jacobson's words: "relaxation is the direct negative of nervous excitement. It is the absence of nerve-muscle impulse. More simply said, to be relaxed is the direct physiological opposite of being excited or disturbed" (Jacobson 1976: vi). Physiological jargon aside, relaxation is simply the contrasting emotional state of anxiety, stress, or threat, which is to say that attaining relaxation depends on the cultural definition of stress. If relaxation is the contrasting emotional state of stress, then in order to provide its customers with the product they demand, the industry of relaxing tourism can never rely on a constant strategy; rather, it must constantly identify current stressors and design a way to bounce them. Relaxation is not only demanded by Club Med customers but explicitly acknowledged by the company as one of the main reasons why "people keep coming back to Club Med" (Club Med website). Considering the firm's reputation, and in light of the overwhelming number of reviews which attest that customers did indeed relax, we can conclude that holiday-making at Club Med resorts does produce relaxation. The question is how.

In order to answer this question, I complemented the historical process research presented mostly in the previous sections with text analysis of Club Med vacationers' reviews posted on tripadvisor.com, a website that provides travel advice and rankings of hotels, restaurants, and attractions based on the aggregation of travelers' rankings and reviews. The sample consists of 55 reviews that were analyzed in two stages. First, I randomly sampled 35 reviews of Club Med vacationers. Through this stage I got acquainted with the holiday experience as reflected ex post by vacationers and found that although "happiness" has been the marketing line of Club Med in the last years, the dominant reference was not to happiness, but to relaxation – both as the incentive for holiday-making and as its outcome. Hence, I decided to focus on the emotional experience of relaxation, and conducted, in a second stage, an in-depth analysis of 20 reviews containing the words relaxation or stress and their declensions. I analyzed the content of the reviews based as much as possible on their literal meaning, concentrating on the operationalization of my theoretical variables, that is, identifying which of the vacation characteristics the reviewer links to the experience of relaxation.[8] I focused systematically on patterns and repetitions, and through the comparison between reviews I highlighted common concepts and used all these as the building blocks of my arguments about the general product, considering them independently as well as evaluating them in the light of theory.

Nonetheless, a significant limitation may derive from the potential bias of the sample, as the population is restricted to those vacationers who had the motivation to post their reviews online, as they might share characteristics that can possibly interact with the variables considered in my theoretical model.[9] Moreover, a problem of credibility exists as firms have a clear incentive to manufacture positive reviews for their products and negative reviews for their competitors. This said, the decision to analyze reviews has also significant methodological advantages for the research at stake, and which contribute to the validity of the findings. First, the scope of TripAdvisor enabled me to access data on a quasi-global level, written by users from different nationalities and backgrounds about several Club Med resorts. Second, being the largest travel community on the Web, TripAdvisor applies fraud detection mechanisms to prevent any kind of manipulations and thus justify its reputation and credibility.[10] Finally, although interviews and participant observations may have higher validity, consumer reviews have important benefits for cultural research. They are a voluntary subjective reflection on a specific experience, usually written not long after the events have occurred, which potentially reveal how individuals make sense of their own experiences, including their emotional and moral factors. Reviewers, similarly to interviewees, expose themselves as producers of culture – of meanings, actions, and reactions. Nevertheless, while interviewees are more likely to be affected by the presence of the interviewer and the wording of the questions, reviews are voluntary and therefore less exposed to research-effect bias. It is also worth noting that the sample analyzed here is mainly meant to work in combination with the historical research, as a way of illustration of the argument, rather than as a way to ground it empirically.

Spatial differentiation

Kevin Meethan states that "unlike other cycles of production/consumption, tourism requires people to travel to the point of production in order to consume ... It is people rather than goods which are imported and exported" (Meethan 2006: 2). Indeed, a Club Med holiday takes place usually at an exotic location in a foreign country. Moreover, unlike ordinary hotels which are mainly a base for the tourist to sleep and occasionally eat in, while engaging in tourist activity for the most part outside the hotel, Club Med resorts are "closed spaces, isolated from their surroundings" (Furlough 1998: 279) which vacationers tend not to leave for several days, usually one week. Interestingly, staying in an enclosed and bounded site does not seem to be interpreted as a limitation, but as a condition for freedom.

Spatiality appears in vacationers' reviews first and foremost in marking the resort and the vacation as a different place, different from the "real world" which was left "back home":

> "Perfect escape from reality ... Peaceful resort on beautiful stretch of virgin beach" (*DrYuri*); "I could not believe that when I woke up this morning that I was not there anymore ... it was a bit sad to be back to reality" (*simbenz*); "We loved our stay and came back refreshed" (*DE1966*).

Noticeably, the emotional transformation requires a physical transition from "reality" to "there" – the location of peace and relaxation. Indeed, physical detachment from routine life is noted in Club Med resorts in many ways. Primarily, as has been previously mentioned, the resorts are located in exotic destinations. Second, the resort – and the experience – is defined and differentiated from its surroundings. The mere transition to a different place generates a feeling of change and novelty and opens the opportunity for detachment from one's daily and ordinary identity. In this context, it is clear that the shift in location constitutes an emotional transformation from routine, stressful, urban life to a new emotional repertoire which includes relaxation, pleasure, and rejuvenation. Illouz shows that spatial limits mark the experience, thus many people leave their daily space in order to intensify emotional experience (romantic, in her context) (Illouz 1997: 115). Her argument can be generalized for other emotions experienced while traveling, as Cohen writes:

> Travelling for pleasure ... beyond the boundaries of one's life-space assumes that there is some experience available "out there," which cannot be found within the life-space, and which makes travel worthwhile. A person who finds relief from tensions within his life space, or does not perceive outside its boundaries any attractions the desire for which he cannot also fulfill at home, will not travel for pleasure.

(Cohen 2004: 68)

Illouz and Cohen denote the spatial quality of emotional states, which is the key for understanding the role of spatial differentiation in the production of relaxation. Given that the emotional charge of different physical locations is socially constructed and historically causal,[11] the emotional significance of the resort environment relies on a previous process in which the already steady distinction between natural and urban environments was emotionally reinforced by gradually attributing stress and anxiety to city life (Berghoff 2002; Simmel 2004 [1903]; Urry 1990, 1995).

Indeed, by the first decades of the twentieth century, the problem of stress was characterized spatially. One of the reactions to industrialization and urbanization was the intellectual movement of anti-urbanism, which criticized city life – seen as chaotic and over-stimulating – for its negative physical (e.g., pollution, dirt, noise), social (e.g., alienation, immoral behavior, delinquency), and psychological effects (e.g., anxiety, nervousness, fatigue) (Bailey 1978: 14–15; Berghoff 2002; Simmel 2004 [1903]). Delimiting the negative emotional state to the urban space made physical distancing a logical cure. Certainly, this was encouraged by the growing accessibility of nature, which made detachment from the city more feasible than ever before thanks to technological developments which made it possible to reach distant locations, eased the journey, and made one's stay in a remote country secure. This was also enabled by the qualities of the capitalist work system: not only because of higher incomes, but also due to the new relation (or rather, lack of relation) between the worker and the workplace. Wage labor, working for someone else, and growing specialization – those factors which Marx argued were responsible for the alienation of the worker from his work, his product, and himself – simultaneously enabled the worker's detachment from the workplace (Burkart and Medlik 1974; Marx 2007 [1844]). That is why holiday-making was not possible in pre-industrial societies.

In addition, since the distinction between nature and urban space had been well established by the nineteenth century, the perception of the city as a stressful space stimulated the contrasting notion of nature as the relaxing alternative. Amongst the multitudinous references to the resorts' surroundings, as well as to their internal design, there is a clear linkage between nature aesthetics and the experience of relaxation:

> "It was without a doubt the most relaxing vacation I have ever had. The biggest contributor to the experience was the beach with the most beautiful turquoise water (*Caymus59*); "The hotel is located by the beach in Agadir, and has its own roped off section to relax" (*VeganEater*); "we just enjoyed relaxing by the sea which is beautifully calm and warm, with fish all around your feet" (*Paul C*).

Club Med resorts are located in natural locations (by the sea or up in the mountains), and the physical and marketing design clearly emphasizes their natural image. However, the question is how this "naturality" produces a sense of relaxation for the vacationers. First, nature could not be associated with a positive emotional state if not for the previous historical process which I named "the emotionalization of nature," as a result of which nature is no longer seen as a threatening space, but as an untouched region, standing outside of time and space, an isle of authenticity and simplicity. A second factor is linked to the holiday resort's cultural ancestors: the spa and the health resort. As illustrated above, the operation of these sites was both based on as well as reinforced by a popular faith in the curative potential of nature, and especially water and sun. The decline of their medical credibility did not erase the related symbolical associations, representations, and myths, since "a tourist space represents the projection into space and time of the ideals and myths of the wider society" (Larrinaga 2005: 89). A third source for the notion of Club Med resorts as relaxing is their explicit portrayal as paradise (Furlough 1993, 1998). This is also a spatial quality, since paradise is usually conceived of as an enclosed site with clear boundaries which have the ability to keep out evil (Walton 2005: 182). But like nature, the meaning of paradise has changed over time. Club Med's "paradise" is based on the specific association of paradise with innocence and tranquility and with a space in which sin, stress, and guilt can be set aside (Ibid.: 181). This idea was fueled by the linkage between a longing for lost paradise and the psychological concept of regression which created the interpretation of a virginal nature fantasy as a defense mechanism, enabling anyone to avoid confrontation with situations of threat and anxiety (Furlough 1993: 68, fn8).

Finally, we must remember that Club Med's "naturality" is limited. Club Med's relaxing atmosphere occurs not in wild nature but in a sanitized site free from possible dangers of nature, such as rip currents or malaria. Although reviewers do not question the authenticity of the beach, the gardens, or the breeze, some of them reveal the synthetic nature of this nature (my emphasis):

> "One GREAT thing about Club Med was the fact that *they did spray the 'village' for mosquitoes twice a day*, so our fear of Malaria was set a bit at ease" (*FCaridade*); "*Worried about malaria scares?* We hardly saw a bug at all and were grateful to have not taken the precautionary medicine that could otherwise have made us sick. And the water? *Purified water was available* everywhere you turned" (*TripAdvisor member 3*); "You *will notice people quietly working to keep the grounds neatly trimmed and clean*. I thought it was pretty well looked after and nice to enjoy. *The beach is regularly looked after to remove seaweed* and to keep sand from getting too piled up in any areas" (*ShaShaShelby*).

Blurring of socio-economic aspects

The "physical mold" discussed in the previous section is complemented by emphasizing the differences between the social ambiences of the departure space and the destination space. A second mechanism operating in Club Med resorts to produce relaxation is thus blurring those aspects of daily life which are generally considered stressful, thereby consolidating the emotional antithetical quality of the vacation.

A first feature is the inducement of an inclusive atmosphere in which there are no social boundaries: an ambience of homogeneity and togetherness. If social classes, social roles, and socio-economic competition are regarded as central causes of stress (Abbott 1990; Pearlin 1989), then we can infer that a classless ambience should help to produce relaxation. Since its early years, the atmosphere in Club Med was "focused around an ethic of liberation from social hierarchies, interpersonal and personal constraints, and stuffy bourgeois attitudes" (Furlough 1998: 277). One can notice the various ways in which life at the resort intends to peel off (some) social conventions and boundaries, particularly regarding economic concerns. The "all inclusive" system is of course a major factor which works to blur socio-economic differences between customers, since they all receive the same amenities in return for a fixed price regardless of their social status. Yet, this is just one of many other ways through which signs of status are dimmed during the vacation.

A significant example from the 1950s and 1960s is that vacationers addressed each other by their given names, as opposed to the official way accepted in the workplace or between strangers "back home" (Ibid.: 279). The club's dress code is another example of the loosening of social chains. Furlough notes that a widespread claim was that "there are no social differences when everyone is in a bathing suit" (Furlough 1993: 70), indicating that the dress code during the vacation was indeed evaluated in contrast to daily life and regarded as correlated to social stratification (Furlough 1998). This correlation is also implied today as evident in this review:

> Club Med offered us the opportunity to relax. There was no pressure to get decked out at night. There were a few who dressed to impress, but just a few. Shorts and T-shirts for men and at the most a sundress for women at night with flip flops. Most of the time I wore a mini skirt with a tank top or shorts with a croped top.
>
> (*simbenz*)

In addition to homogeneity and equality, a sense of togetherness is created, for example, through communal sitting in meal time, following the declared ethos stated on the website: "the happiness of living together." Although some reviewers express skepticism about the practice of dining together, in fact those who mentioned it find it to be a good experience:

> "At first, I did not like being seated with strangers, but after a couple of days, we started talking to the people sitting with us and I found it was a great way to meet others" (*MersKouk*); "It was fun sharing a table with people from all over the place" (*fiveinthefamily*); "For all meals, you are seated with different people so it is very easy to get to know other vacationers" (*TripAdvisor member 5*).

The second socio-economic feature is the liberation from money and work, expressed both through the reduction in the vacationer's direct connection with work and money, and in the general concealment of work. The "all inclusive" concept is the clearest feature of the first strategy. Although the concept itself was not created by Club Med but by the British holiday camps in the 1930s, Club Med made the concept internationally popular. In addition, while British holiday camps were not totally "cash-less," in Club Med the objective is to eliminate any "extra charges that can sour the sweetest of vacations" (Issa and Jayawardena 2003: 167). Relaxation is produced, thus, through the abstention from continuous use of money and calculations and through the "all inclusive" philosophy which sanctifies consistency, quality, and "no surprises (unless surprise is part of the program), especially unexpected costs" (Ibid.).

Unlike other forms of tourism, in Club Med the vacationer expects that the crew will take care of everything (Furlough 1993: 71). The correlation of "all inclusive" and relaxation is actually noted explicitly on Club Med's website where the link "All inclusive by Club Med" leads to a new screen in which the headline "It is all included – without the stress" is displayed. Indeed, vacationers' reviews also express the link between the "all inclusive" logic and the relaxing experience:

"We chose club med for a summer Caribbean destination as a way to relax without needing much planning" (*Mike_J1963*); "Most relaxing and stress free holiday ever ... For once not having to think about or pay for anything ... Not having to put our hands in our pockets every time we had a drink or snack at the pool or sign for anything made it a true vacation!" (*Pat N*); "you don't have to worry about getting extra payments" (*coolbs*. My translation from Spanish).

A second way in which the connection to work is diminished is the attempt to release the vacationer from any kind of work, e.g., buying food and cooking, taking care of children, or renting sports equipment. Many of these are seen as part of daily obligations, and are mostly female tasks, and that is why transferring them to the resort's staff serves to mark the division between stressful routine and relaxed vacation (Berghoff 2002: 166–167; Furlough 1998: 271–272).

Babysitter services are mentioned many times in the reviews as one of the essential features for the vacation's success:

"If you want a place to relax and enjoy while your children are being looked after, this place is great" (*ShaShaShelby*); "Punta Cana offers a great kids club (that costs no extra $)" (*fiveinthefamily*); "they took such good care of the kids here, that they weren't screaming in my face during my whole vacation" (*MersKouk*); "The GO's of The babyclub are EXCELLENT! Special Thanks to Them ... You don't need to Bring a luggage full of pampers/babyfood/etc (like i did) They have everything!" (*Liesbeth80*).

The clearest manifestation of the second strategy – hiding the general concept of work – is the resort staff: *Gentils Organisateurs* or GOs. The function of the GOs is a perfect example of Hochschild's (2003) concept of "emotional labor" – they are paid to constantly manage their emotional performance according to Club Med's demands in order to create an agreeable, friendly, and fun ambience for the customers. Emotional labor is significant here in an indirect way, as the GOs' work style essentially blurs the very presence of labor. As Furlough notes, "even the labor of the GOs was constructed so they would not appear to be working, and all reminders of work, such as cooking and service facilities were carefully tucked away from view" (Furlough 1998: 280). All signs of power relations, hierarchy, or exploitation were removed as well: "the 'natives' were not really exploited and workers did not really work" (Ibid.: 282). Reading the reviews one easily notes the tensions in reference to the GOs: between labor and play, hard work and fun, service and friendship:

> "They seemed to be working while playing and playing while working! … They were always available and smiling, even after a long day!" (*Dmam22*); "They are happy, friendly, will say hi around the village and it makes for a nice environment" (*ShaShaShelby*); "Entertainment staff were kind, patient, always with a smile and it was so nice to see that they enjoy their work" (*lazaromy*); "The staff are very friendly and do their best to please you" (*Roger S*); "She will join you for dinner, on the sofa or at the dance floor and will surely make you laugh" (*LisaCorone*); "we felt like we were leaving our family when we left" (*Rob S*); "GOs are friendly and always are keen to make your stay joyful" (*ivandk*).

These aspects of the GOs' working system contribute to the relaxing atmosphere by providing security and confidence for the vacationers and fulfilling their desires behind a smoke screen which helps both to dull flashbacks of the stressful "real world," such as labor and hierarchy, and to avoid the potential awkwardness of being served.

Focus on the individual

The physical (spatial) and cultural (socio-economic) detachment from daily life is especially effective in Club Med vacations because the vacationer is related to as a singular individual. In particular, there are two notable expressions of the emphasis on the individual in Club Med: attention to the individual body, and the active participation of the individual in producing the experience.

A Club Med holiday gives a lot of attention to the body. From the outset, Blitz wished to distinguish his project from previous forms of tourism by creating an *ethos* of satisfaction of physical desires in order to allow the vacationer the opportunity for relaxation, recovery, and recreation. This ethos is expressed in various activities (or non-activities) which are all highlighted in Club Med's advertisement and literature: sports, spa and massage services, yoga, fitness and stretching (classified on the website as "relaxation activities"), and lying on the beach or by the pool. According to a caption from the website, "Club Med will take care of your body in perfect conditions [sic]. Between relaxation and exercise sessions, choose the pace that suits you, to get your fill of well-being during your holiday." For many vacationers, the Club Med experience consists of intensive physical activity in addition to merely lying on the beach. This is mentioned as a way to "*stretch yourself*" (*TripAdvisor member 6*) and to "*come to be active and healthy again, bringing normalcy back to an achy body that's been too long at a desk*" (*COCOFromOttawa*). However, contrary to my expectations, none of the reviews I read made a straightforward link between physical activity and relaxation.

A second example of the way in which Club Med focuses on the individual is its unique expression of individual free choice. "All inclusive, all exclusive, all yours" states one of the captions on the website, emphasizing not only that "all" is yours, but that this "all" is a lot. The company boasts about the diverse range of activities in their resorts and about the culinary variety, and this abundance is reflected again and again in the reviews:

> "There is literally not enough time to do everything there is! Sailing boat, dancing, fitness, meeting great people, you have everything you desire within reach" (*Pascal L*); "As always the activities at the Club Med are the big draw – everything is included" (*pyegirl*); "there are a thousand things to do here – golf/tennis/archery/beach volley/scuba/sailing etc,etc." (*Paul C*); "They have many activities to keep you busy thru the day" (*FCaridade*).

Theoretically, a wide variety like this seems to jeopardize the intention of sparing the tourist irritating decisions and could easily make one more anxious than relaxed (MacCannell 1976: 49; Simmel 2004 [1903]). However, these potential contradictions dissolve if we consider the wider ecology of the vacationer's choice. Everyday decision-making may lead to stress, especially when made under time pressure, based on incomplete information, and considering the opportunity cost (Payne *et al.* 1996). Under the "all inclusive" logic, these three factors are modified: there are no strict deadlines to the decision so there is no significant potential opportunity cost to delaying decisions; all the options are known; and the opportunity cost is reduced since paying the fixed price in advance annuls the uncertainty regarding the "real price" of a specific option, sparing the vacationer the need to compare prices. Furthermore, the option of choosing not to choose and "do nothing" is constantly presented as legitimate, meaning that no pressure is applied on the customer to exhaust all the possibilities.

Club Med literature emphasizes the concept of free choice and asserts that "how you fill your time is your business" (Furlough 1993: 71). This is also reflected in many reviews (my emphasis):

"lots to do *if you want to. You have the option* to join in with sporting activities *or* just lounge by the pool or the beach" (*herstory1*); "Great fun place where *you can do anything you want, or nothing at all*" (*Caymus59*); "so much to do, *or if it is your choice – do nothing!*" (*Schavefamily*); "there are many activities to do ... and *you can choose to just float on your back and nothing more* (*Sebastian L.* My translation from Spanish); "you can relax or party, *it's up to you*" (*MersKouk*).

Finally, the abundance of possibilities and options offered at Club Med counteracts the sensation of homogenization and coercion, transforming the vacation into a self-customized commodity. As mentioned above, one of late capitalism's strengths is its ability to use a standardized industry to produce commodities with endless non-identical reproductions, satisfying the growing expectation of consumers to have unique and singular end products and experiences. By choosing from a variety of options, the Club Med vacationer designs her own singular product/experience, translating the economic activity to a component of her biography, personality, and self-identity. This is also reflected in the words of Sabine Sitruk, one of Club Med's marketing managers, who declared that for the relaunch campaign of Club Med Arziv she "would ask people to tell their personal stories of Arziv" (quoted in Lagerquist 2006: 52).

So far I have demonstrated how relaxation is created at the resort as a result of its physical and symbolical contrast to what is perceived as stressful in daily life. Nonetheless, the issue of singularity exposes an additional mode of production: the customer. Consider for example this review:

> I think the only thing you have to realize is that Club Med is all about trying things, having fun, and not being too serious about it. So if you super serious about any particular activity, this isn't the place to hone that skil.
>
> (*pyegirl*)

These words reflect a mentality of responsibilization, since they ascribe the individual consumer with the responsibility for the content of her experience. In "The Body in Consumer Culture" (1991), Mike Featherstone points to a similar trend in many fitness, health, and leisure industries, highlighting the moral demand which binds individuals with "increasing self-responsibility for their health, body shape and appearance" (Featherstone 2001: 89). The same is true for emotional competence, thanks in particular to both the professional and the popular therapeutic discourse (Cabanas, in this volume; Illouz 2008); and specifically, in literature concerned with stress, as can be seen in this "professional" recommendation to "find ways to stimulate individuals to take care of their own problems" (Elliott and Eisdorfer 1982: 137, quoted in: Abbott 1990: 448).

The moral demand emphasized in the review above can be found in many other reviews, which almost warn potential vacationers that the emotional experience depends on their own collaboration:

"If you are spending time in your room other than to shower and sleep, then you are not there to share the Club Med experience ... If you are willing to meet people, participate in activities, get on the dance floor, etc. then your experience and those of others will make your vacation more rewarding. It is all about you and what you are willing to do" (*Clubmednorm*); "Even if you don't have rhythm, you have to try your hand at the salsa and merengue classes (otherwise you will miss out on some of the evening festivities going on by the bar)" (*TripAdvisor member 3*).

From this perspective, the resort can be regarded as a platform, in the same sense as the word is used to describe an iPhone or a psychotherapy meeting: Club Med provides the consumer with the place and the facilities, but the consumer is expected to take his part in the manufacture of the product. Club Med promises relaxation, happiness, and fun; yet, as we see, the company cannot ensure its supply: that is down to the consumer. This is a clear manifestation of the co-productional characteristic of Emodities, namely that the consumer has an essential role in the process of the production of the object s/he has paid for (Ramirez 1999; Vargo and Lusch 2004). Interestingly, this seems to work against the constant effort to spare the vacationer from work. True, the vacationer does not need to search for attractions, cook, or amuse the children – all this is taken care of by the GOs. The consumer is thus also experiencing a dimension of emotional work (Hochschild 2003).

Conclusion

Before I left I made a 20 second video of the beach on my phone with the sound of the waves. Whenever I get stressed out I play the video, watch and hear the waves, and instantly am transported back to this vacation.

(*P-and-R1976*)

After a number of days, the holiday ends. The vacationers return to their normal lives, to their homes, to their occupations. True, some love their work and see it as their sphere of self-fulfillment and joy, just as some cannot stand the kind of vacation offered in places such as Club Med. Nevertheless, for many, holidays operate as a steam release mechanism which enables them to go back to their stressful routine until the next vacation. Yet, this chapter did not follow the line of critique of tourism as a disciplining tool that "keeps the system going." Instead, it has documented the conditions and techniques required for achieving emotional alternation in holiday-making – a question overlooked so far – showing that it is within the capitalist economy (e.g., the workplace, the tourism industry) that emotions, positive as well as negative, are produced and experienced. Emotional alternation is enabled through a reciprocal process where culture, economy, and emotion shape each other.

The industry, i.e., Club Med, produces an experience of relaxation by reacting to established emotional features of the consumer's daily life. The cultural notions of the capitalistic routine and workplace, and the therapeutic discourse which translated these into emotional and semi-pathological spaces, played a crucial role in the shift of the emotional-motivational core of holiday-making from physical health to emotional alternation, as well as in the process of constituting emotions as exchangeable objects. The generation of a relaxing emotional experience is a reflection of a priori social processes, such as the differentiation between work and leisure, and it is shaped by the cultural meaning attached previously to objects (the use of money is stressful, therefore the all inclusive system is relaxing) and atmospheres (lying on a white sand beach is so relaxing).

Relaxation is proclaimed by Club Med to be a central component of the holiday in its resorts, and vacationers' feedback indicates both that there is indeed a demand for relaxation and that the resorts are able to supply it. This is an essential feature of Emodities. Where in branding emotions are manipulated by the industry strategically, and in the case of affective economy emotions are turned into value (Illouz and Benger 2015), in the case of emotional commodities, as illustrated throughout this book, the emotional experience is consciously demanded by – and actually delivered to the customer (see also Illouz, Introduction to this volume; Schwarz and Gilon, both this volume). It is therefore impossible to evaluate the authenticity of emotions as a category external to capitalism.

Many experience anxiety, boredom, or degradation in their workplace. Many seek relief in their holidays. But the authenticity of the emotional experience does not mean that we should accept it as the right and proper solution to their agony. The general acceptance of the work-vacation-work (or stress-relaxation-stress) cycle is an expression of the tendency of the psychological industry to reconcile some problematic aspects of capitalist society. In this sense, the "professional" advice (e.g., Buettner *et al*. 2011) to go on holiday in order to relax not only bolsters the tourist industry, but preserves the social order, which is at the same time regarded as the source of the "disease."

The popular perception of holiday-making as a necessary break from work, the aim of which is to regain energy in order to cope with routine life again, should raise some critical questions: Are we to accept that it is physicians and psychologists to whom we turn when we suffer in our routine life, and that it is economists and businessman who produce our emotional refuges? Moreover, should we simply accept that for so many people "daily life" is so hard and stressful that they need a holiday at least once a year? This means also accepting that for many people the way to relax includes contributing to pollution by airplanes, adding to the profit of the holiday corporations, and exploiting the population and environment of the destination country. It means overlooking the fact that most people on earth never get the opportunity to "have a break" and relax.

If our emotional fabric is in itself a product of the capitalist culture and industry, then the modern bonding of subjective authenticity and morality must be challenged. The authenticity of emotional experiences should not stop us from questioning, scrutinizing, and criticizing the existing social order.

Notes

1 All reviews are taken from tripadvisor.com website. The reference to the authors is by their user names. The exact wording of the original reviews including spelling mistakes and orthographic errors is preserved. The complete data, consisting of links to the users and their reviews, is available at: http://hdl.handle.net/11858/00-001M-0000-002C-25A6-C.

2 The United Nations World Tourism Organization states that 980 million tourists traveled internationally in 2011 and that tourism is "one of the fastest growing economic sectors in the world" (World Tourism Organization website)

3 For a detailed review of the different definitions of tourism, see Urry, 1990, 1995; Wang 2000; Cohen 2004.

4 Studies of the emotional components of tourism are plentiful, especially from the fields of history, anthropology, and psychology (e.g., Picard and Robinson 2012; Ryan 2002; Ross 1994). Nevertheless, they do not offer a broad social and cultural context to the link between emotions and tourism. Moreover, to the best of my knowledge, they do not conceptualize their founding under theories of commodification. Current marketing and business literature, on the other hand, is deeply concerned with the emotional impact of the tourist industry (e.g., Ibrahim and Gill 2005; Kozak 2006; Krippendorf 1987), but not critically or self-reflectively, in the sociological sense.

5 This is definitely not the case in Chinese culture. For example, as Dan Daor shows, poems describing nature and clearly reflecting its emotional effect on the writer can be traced back to the fifth century. An equivalent style appeared in Europe only with the rise of Romanticism (Daor 2001).

6 In fact, the research and treatment of neurasthenia were an early step in the evolution of psychology as an independent discipline that was in many ways an offspring of neurology and psychiatry (Pietikainen 2007).

7 In the Club Med jargon, GM or Gentil Membre is the vacationer, the customer of Club Med, and the GO or Gentil Organisateur is "the Club Med employee . . . the ambassador of the Club Med spirit and upholds the company's 5 values: kindness, freedom, responsibility, pioneer, multiculturalism" (Club Med website).

8 Albeit the potential contribution of considering the influences of other variables such as gender or class, as this data is not always available, I restricted the analysis to the site (Club Med seaside resorts) and the emotional experience (relaxation, stress). It should be noted that the sample includes both positive and negative reviews.

9 As for the relatively small sample, enough had been written on the limitations of applying statistical standards of generalization for cultural research and on the qualitative alternatives to this issue (e.g., Geertz 1973: 9–10; Illouz 1997: 19; Marshall 1996; Maxwell and Chmiel 2013; Polit and Tatano 2010).

10 A recent study further shows, that a policy of posting manipulative reviews is less likely to be conducted by branded chain companies primarily because of their higher potential damage (Mayzlin *et al.* 2014).

11 These processes are not necessarily correlated, but they might – temporally at least – influence each other. Thus, the evolution of any identified correlation between space and emotion should be examined individually.

Bibliography

Abbott, Andrew. 1990. "Positivism and interpretation in sociology: Lessons for sociologists from the history of stress research." *Sociological Forum* 5(3):435–458.

Adams, Jane M. 2015. *Healing with Water: English Spas and the Water Cure, 1840–1960.* Manchester, UK: Manchester University Press.

Bailey, Peter. 1978. *Leisure and Class in Victorian England: Rational Recreation and the Contest for Control, 1830–1885*. Buffalo, NY: Routledge & Kegan Paul Books.

Beckerson, John and John K. Walton. 2005. "Selling air: Marketing the intangible at British resorts." In *Histories of Tourism: Representation, Identity and Conflict*, edited by John K. Walton, 55–68. Bristol, UK: Channel View Publications.

Bell, Claudia and John Lyall. 2002. *The Accelerated Sublime: Landscape, Tourism and Identity*. Westport, CT: Greenwood Publishing Group.

Benger Alaluf, Yaara. 2017. "The emotional economy of British seaside holiday-making 1870–1918." PhD dissertation, Department of History and Cultural Studies, Free University of Berlin. Manuscript in preparation.

Berghoff, Hartmut. 2002. "From privilege to commodity? Modern tourism and the rise of the consumer society." In *The Making of Modern Tourism: The Cultural History of the British Experience*, 1600–2000, edited by Hartmut Berghoff *et al.*, 159–179. Basingstoke, UK: Palgrave Macmillan.

Buettner, Linda, Mona Shattell and Madeleine Reber. 2011. "Working hard to relax: Improving engagement in leisure time activities for a healthier work-life balance." *Issues in Mental Health Nursing* 32(4):269–270.

Burkart, A. J. and S. Medlik. 1974. *Tourism: Past, Present and Future*. London: William Heinemann.

Chen, Joseph S. 2007. "Wellness tourism: Measuring consumers' quality of life." In *Proceedings of the First Hospitality and Leisure: Business Advances and Applied Research Conference*, edited by Joseph S. Chen *et al.*, 32–38. Lausanne, Switzerland: Ecole Hôtelière de Lausanne.

Club Med. n.d. Retrieved May 15, 2017. (www.clubmedjobs.uscom/knowing-us-better/our-story/happiness-maker-1950).

Cohen, Erik H. 2004. *Contemporary Tourism: Diversity and Change*. Bingley, UK: Emerald Group Publishing.

Coleman, Simon and Mike Crang. 2002. *Tourism: Between Place and Performance*. New York: Berghahn Books.

Cooper, Cary L. and Philip Dewe. 2008. *Stress: A Brief History*. London: John Wiley & Sons.

Corbin, Alain. 1994. *The Lure of the Sea: The Discovery of the Seaside in the Western World, 1750–1840*. Berkeley, CA: University of California Press.

Cross, Gary and John K. Walton. 2005. *The Playful Crowd*. New York: Columbia University Press.

Daor, Dan. 2001. *108 Poems: Anthology of Classical Chinese Poetry*. Tel-Aviv, Israel: Xargol [Hebrew].

Daston, Lorraine. 2004. "Attention and the values of nature in the Enlightenment." In *The Moral Authority of Nature*, edited by Lorraine Daston and Fernando Vidal, 100–126. Chicago, IL: University of Chicago Press.

Featherstone, Mike, 2001. "The body in consumer culture." In *The American Body in Context: An Anthology*, edited by Jessica R. Johnston, 79–102. Wilmington, DE: Scholarly Resources Inc.

Friedberg, Anne. 1993. *Window Shopping: Cinema and the Postmodern*. Berkeley, CA: University of California Press.

Furlough, Ellen. 1993. "Packaging pleasures: Club Mediterranee and French consumer culture, 1950–1968." *French Historical Studies* 18(1):65–81.

Furlough, Ellen 1998. "Making mass vacations: Tourism and consumer culture in France, 1930s to 1970s." *Comparative Studies in Society and History* 40(2): 247–286.

Geertz, Clifford. 1973. *The Interpretation of Cultures: Selected Essays*. New York: Basic Books.

Gijswijt-Hofstra, Marijke and Porter, Roy, eds. 2001. *Cultures of Neurasthenia from Beard to the First World War*. Amsterdam: Rodopi.

Hochschild, Arlie Russell. 2003. *The Managed Heart Commercialization of Human Feeling, Twentieth Anniversary Edition, With a New Afterword*. Berkeley, CA: University of California Press.

Ibrahim, Essam E. and Jacqueline Gill. 2005. "A positioning strategy for a tourist destination, based on analysis of customers' perceptions and satisfactions." *Marketing Intelligence & Planning* 23(2):172–188.

Illouz, Eva. 1997. *Consuming the Romantic Utopia: Love and the Cultural Contradictions of Capitalism*. Berkeley, CA: University of California Press.

Illouz, Eva. 2008. *Saving the Modern Soul: Therapy, Emotions, and the Culture of Self-Help*. Berkeley, CA: University of California Press.

Illouz, Eva and Yaara Benger. 2015. "Emotions and Consumption." In *The Wiley Blackwell Encyclopedia of Consumption and Consumer Studies*, edited by Daniel Cook and J. Michael Ryan, 263–268. London: John Wiley & Sons.

Issa, John J. and Chandana Jayawardena. 2003. "The 'all-inclusive' concept in the Caribbean." *International Journal of Contemporary Hospitality Management* 15(3):167–171.

Jacobson, Edmund. 1976. *You Must Relax*. New York: McGraw-Hill Companies.

Kozak, Metin. 2006. *Progress in Tourism Marketing*. Amsterdam: Elsevier Science.

Krippendorf, Jost. 1987. *The Holiday Makers: Understanding the Impact of Leisure and Travel*. London: Heinemann Educational Books.

Lagerquist, Peter. 2006. "Vacation from history: ethnic cleansing as the Club Med experience." *Journal of Palestine Studies* 36(1):43–53.

Larrinaga, Carlos. 2005. "A century of tourism in Northern Spain: The development of high-quality provision between 1815 and 1914." In *Histories of Tourism: Representation, Identity and Conflict*, edited by John K. Walton, 88–103. Bristol, UK: Channel View Publications.

Lash, Scott and Celia Lury. 2007. *Global Culture Industry: The Mediation of Things*. Cambridge, UK: Polity Press.

MacCannell, Dean. 1976. *The Tourist: A New Theory of the Leisure Class*. Berkeley, CA: University of California Press.

Marshall, Martin N. 1996. "Sampling for qualitative research." *Family Practice* 13(6): 522–526.

Marx, Karl. 2007 [1844]. *Economic and Philosophic Manuscripts of 1844*. Mineola, NY: Dover Publications.

Maxwell, Joseph A. and M. Chmiel. 2013. "Generalization in and from qualitative analysis." In *The SAGE Handbook of Qualitative Data Analysis*, edited by Uwe Flick, 540–553. London: SAGE.

Mayzlin, Dina, Yaniv Dover and Judith Chevalier. 2014. "Promotional reviews: An empirical investigation of online review manipulation." *The American Economic Review* 104(8): 2421–2455.

Meethan, Kevin. 2006. "Introduction: Narratives of place and self." In *Tourism Consumption and Representation: Narratives of Place and Self*, edited by Kevin Meethan *et al.*, 1–23. Cambridge: CABI.

Meller, Helen. 2013. *Leisure and the Changing City 1870–1914*. Oxford, UK: Routledge.

Payne, John W., James R. Bettman and Mary Frances Luce. 1996. "When time is money: Decision behavior under opportunity-cost time pressure." *Organizational Behavior and Human Decision Processes* 66(2):131–152.

Pearlin, Leonard I. 1989. "The sociological study of stress." *Journal of Health and Social Behavior* 30(3):241–256.

Picard, David and Mike Robinson. 2012. *Emotion in Motion: Tourism, Affect and Transformation.* Farnham, UK: Ashgate Publishing.

Pietikainen, Petteri. 2007. *Neurosis and Modernity: The Age of Nervousness in Sweden.* Leiden, The Netherlands: Brill.

Polit, Denise F. and Cheryl Tatano Beck. 2010. "Generalization in quantitative and qualitative research: Myths and strategies." *International Journal of Nursing Studies* 47(11): 1451–1458.

Rabinbach, Anson. 1992. *The Human Motor: Energy, Fatigue, and the Origins of Modernity.* Berkeley, CA: University of California Press.

Ramirez, Rafael. 1999. "Value co-production: Intellectual origins and implications for practice and research." *Strategic Management Journal* 20(1): 49–65.

Ross, Glenn F. 1994. *The Psychology of Tourism.* Melbourne: Hospitality Press

Ryan, Chris. 2002. *The Tourist Experience: A New Introduction.* London: CENGAGE Learning Business Press.

Simmel, Georg. 2004 [1903]. "The Metropolis and Mental Life." In *The City Cultures Reader*, edited by M. Malcolm *et al.*, 12–19. London: Routledge.

Stearns, Peter N. 2001. *Consumerism in World History: The Global Transformation of Desire.* New York: Routledge.

TripAdvisor. Retrieved May 6, 2015 (www.tripadvisor.com).

Urry, John. 1990. *The Tourist Gaze: Leisure and Travel in Contemporary Societies.* London: SAGE Publications.

Urry, John. 1995. *Consuming Places.* New York: Taylor & Francis.

Vargo, Stephen L. and Robert F. Lusch. 2004. "Evolving to a new dominant logic for marketing." *Journal of Marketing* 68(1): 1–17.

Walton, John. K. 2005. "Paradise lost and found: Tourists and expatriates in El Terreno, Palma de Mallorca, from the 1920s to the 1950s." In *Histories of Tourism: Representation, Identity and Conflict* edited by John K. Walton, 179–194. Clevedon, UK: Cromwell Press.

Wang, Ning. 2000. *Tourism and Modernity: A Sociological Analysis.* Amsterdam: Pergamon.

Watson, G. Llewellyn and Joseph P. Kopachevsky. 1994. "Interpretations of tourism as commodity." *Annals of Tourism Research* 21(3):643–660.

Weber, Janice Gauthier G. 2010. *Individual and Family Stress and Crises.* Los Angeles, CA: SAGE Publications.

Weisz, George. 2001. "Spas, mineral waters, and hydrological science in twentieth-century France." *Isis* 92(3):451–483.

Weisz, George. 2011. "Historical reflections on medical travel." *Anthropology & Medicine* 18(1): 137–144.

WTO. 2002a. "World Tourism Organization: Sport and Tourism, Introductory Report." Retrieved May 6, 2016. (http://sete.gr/files/Media/Ebook/110301_Sport%20&%20 Tourism.pdf).

WTO. 2002b. "World Tourism Organization: Why Tourism." Retrieved May 6, 2015. (www2.unwto.org/en/content/why-tourism).

Chapter 2

Emotional ear drops

The music industry and technologies of emotional management

Ori Schwarz

The belief that music has power over our emotions is as at least as old as Aristotle (Politics, 8), and probably even older, and composers have long explored the emotional effects of music and exploited them (DeNora 2000:13); yet for most of human history music was not available for private consumption. Until the emergence of music recording technologies, music was consumed as a social event (the nineteenth-century concert), or accompanied other social events (masses and prayers, weddings and funerals, processions and receptions, public dancing and social drinking; see e.g. Garrioch 2003) which it helped to characterize and bestow the right emotional colouring or 'mood'. It was rarely available to individuals within their private space to shape their individual feelings, their 'inner' world, independently of external events. It was recording technologies that turned music into a 'thing'; but even after the invention of the phonograph, it took some time before consumers got used to collecting records (extending the library model to these new objects) rather than disposing of them after a few listenings (Maisonneuve 2001).

This transformation of music into objects had several consequences. First and most obviously, objectification helped to commodify music: both packaged music as a concrete material object (the record) and the abstract legal rights to play it (on the radio or in public places) have been exchanged for money (for a review see Roy and Dowd 2010: 185–186). Second, objectification encouraged the development of both a collective cannon ('classical' music) and of elaborated personal musical tastes (Maisonneuve 2001), the main research object of the sociology of music. Third, it dissociated music from its context. Evan Eisenberg claims that recorded music technologies are liberal technologies of individual empowerment *par excellence*: they enable individuals to choose freely which music to listen to in their private homes (and since the invention of mobile stereos, even outside them). When Christmas songs can be played at Easter (Eisenberg 2005) and a philharmonic orchestra can squeeze into the tiniest bathroom as a soundtrack to shaving, music listening becomes both *interior design* (choosing the right music to accompany shaving, eating, love-making, house chores, conversations, and many other domestic activities: Eisenberg 2005: 37–38) and *interiority design*, a technique for manipulating one's emotional interiority.

While some attention was given to the ways in which individuals appropriate music in their emotional self-constitution (DeNora 2000; also: Brownlie 2014; Bull 2000; Chen 1998; Juslin and Laukka 2004; Simun 2009), the existing literature fails to associate these everyday micropractices at the individual level with wider cultural transformations and technological developments on which they rely; as well as with wider shifts in the interrelations of capitalism and emotions.

This chapter tells the story of the modern music industry and music consumption from an unusual angle: as the story of the rise of a new set of practices for emotional management, in which music is both produced and consumed as an emodity. Since its very dawn, the record industry has been producing emotions, while its customers have engaged in consuming emotions, using music both to manipulate their pre-existing emotions (that is, as instruments for emotional management) and to indulge hedonistically in bracketed emotional experiences (that is, music as a packaged emotional experience). These new consumption techniques (Schwarz 2013a) did not escape the attention of the music industry, which identified their business potential, encouraged them, catered to them and transformed them.

The chapter offers a genealogical analysis of contemporary practices of music consumption for emotional navigation, exploring their enabling conditions and portraying their evolution, while stressing the constitutive role of the record industry (alongside the electronics and film industries). I will first present my object of study, culturally and historically specific listening techniques, ways of attending to music, and their emergence, while distinguishing my work from both traditional sociology of taste and media psychology research into mood modification. I will then briefly discuss wider cultural trends that enabled the emergence of music listening for emotional management: changes in the cultural understanding of and attitudes towards emotions (their reification and the rise of emotional reflexivity); and earlier models of cultural consumption (emotionalized novel reading). These trends may explain why music consumers used music for emotional consumption, even before the industry encouraged them to do so. I then offer a short historical review of the contribution of the record industry to the emergence of the pharmaceutical usage of music through research, cultural production and marketing. I also address other factors that are likely to have contributed to shaping contemporary emotional listening practices: musical soundtracks in the cinema industry, the invention of mobile stereos and the digitization of music. Finally, I discuss the increasing legitimation of emotional listening, as this practice has moved upward in social space. The analysis mainly relies on reinterpretation of existing literatures, which is supplemented by analysis of mood compilation cover texts, emotional playlists published in popular magazines online and offline, and interviews conducted with radio presenters and music directors.[1]

From the sociology of taste to consumption techniques

In order to understand the music industry as an emotional industry, that is, to study cultural objects as both commodities and affective objects, we must concentrate on *consumption techniques* and *modes of attention* (Schwarz 2013a, 2013b), the practices that produce these effects. Studying the emergence and evolution of these culturally and historically specific practices reveals the link between macro-level analysis of capitalism and micro-sociological analysis of emotions in everyday life.

This focus departs from the main focus of the sociology of music, that is, taste and cultural stratification (e.g. Bennett *et al*. 2009; Bourdieu 1984; Bryson 1996; Peterson and Kern 1996). Music sociology constituted reified tastes (durable preferences for particular genres and performers) as its main object, and has studied their connection to class positions, social identities and cultural identifications. That musical likes and dislikes are shaped by social structures and intergroup relations has been demonstrated by sundry studies. These studies explain tastes (high- or low-brow, omnivore or univore) as shaped by objective life conditions (differential capacities to invest in acquiring exquisite taste: Bourdieu 1984) or stratification from above by cultural producers and mediators (the record industry and music critics: Roy 2004; Roy and Dowd 2010). They explore the role of musical tastes as status cues or identity claims which reflect social position, group membership and collective values of class, ethnic, life-style, sub-culture or age groups, and used in vertical or horizontal distinction (Bennett *et al*. 2009; Bourdieu 1984; Frith 1981; Hebdige 1979; Willis 1978); but also as a factor which creates social identities based on these shared tastes (Negus and Velázquez 2002).

Studying musical stratification has yielded important sociological insights, but this focus has two important drawbacks. First, by assuming that individuals have reified, stable 'tastes' and asking what kinds of people have which kinds of tastes, sociologists are distracted from a no less interesting question, namely, how people make musical choices within the range of their 'taste', that is, to which music they choose to listen in any particular moment, and why. Even worse, the focus on the semiotics of taste, on its role as a readable identity marker, gives the impression that people listen to music *in order* to make identity claims, that is, *that music listening is directed mainly at the ears of others rather than those of the listener.* While taste surely has semiotics, we should avoid the *semiotic fallacy* that reduces the world into a text and human existence into encoding and decoding. This semiotic gaze ignores the world as praxis: people manipulate not only signs and meanings, but also objects and bodies in the world, including their own bodies. Cultural consumption is not merely communicative but also affective. In Michel Foucault's terms, they employ not only 'technologies of sign systems', but also 'technologies of the self' (Foucault 1997: 225). As DeNora (2000) demonstrated, when contemporary individuals choose whether to listen to music and what music to listen to, they take into consideration the effects of music on their body and the ways in which it shapes social interaction, as well as its emotional effects.

However, these are not the effects of music on passive objects, but rather achieved by culturally specific ways of engaging with music. Reifying these culturally and historically specific ways in which people engage with music would allow complementing DeNora's microsociology with a macro-level account of their genesis, transformation and diffusion.

This focus on the historical and cultural specificity of these practices stands in stark contrast with the universalizing interpretation of music psychologists. Psychologists have studied empirically the use of music for mood modification. Unlike 'emotional management', mood modification need not necessarily be conscious. Thus, a study by Knobloch and Zillmann (2002) demonstrated that people tend to choose more energetic and joyful music when they are in a bad mood. Psychologists often understand such preferences to be not only unconscious, but also universal. The classical theory of mood optimization suggested that media consumption is guided by an (often unconscious) effort to improve and balance emotional states (Zillmann 1988). According to this model, people are 'natural hedonists' who naturally seek eternal cheerfulness. However, cultural studies research has identified this emotional style as anything but universal, and highly unique to twentieth-century USA (Kotchemidova 2005). Knobloch (2003) has refined mood optimization theory, suggesting that media consumers are indeed usually motivated by the wish to feel good ('mood enhancement'), but occasionally choose media which might help them prepare for desirable paths of future action ('anticipatory regulation'). Thus, people have different music preferences while preparing to play a game than while preparing to do a work-related task (Knobloch 2003). Similarly, angry men have different media preferences from angry women: since gender norms expect men to assertively demonstrate anger and women to suppress it, men choose media which is likely to intensify their anger, while women prefer media that would soothe it (Knobloch-Westerwick and Alter 2006). While the introduction of cultural expectations and social roles makes Knobloch's later formulation much more sensitive to culture than Zillmann's earlier one, it still implicitly assumes that anyone with access to media technologies will use them for mood enhancement and anticipatory mood regulation. Media usage for mood modification is thus assumed to be determined by universal psychological dispositions and technological affordances. The only 'cultural' factor in the model is the culturally specific emotional scripts to which people try to adapt by unreflexive media consumption choices.

Against this physiological-cum-technological determinism, I suggest that using music to manipulate emotions relies on particular modes of attention to music, and on particular attitudes towards media, emotions and interiority, which have both developed historically. Music listeners are not passive objects on whom music has a pre-determined effect: rather, the embodied mental experience of listeners is shaped by the way in which they attend to music with their bodies and minds. As Merleau-Ponty (2002) has taught us, objects of sensuous attention do not even exist prior to active, embodied attending which constitutes them qua objects, and this insight has enlightened phenomenologically oriented social sciences from

Schutz (1967) to Csordas (2002) and beyond. Even closing one's eyes while listening to music changes both the perceived emotional intensity of the cultural experience and the related brain activity as represented in neuroimaging (Lerner *et al.*, 2009).[2] The mental effect of music depends on the 'technique of art tasting' (Schwarz 2013a) applied by the listener, that is, 'a sequence of actions conducted by the art taster, which directs the operation of her body, mind, and sensuous attention while interacting with the artwork in order to achieve a certain experience, feeling, or understanding' (p.416). James Johnson's historical research attentively portrays the shift from the disengaged music listening practices of Mozart's time, when music was mere decoration or background for social interaction among the elites, to the new norms of Beethoven's time, when holding a conversation during a concert was no longer a socially acceptable option. This new tasting technique consisted of attentive, absorbed (preferably with eyes closed), silent and emotionally involved listening. The new ideal of intensified emotional experience required transformations of every dimension of music listening, including hall design, lighting, the listener's posture, mental attention and decorum (Johnson 1995).[3] This emotional intensification was first restricted to the most sacred music (Beethoven) and should not be confused with contemporary music listening patterns: the romantic concert was a sacred *event*, a spiritual experience, not an aide for mundane emotional management.

It is also important not to study culture consumption techniques in isolation from one another: even genre-specific techniques that may seem extremely different at first glance (blasting punk while whipping one's hair vs. listening to classical music with one's eyes closed) may actually partake in a single cultural ecology and follow a single coherent logic. Thus, throughout this book, we suggest that different kinds of 'cultural' and 'non-cultural' commodities (including different kinds of music) have turned into emodities and are consumed qua emotions or emotional management aides.

Emotional reflexivity

Unlike unconscious emotional modification studied by psychologists, conscious emotional management through cultural consumption assumes the reification of one's 'emotions' or 'mood'[4] and their monitoring: people must first believe they have a specific emotional state or mood at any given moment (not unlike our common belief that we have blood pressure even while not attending to this fact), as an empirical variable which they have privileged access to, and ask themselves rather often what the value of this variable is ('how do I feel?'), and whether and how they want its value to change.[5] In other words, they must develop *emotional reflexivity*: reify emotions and moods and construct them as objects of reflection, monitoring, interpretation and manipulation.[6] This state of emotional reflexivity is indispensable for both modern utilitarian morality (in Bentham's version) which quantifies justice in emotionalized terms of utility qua happiness (cf. Duncan 2007), and for significant trends in psychology which have preached the imperative of being aware of one's emotions as a way towards self-knowledge, self-understanding and self-change.[7]

These significant components of modern culture not only entail the reification of emotions: the very modern notion of emotion which has emerged since the eighteenth century is of an *entity* which is located within us, intimately related to individual uniqueness, identity and moral composure, and yet influenced by certain privileged, sublime objects – music, art and nature – which owe much of their sacred status to their emotional efficacy (Taylor, 1989). However, it may be wise to add a finer distinction between the romantic reification of 'emotions' – or even the psychological reification of the 'emotional core' or subjective 'emotionality' – and the reification of one's 'emotional state', or 'mood': the latter is the ever-changing yet constantly existing adjective of a durable psyche; although changing it is always there. The reification of one's mood (rather than emotions as such) is what makes modern emotionality so susceptible to rationalization and exploitation by capitalist entrepreneurs. This unique modern attitude has influenced cultural production immensely: since the nineteenth century, music, paintings, books and even gardens have been evaluated for their emotional efficacy on the interiority of their consumers (Taylor 1989). The romantic mode of attention engages with these sacred objects *in order* to experience emotions. This sacred romantic model with its unique ontology of emotions was quickly succeeded by a secularized, hedonistic/mechanistic version, represented by the cubist painter Amédée Ozenfant's definition of the work of art as 'a machine for evoking emotions' (quoted in Naegele 1998). Only once music listeners have reified their 'mood' and developed emotional reflexivity can they exercise 'aesthetic agency' (DeNora 2000; or more accurately, 'aesthetic-emotional agency') and manipulate their mood through music.

The culturally specific techniques through which people 'navigate' their emotions have been famously studied by historian William Reddy (2001), who coined the term 'emotives' for the culturally and historically variable vocabularies used to describe, explore, process and mould emotions. Reddy made the strong case that by talking or thinking about emotions or paying attention to them people navigate them, and change them in culturally patterned desired (and incidentally unintended and undesired) directions. My intention is to expand Reddy's discussion to the use of non-verbal technologies for the navigation of emotions. The consumption of music for emotional navigation is inseparably intertwined with culturally specific models and vocabularies of emotionality, but also with the materiality of music and recorded music technologies. This is where the sociology of culture should follow Bruno Latour and retreat from the vain attempt to purify the symbolic realm of culture from any trace of the material world.

This modern technique – the consumption of music for its emotional effect – follows in the footsteps of an older cultural model: that of reading fictional literature. Early modern female fiction readers were the first to entrust their emotions to cultural objects through their individualistic consumption. Private, silent reading, in which a single reader immerses herself in reading and 'gets lost in a book', is an emphatically modern phenomenon. Its first carriers were female readers of fiction novels. Some scholars (e.g. Chartier 1994; Spacks 2003) date this as early as the sixteenth or even late fifteenth century, while others (e.g. Jagodzinski 1999; Saenger 1997) date it as late as the eighteenth century; however, by the time the phonograph had been invented, this modern reading practice had already reached its zenith. Private reading was initially considered a public threat, precisely because of its alleged emotional, moral, physiological, mental and sexual influence on readers. Readers were believed to be passive and vulnerable vis-à-vis the power of the text to allure them (Young 2008): literary texts were believed to have strong intellectual and emotional effects (Chartier 1994), spiritual as well as somatic (e.g. moving readers to sobs: Taylor 1989: 295). Books allegedly caused readers to withdraw from the world and abandon themselves in reveries. Beyond their transient emotional effects, books were also believed to foster sensibility and emotional refinement (which were highly valued in the late eighteenth century), that is, to hone the readers' emotional core. Reading novels entailed both fostering intimacy and empathy (with the protagonist) and emotional engrossment (Wittmann 1999). Books were believed to be so suggestive they could lead readers to end their lives (as in the famous case of Goethe's Werther). Early modern fiction reading was thus a powerful emotional technology.

However, the length and complexity of novels rendered the emotional experience of reading fiction significantly different from that of listening to recorded music. Reading a novel meant diving into a parallel world, rich in *multiple* emotions that succeeded one another throughout the novel. Similarly, the structure of classical musical forms such as the sonata, the concerto and the symphony is based on changes in mood and pace between the movements (an allegro followed by an adagio or a largo, etc.). This is still very different from the consumption of emotionally uniform musical units for the creation of a planned, desired effect, which is typical of much contemporary music consumption. When and how did this transformation take place? Answering this question requires shifting our attention from individual consumers towards the record industry.

Edison's mission

In 1921, Thomas Edison announced an experimental programme to record music which would engender 'moods'. To realize this goal, Thomas A. Edison, Inc. contracted a team of psychologists who conducted listening experiments with hundreds of participants and a survey among 2,644 American phonograph users, and consequently developed a classification system that classified Edison records into 12 categories according to the emotions they induced: records bringing 'joy' or 'wistfulness', 'true devotion' or 'love'. The explicit goal of the team was to teach Edison how to produce emodities – records that would push the right emotional buttons in order to stimulate these emotions (Kenney 1999). The explicit motivation was the belief that 'best sellers are the selections that exert the strongest effects on the emotions, mood and actions of the listener'. Thus, similar to the case of horror films (Gilon, this volume), expert knowledge and market research played a key role in the emergence of emodities.

The team, led by Carnegie psychologist Dr Walter Bingham, used 589 different recordings in their experiments. Subjects were asked to document their mood on 'Mood-Change Chart' forms, before and after listening to a selected piece (Selfridge-Field 1997). Of these, 135 recordings were found to have an intense and uniform effect on all listeners (Wheeler 1927). These patterned, uniform reactions to music were interpreted as a business opportunity to capitalize on music's emotional efficacy by consciously offering for sale packaged emotional experiences.

Bingham defined his goal as 'bringing the public to . . . want these emotional effects of music which Mr Edison has made accessible to them', while vice president William Maxwell stated that his goal was to 'thoroughly sell the idea that the big thing about music is how it makes you feel' (Selfridge-Field 1997: 297–298).

The 1921 survey data on actual patterns of phonograph use showed that by that time, many Americans were already using the phonograph for emotional management before being seduced into doing so by the industry. However, their mood management mainly took place at the family level: music served for the design of *emotional atmospheres*, rather than for the consumption of personal, internal emotional experiences. Thus, many female respondents reported using the phonograph when someone was blue or when family relations became brittle in the afternoon hours: upon playing a merry song, 'at once everybody smiles and the white flag waves' (Kenney 1999: 11). Women also used recorded music to soothe their tired mates by playing calming or uplifting records, in a modern take on the piano-playing 'angel of the household' (Ibid).[8] Yet, using phonographs as technological aides for female domestic emotional work is still remote from the emotional navigation practices that Bingham envisaged or those DeNora (2000) explored.

Bingham was not the first to classify short musical pieces based on their 'mood': the film industry had started employing a similar classification system a few years earlier, offering another cultural model for emotional listening.[9] In 1912, Max Winkler, a clerk who sold sheet music in the shop of a large New York publishing house, contacted Universal Studio, offering them his new invention: cue sheets. These were instructions for film theatre musicians, aimed at assisting them to avoid emotional mismatches between the visual and the music. The idea was simple: Winkler knew that in sheet music catalogues (such as the catalogues of his employer) there was 'music for every mood'. He scanned catalogues and sorted pieces and excerpts according to their moods (sinister, chase, sad, mysterious, furious, majestic) in order to wed them to silent films, without hesitating to tear emotionally uniform excerpts out of their original, organic context within sacred classical musical pieces. As early as 1915, Winkler's invention was used commercially (Cooke 2010; Frith 1984; Wierzbicki 2009). Bingham's mission was to offer families emotionally laden soundtracks to accompany their everyday lives, beyond the circumscribed screening event, thus enabling them to develop new modes of aesthetic-emotional agency.

In a *Popular Science* story from 1927 the author tells about his friend who used Bingham's classification system in order to choose the right music depending on the desired emotional effect: uplifting, soothing anxiety, etc. (Wheeler 1927). However, the 1921 survey is significant not for its direct impact on listening patterns (Wheeler's friend was idiosyncratic in using music pharmaceutically in such a conscious manner), but rather in showing that these new uses started to develop 'from below' quite early, and that the emerging industry was aware of them and looked for ways to foster them, capitalize on them and cater to them.

The record industry has further elaborated its ways of capitalizing on the potential of music for emotional management since the 1950s by offering mood compilations. Unlike earlier compilations (which usually celebrated the anniversary of a single composer: Maisonneuve 2001), these later LP compilations were playlists characterized by their consistent emotional tone and marketed as emodities. These compilations have been explicitly marketed and consumed as 'legal mood-manipulators' (DeNora 2000), organizing music around emotional themes such as 'relaxation', 'romance', 'nostalgia' and 'melancholy'. Unlike most classical pieces (and rock albums), they contain no shifts between different tempos, moods and emotions through the album. These music compilations also differ from mood music used in the film industry or played as Muzak in shops and restaurants, since they were addressed at individual subjects who have *consciously chosen* to consume music in order to express or manipulate their emotions, rather than being manipulated by others through the unconscious influence of music.

The language used in the marketing of early mood compilations is very revealing indeed. The first mood compilations were Jackie Gleason's instrumental LPs, printed in the 1950s in the US (Lanza 2004) with titles such as 'Music for Lovers Only', 'Lonesome Echo' or 'Music to Make You Misty'. Gleason's albums immediately became bestsellers ('Music for Lovers Only' remained on Billboard's Top 10 Chart for a record period of almost three years). These compilations were accompanied by listening instructions, such as 'This is the music that says relax . . . close your eyes . . . remember . . .'; these are the words printed on the back cover of Lonesome Echo, a formulation that reminded music historian Joseph Lanza (2004:7 6) of 'advice from a sound psychoanalyst'. This comparison is noteworthy: processing emotions, absorption in reflection and emotional management are at the core of what psychology offers its customers. The compilation is explicitly offered as an aide in techniques of mood management, mixing therapeutic undertones with promises of hedonistic indulgence in desired feelings. The back cover text further describes the album as having a 'nostalgic, lonely quality' and haunting melancholy thoughtfully achieved by the arrangements. Similarly, the cover of 'Music to Make You Misty' promises it 'can evoke sentimental memories', and 'bring back the tender moments of *everyone's* romance' (emphasis added). Not only did Capitol Records sell emotions and memories, it guaranteed universal efficacy. This is an emphatically pharmaceutical use (and marketing) of music.

While these two albums were explicitly offered for lonesome men who wish to 'evoke' sentimental emotions and the memories of their beloved girls, or indulge in reminiscence, 'Music for Lovers Only' was explicitly aimed at couples, and promised to function as a part of 'love's entrancing setting', together with soft lights, the tinkle of glasses and hushed whisper – a 'sentimental music for your most relaxed listening moments'. While the first two albums are pharmaceutical (aimed to work upon the individual psyche), the third is aimed at shaping interpersonal interaction, like other commodities used for the socioemotional construction of 'romance' (Illouz 1997). While Gleason's target audience was mainly men, DeNora (2000) demonstrates it is often women who prefer to play soft, sentimental music in intimate interactions, not only to imbue them with romance and sentimentality but also to orchestrate and slow down the interactions.

A straight line connects Edison Inc.'s mission of making the public 'want these emotional effects of music' and the marketing language of Jackie Gleason's back covers: the attempts by the industry to capitalize on the power of music to work on the emotional interiority of the listener or to design an emotional atmosphere with a benevolent influence on social interaction. Mood compilations have been produced ever since (a prominent example would be K-Tel's mood compilations, which included remakes of hit ballads and were a commercial success in 1970s Europe). The major record labels today still offer post-breakup compilations, sad songs compilations, music for relaxation, love music and so on. While the popularity of mood compilations has subsided, emotional and therapeutic music consumption has spilled over beyond the boundary of the genre. Here I mean not only the emergence of new therapeutic genres, most prominently popular new-age 'music for relaxation' which emerged in the 1980s, with its slow, repetitive music, the texture of which consists of nature sounds (dolphins, songbirds, ocean waves, babbling brooks), synthesized sounds and East-Asian motifs. More significant is the emotionalization of music consumption at large due to socio-cultural changes in consumption techniques and modes of attention to music, which is the topic of the next section.

Playlist medicine becoming obvious

When first offered by Bingham in the 1920s, the pharmaceutical usage of music to optimize mood with its scientific pretensions was hardly more than a curiosity. Ninety years later, however, it has become a viable cultural option. In 2012 Columbia psychiatrist Galina Mindlin co-authored a self-help book entitled *Your Playlist Can Change Your Life*. The book's main argument is that by carefully identifying one's emotional needs and catering for them with the right playlist, people can avoid self-destruction, improve their mood, and get over anxieties and crises. By using music wisely, the authors maintain, people can regulate the levels of dopamine and other chemicals in their brain. All we need to do in order to benefit from this 'playlist medicine' (as they call it) is diagnose our needs and carefully select the right songs in the right order. Readers are advised to improve a mildly low mood by moving in small steps, with each song merrier than the last; to listen to cathartic music to cope with the pain of loss; to use particular soothing tracks to expel anxiety; to listen to funny children's songs after a romantic break-up; and to use fast dance music to promote the release of endorphins and experience pleasure without resorting to self-destruction, or to mitigate a sudden drop in dopamine levels which may lead to irresponsible behaviour. Readers are warned that listening to their regular morning playlist after a quarrel with their partner, or listening to romantic music after a break-up, may have significant negative implications on their emotional and mental well-being (Mindlin *et al.* 2012).[10] The book received some media attention, including an item on NBC's *Today's Show* and a review in the *Los Angeles Times*. It did not become a bestseller, but unlike Bingham's pharmaceutical classification, it did not seem extraordinary to readers. While a few readers praised the book in their Amazon reviews, one disappointed reader commented: 'I did not learn too much new that did not seem obvious to me before I read the book'.

The research literature offers more indications that while most readers may be unfamiliar with the quasi-scientific language of 'dopamine levels' and 'endorphins drop', they might have engaged in some practices similar to those Mindlin preaches. Evan Eisenberg suggested as early as 1987 that 'amateurs of the phonograph know well the art of matching music to a mood' (Eisenberg 2005 [1987]: 157), and offered a helpful distinction between two common strategies of emotional management, *Platonic sympathy* and *Aristotelian catharsis*. In the former, the listener selects music characterized by a different mood than her own (calmer or merrier) in order to assimilate her internal mood to that of the external music. In the latter, the listener chooses music that *expresses* her negative feelings (such as rock music while feeling anger, blues while feeling sad, or jazz for melancholy). Listening then expels these emotions by giving them objective existence external to the listener, and the listener is purified.

More recent studies show that American students use music to improve their mood and expel negative emotions, avoid feeling lonely, change energy levels, experience excitement and enhance feelings they already feel (Chen 1998; Wells 1990). Mobile stereos make these strategies constantly available, promoting a 'pattern of uninhibited effort to gratify emotional needs' (Chen 1998: 257). In a questionnaire study among adult Swedish music listeners, 47 per cent reported listening to music 'to express, release, and influence emotions', and 33 per cent to 'relax and settle down'. They reported that experiencing emotions to music is more typical of listening alone than of social listening (Juslin and Laukka 2004). The most thorough account of music's pragmatic roles in everyday life is offered by sociologist Tia DeNora (2000), who meticulously portrays the multiple self-regulatory techniques through which her interviewees manage and express their emotions, and shape the emotional atmospheres in which they interact with others. They report listening to aggressive music (such as punk-rock) or to very loud music in order to 'vent' anger and cope with aggression; choosing the right music to promote romantic intimacy in an evening with a partner; and generally reflectively choosing the music they believe they 'need' in terms of energy level and emotional colouring (ibid. Also see Brownlie 2014: 163ff.). Thus, while mood compilations have diminished in popularity since the 1950s, the pharmaceutical attitude to music listening promoted by Gleason's back covers has extended way beyond the limits of the genre. But why?

The remaining pages of this chapter are dedicated to four technological and cultural factors which may explain this cultural transformation in modes of attention to music and listening techniques: the cinema soundtrack, the mobile stereo, the digitization of music and the secularization of music listening.

Mundane soundtracks

Background music plays a crucial role in films from a very early stage. The lives of film characters are almost constantly accompanied by music. As sociomusicologist Simon Frith remarks, this background music is not realistic, yet 'audiences take it for granted that strings accompany a clinch. Indeed, a clinch without strings may seem less real, though another film convention is to climax a sex scene with silence – as if to register its "privacy"' (Frith 1984: 83). The role of film music ever since the silent film era is to fix the emotional meaning of an often polysemic visual narrative. Film music, as Frith suggests, makes the invisible reality audible, conveying and clarifying 'the emotional significance of a scene, the true, "real" feelings of the characters involved in it'. In this sense, its role is similar to that of the omniscient narrator in a novel: it gives viewers access to the interiority of the characters, to the emotional dimension of their subjectivity, and fosters emotional identification of the viewers with the characters. Contemporary filmmakers not only rely on a stabilized repertoire of musical cues to evoke emotions such as suspense and serenity, fear and joy but also use popular songs to accompany different scenes. The pattern of background music which expresses the interiority and the emotional colouring of the interaction is to a high degree a cinematic pattern which has been carried over into everyday life. However, this only happened at a later stage, as indicated by DeNora's data: unlike her younger interviewees, her older interviewees hardly ever listen to music while doing something else, as an emotionally charged background.

Michael Bull's studies (Bull 2000, 2007, 2012) show that personal stereo users often understand their music as the 'soundtrack' of their lives (an expression they repeated often), which awards their lives with a cinematic aura ('It's sort of like making my life a film. Like you have the sound, the soundtrack in the back': Bull 2000: 91). This soundtrack transforms movement through the urban space, as 'the street becomes a function of their mood and imagination mediated through the iPod'. IPod users listen to music which expresses their emotions and experience the urban landscape itself as the externalization of their subjective emotions (Bull 2012: 533–534). However, the 'soundtrack' metaphor is not restricted to the isolated experience of the headphones-wearing late-modern flâneur: it is often used by people to describe the music accompanying their everyday interactions, such as love-making (e.g. DeNora 2000: 117). Here the choice of soundtrack expresses emotions (telling the interaction partner what I feel), but also 'navigates' emotions (in Reddy's sense of the word, as any expression of emotions is likely to transform them, not merely verbal ones), enhances them and manipulates them, as people are not merely the protagonists of their lives, but their directors as well. While Frith claimed that the soundtrack is 'non-realist', reality may gradually align with representation, particularly with the norm of expressing interior emotions through external background music. The affordances of the technologies discussed later made this alignment possible, and even easy.

Out of context

While the first American gramophone owners used them mainly for collective listening and for mood management at the level of the family, later generations have increasingly engaged in emotional management at the level of the individual. This trend was fostered by technological developments. Two such developments in particular deserve our attention: the personal stereo ('Walkman'), marketed since 1979; and the MP3 digital encoding format for digital compression of music (developed in the early 1990s, and incorporated into digital stereos since 1998). These two technologies have liberated listening from two contexts that used to shape it: the spatial context and the context of the pre-sequenced album.

Personal stereos enable their users to withdraw sonically from the physical spaces they inhabit, thus bringing music listening closer to the private, isolated withdrawal from the world into an internal parallel world traditionally associated with reading. It is used mainly in public spaces such as streets and public transport. With personal stereos, emotional management has gone mobile, and unwanted feelings can be fended off on the move. 'Personal stereos are mood managers that minimize the contingency of users' thoughts, moods and emotions' (Bull 2000: 189), as commuters gain control over their auditory environment and, consequently, over their interiority and emotionality. They are protected from both external sonic intrusions and internal unwanted feelings, which can be pushed away with music (Bull 2000: 192). At will, they select music which is in harmony with their internal feelings (Bull 2012: 533); at will they engage in emotional management, e.g. to stop feeling depressed (Bull 2000: 33). As Bull's and Chen's (1998) works demonstrate, with the rise of personal stereos, having a personal soundtrack becomes the default, and hence emotional management turns into a mundane experience.

However, the material affordances of the analogue Walkman render it still a limited tool for emotional management: first, data is cumbersome, hence users must plan which albums to take before hitting the road. Even worse, analogue data is organized into pre-programmed sequences, 'albums', which are often emotionally diverse. Indeed, the music industry catered for the need for emotional management by producing emotionally consistent albums (mood compilations and others).

However, the digitization of music has paved the way for a significant change in the ways music is consumed, as it has liberated tracks for the first time from the context of the album (be it an original album or a compilation). First, it allows users to constantly carry their whole music library, where they can find a song that will precisely fit each mood or emotional need. Thus, for a London-based 38-year-old recruitment consultant, the MP3 player is 'more personal' since 'I've got loads and loads [of music on my MP3 player], whatever I want to listen to, whatever mood I'm in, whatever I want to do' (Simun 2009: 922). Similarly, a 20-year-old MP3 player user claimed that:

> [y]ou need to have music to fit all of your moods ... I can use it cathartically, so if I want to think about a relationship, I can choose music that will remind me of that and it will bring out emotion ... you can psyche yourself up for things.
>
> (Ibid: 924)

Furthermore, just as the personal stereo had liberated individual music listeners from their spatial and sonic contexts, digitization has liberated the individual track from its sequential context. Unlike analogue data, digital data is organized in paradigmatic databases ('folders') rather than syntagmatic narratives (Manovich 2001). Digital tracks are stored on computer drives and digital players, where users are free to organize and re-organize them into categories as they wish. Admittedly, users often tend to avoid spending unnecessary time on classification, and have a folder for each album. Yet classification systems may be highly personal and idiosyncratic, and the literature suggests that emotional mood is one of the criteria used to organize personal music libraries. When users classify songs into folders such as 'sad', 'I hate men' or 'feel good' (Bentley *et al.* 2006; cf. Kim and Belkin 2002), they actually compile their own private version of Winkler's or Bingham's mood classifications, which enable them to engage in emotional, pharmaceutical consumption of music. They also use the same methods Winkler used: bracketing songs out of their original context.

Not only can users flexibly organize tracks of various artists in unordered folders, they may also control the sequence in which they are played, creating DIY ordered playlists which may be disposed of after a single use or saved for future use.[11] Thus, a London-based student told Miriam Simun in a research interview that she loves her iPod because she 'can customize my playlist ... I can say, hmmm, none of the playlists are doing it for me, I'll make one'. Even more than folders, playlists are often organized based on their emotional efficacy, turning into DIY mood compilations. This is the 'playlist medicine' preached by Mindlin and her collaborators which was considered 'obvious' by their Amazon reviewer. And indeed, 'playlist medicine' prescriptions can be found in magazines of all kinds, which offer their readers suggested playlists for emotional management. A particularly popular genre of playlists is prescribed for coping with divorce or emotional break-up. Such playlists have been offered over the last few years in magazines as diverse as *Cosmopolitan, TimeOut New York*, the *Huffington Post* and *Seventeen*. These lists all participate in the emotion economy: musical prescriptions for emotional management, like all content published in magazines, enable magazines to attract a readership who may be sold to advertisers (Smythe 1994), and (if reading offline) pay for their copies. These playlists may also assist the marketing efforts of the music industry, either indirectly (by accentuating the emotional use value of its products) or directly: one of the break-up playlists on the *Cosmopolitan* websites went as far as accompanying each and every song on the playlist with a link to buy the song as a digital file from the virtual shop iTunes. Online radio channels which specialize in music for selected moods are another way in which late capitalism tries to capitalize on the demand for music for emotional consumption.

Break-up and divorce playlists promise to help users cope with negative emotions such as sadness, anger and pain, and to achieve empowerment and emotional resilience, while echoing the therapeutic discourse of the psy-experts. Thus, one list offered different songs for each one of the stages of grief: that is, different songs for the denial stage, the anger stage, sad songs for the depression stage, and eventually 'healing music good for the acceptance stage'. Similar playlists are offered by magazines for romance, love-making and other emotionally laden situations. The fact that alongside the playlists offered on magazines there are many similar DIY playlists published online by ordinary people demonstrates how popular the practice of emotional management through music has become.

Users of music in digital formats do not always pay for the music which they listen to, yet their consumption is usually embedded in the market economy (e.g. by listening to music, including self-made playlists, on ad-supported websites; or by buying digital players to support their emotional management needs). Some of Simun's interviewees have shown little interest in the music in itself beyond its role as an effect inducer: their music consumption was mainly a tool for emotional management. Discrepancies between one's emotional repertoire and one's music collection further intensify consumption of new music: 'Because you need to have music to fit all of your moods, you identify holes in your music collection' (Simun 2009: 935). Compared with Gleason's audience, the readers of Mindlin and the interviewees of Simun, Chen and Bull are active *prosumers*: the music files they buy (or download illegally) are only the raw materials they use for their active engagement with sophisticated emotional management techniques, comparable with raw food products bought at the supermarket for cooking. Magazines offer useful playlists just as they offer their readers recipes, yet savvy home cooks often appropriate these recipes by improvising upon them, creating their own personal versions. The emotional efficacy of music is a main motor of consumption, yet emotional consumption is not fully or even mostly orchestrated by the industry, and takes place even where the industry cannot capitalize on it. The music industry's product is no longer 'albums' (a finished product) but rather tracks, raw materials for emotional management and other demonstrations of aesthetic-emotional agency.

Adorno's scorn

The philosopher Theodor Adorno did not think highly of emotional listeners. In his typology of listeners, the practices of the 'emotional listener' are minutely portrayed in order to condemn them (Adorno 1976, 1990). The 'emotional listener' employs both of Eisenberg's methods: Platonic sympathy (changing one's original emotional state through identification with emotions that originate in the music) and Aristotelian catharsis. For Adorno, this 'catharsis for the masses' (Adorno 1990: 314) is artistically unrespectable and politically debilitating (through emotional listening, music listeners are distracted from their own alienation and become addicted to gratifications). Listening of this kind is typically exercised by those actors who lack the education required to understand music and its formal structure: Adorno associated this low-brow listening style which emerged in late Romanticism with the working-classes, women and the Slavic peoples, the most naïve and sentimental listeners who could not distinguish high art from kitsch. Middle-class Western European men knew better how music should be listened to. Adorno even pathologized emotional listening, suggesting it might attest to psychological deficits. While some of Adorno's formulations emerge from his unique philosophy, his general negative sentiments towards emotional listening were shared by many members of his class and generation. Like Adorno, they often felt that artistic music was too sacred to serve the economy of drives (*Triebökonomie*).

His scornful remarks may surprise contemporary readers, not only for their elitist, anti-democratic tone, but also since the practice of emotional listening has since been universalized, and gained ground among wider gender, class, age, ethnic and education groups. Although genre hierarchies still rely on their degree of corporeality, that is, the immediacy of their effect on the consumer's body (Dyer 1985), today 'high art', like lower genres, is also expected to excite and stir emotions: as Linda Williams claims, since Turner's time 'commodified images and high art both seduce and excite the body – though in different ways' (Williams 1995; cf. Gomart and Hennion 1999). The social agents most associated with this transformation are the new, creative middle classes with their hedonistic ethic of experience (Bourdieu 1984: 365ff.), those most close to Bauman's post-modern ideal type of the 'sensation gatherer' (Bauman 1995). In late capitalism, as many commodities are re-conceptualized in terms of experiences (cf. Pine and Gilmore 1999), the value of high art is also re-conceptualized in terms of its experiential and emotional effects on the bodies and souls of art consumers. Mood compilations or new-age music for relaxation did not challenge the cultural hierarchies: these have always been 'low' genres with no pretensions, far removed from the consecrated classical, jazz or even rock genres. Much more interesting is the evidence for the growing emotionalization of listening to high genres, which Adorno associated with 'higher' listening styles. The legitimacy of the consumption of emotions qua art has increased, even – and maybe especially – among the elites.

DeNora notes that while her younger interviewees often used music in their everyday life, to most of the respondents over seventy and to those who were professionally trained musicians, the idea of music as 'background' to nearly any-thing was antithetical. Music is something one either makes or listens to intently. For example, Eleanor (born ca. 1922), a church organist and highly active ama-teur musician, describes how she would *never* attempt to listen to music if she were doing paperwork, studying chess or otherwise needing to concentrate:

> No. Because the music I have is not background music, the music that I love is something that is wonderful to me, you know, and when I listen to music I listen to the music and, well, I might sometimes put it on in breakfast time but then I can't really concentrate. I use the time during breakfast time doing two crossword puzzles, two cryptograms. It gets my brain going [laughs].
>
> (DeNora 2000: 61)

However, there is evidence that for younger people, formal musical education does not preclude emotional listening – on the contrary. A study in Serbia sug-gests that music academy graduates and students are *more* likely to choose which music to listen to according to their mood rather than the event. They are more likely to fit classical music to their mood than non-musicians of their age group are likely to fit pop music to their emotional state (Prnjat 2010).[12] These are no longer the abstract, pure, disinterested and supra-individual emotions associated with noble music in the tradition of Kant and Schopenhauer. Uses of music which were sacrilegious for Adorno and for DeNora's older interviewees may now be considered evidence for the quality of music, hinting at a transformation of the criteria used for aesthetic evaluation.

This shift may shed light on a recent trend widely discussed in cultural soci-ology, that is, the (alleged) shift from distinction to cultural omnivorousness (e.g. Bryson 1996; Erickson 1996; Peterson and Kern 1996; Warde *et al.* 1999). The shift of the educated strata from Adorno's cerebral 'expert' or 'good' listen-ing to sacred pieces into a more experience-driven listening aimed at emotional management might have contributed to the shift from distinction to omnivorous-ness. We may speculate that the music listening patterns of the dominant classes might have become less directed at the public demonstration of social identity and distinction as suggested by Bourdieu (1984), and more at subjectively feeling different emotions (possibly including social distinction), that is, at the care of the self and its emotional management. If this hypothesis is correct, then music consumption instantiates a wider shift from prestige economy to narcissistic consumption (Featherstone 2007: 27).

The interviews I conducted with Israeli radio presenters and music directors may also indicate that Prnjat's findings apply more generally, and that emotional management is no longer contrasted with musical and general education. Boaz Cohen, presenter of a personal programme at the middle-high-brow state-owned Israeli station 88fm, stressed the emotional and therapeutic value of his program for his audience: listeners want the music to 'comfort' and 'envelope' them, and give them 'strength to get through the day'. For him, success means 'moving' listeners with the music he chooses to play, while the professional challenge of creating a playlist for a program lies in weaving together songs from different countries and styles into 'a single statement that makes sense, and also creates a mood'. During each program he attempts to gradually raise the listeners' energy level and mood, arriving at a peak and then landing softly.[13] By contrast, Dandan Matyuk, music director at Israel's most popular radio station, stressed different professional guidelines: each 'snapshot' of 3–4 songs in a row should be representative of the diversity of the whole station, each song addressing a different segment of the audience in terms of age and cultural capital. Diversity of mood is also desired in order to cater for the broadest audience possible. He claims that listeners are so accustomed to this diversity that playing a few quiet songs in a row makes listeners call in to ask whether something terrible, such as a terror attack, has occurred. These two very different attitudes towards the emotionality of music demonstrate that emotional listeners are no longer mainly low-brow. Eventually, high-brow cultural mediators and consumers have come to understand music consumption as revolving around the care of one's emotions. As this cultural consumption technique moves upwards in the social space, it changes its social meaning in terms of distinction.

Emotional listening as a mode of attention to music or consumption technique has changed its status considerably from a stigmatized technique into a hegemonic practice legitimized by cultural elites. In Bourdieu's terms, it shifted beyond large-scale production into the prestigious field of restricted production. Taking music *seriously* now means attending to it emotionally and using it for emotional navigation. This legitimation of formerly sacrilegious pharmaceutical listening reflects a wider cultural transformation in the attitude towards emotions in general, the rise of a new emotional habitus,[14] which capitalism has both encouraged and exploited. Music as both a sacred art and an industry branch was re-conceptualized around the production of emotions for individual consumption. Over a few decades, Adorno's moralist words became obsolete and strange like relics from a bygone age.

Conclusion

The story of emotional music consumption in the twentieth century is thus a complex one: first, the reification of 'mood' has constructed a stable object of self-knowledge, monitoring, care and manipulation. Thanks to this increased reflexivity, modern people may constantly consider themselves to 'have' some kind of mood, even while not feeling anything unusual. Second, recording technologies have turned music from an event into a stable object: the record is always available for consumption, and it always sounds exactly the same. This double objectivation of emotion and music has paved the way to the systematic use of music for emotional management, as the emotional effect of music on emotions has been known since time immemorial. Thus, new music consumption techniques emerged which partly relied on the older techniques of fiction reading, but have gradually developed their own peculiar character, which was increasingly pharmaceutical: one that isolates active ingredients and uses them to achieve a desired effect on the emotionalized self.

However, therapeutic (or better, pharmaceutical) uses of music have developed gradually. It is a new consumption technique: that is, a new way to attend to music and use it to evoke desired feelings, cope with undesired moods as well as with emotional crises on a larger scale, and transform one's mood. The creativity of users from below, efforts of the music industry from above, and changes in the material affordances of music players (such as the double de-contextualization of listeners and tracks fostered by the personal MP3 player), have all contributed to the emergence of the emotional consumption of music as we know it. This new consumption technique was first stigmatized, but later climbed upward in social space. If early emotional consumption of music usually took place at the level of the household, contemporary emotional consumption of music is at the level of the individual. While real people often attempt to play music to match and express their feeling, the cinema offered a similar aesthetic convention in which music is played in the background of a scene to inform viewers about the subjective, interior experience of the characters and evoke their identification. While it would be imprudent to point at the direction of causality, it is highly plausible that these two cultural models have developed in tandem and might have influenced each other.

The study of the emotional consumption of music demonstrates the significant sociological gains of going beyond distinction to study the genealogy of consumption techniques (Schwarz 2013a). Emotional listening goes beyond Bourdieu's model, as people consume music not merely to *express* their social identity, but also in order to *act on* their self and navigate it emotionally. While the constant availability of an abundance of tracks which cover the consumer's whole emotional spectrum makes this second project viable, it also relies on a different subjectivity.

Consumer capitalism, a psychological model of the human psyche and a set of technological affordances have all been important enabling conditions for the emergence of contemporary emotional music consumption as documented and evidenced in the literature (Bull 2000, 2012; Chen 1998; DeNora 2000; Mindlin *et al.* 2012; Simun 2009; Wells 1990). The music industry has packaged catharsis, and is now offering emotional ear drops for a plethora of different needs: tracks to be consumed as raw materials for the late-modern emotional care of self. In doing so, the music industry (together with the electronics industry) has contributed significantly to the rationalization of emotional management in everyday life.

Notes

1 I have conducted interviews with four leading figures, all of which are renowned and centrally positioned in the Israeli radio field, yet each representing a distinct style of radio.
2 Similarly, the context and mode of attending to nude images is responsible for their pornification and de-pornification, and distinguishes between high art and low pornography: Kimmel 2005; Nead 1992.

3 Kesner (2006) has described the parallel intensified, absorbed attention in the sanctified visual arts and the unique cognitive style of 'good' art museum visitors.

4 'Mood' as an *emic* category, which constitutes the object of emotional reflexivity, is an emotional state ascribed to an individual in a particular time. Unlike emotions, moods are often not assumed to have an external referent and are assumed to be ubiquitous (we are allegedly always in a certain mood).

5 Some of the wider consequences of this modern ontology of emotions are discussed in Illouz, Conclusion to this volume.

6 This use of the term 'emotional reflexivity' as a culturally and historically specific phenomenon should not be confused with that of scholars such as Burkit (2012) and Holmes (2010), who use it to refer to the universal emotional and relational dimensions of reflexivity. Faithful to this definition, using music to 'still emotion' is not the *opposite* of reflexivity as suggested by Brownlie (2014); it is not any less reflexive than using music as a means of venting emotions or working through them.

7 However, I am not suggesting here that either psychology or utilitarianism are the historical *causes* of the rise of emotional reflexivity: exploring the direction of causality lies beyond the scope of this chapter.

8 Sterne (2003) maintains that even in its earliest stages, collective phonograph listening was still directed towards the individual internal experience of the listeners, who listened 'together alone'. However, the validity of this claim is doubtful, as it relies on normative rather than descriptive sources: that is, early advertisements, the illustrations of which show listeners sitting in groups while avoiding eye contact with one another in order to concentrate on the music.

9 For more on the subject of music and sound to engender emotion in film audiences, see Gilon, Chapter 3 this volume.

10 The book even suggests that music can help people diagnose, identify and clarify, that is, reify their emotions by trying songs and exploring their reaction and degree of emotional identification.

11 Since the 1980s double-cassette tape-recorders have been used to produce home-made compilations, yet unlike digital playlists the production of these analogue compilations was time consuming, their sound quality deteriorated and the compilations themselves were not flexible.

12 Similarly, Jörg Rössel (2011) demonstrated that emotional listening among opera audiences is typical of the more highly educated and affluent.

13 Cohen also described his own private music consumption as derived from the needs to experience a particular experience at a particular time ('now I need strings, or rock; now I desire to be in a green meadow by the river').

14 There are obvious similarities between pharmaceutical music consumption and other therapeutic practices which are especially common among the dominant classes. Cf. Shachack, Chapter 6, this volume.

Bibliography

Adorno, Theodor W. 1976. *Introduction to the Sociology of Music*. New York: Continuum.

Adorno, Theodor W. 1990. "On popular music." In *On Record, Rock Pop and the Written Word*, edited by Simon Frith and Andrew Godwin, 301–314. London: Routledge.

Aristotle. 1943. *Aristotle's Politics* (trans. Benjamin Jowett). New York: Modern Library.

Bauman, Zygmunt. 1995. *Life in Fragments*. Oxford, UK: Blackwell.

Bennett Tony, Mike Savage, Elizabeth Silva, Alan Warde and Modesto Gayo-Cal. 2009. *Culture, Class, Distinction*. London: Routledge.

Bentley, Frank, Crysta Metcalf and Gunnar Harboe. 2006. "Personal vs. commercial content: The similarities between consumer use of photos and music." In *Proceedings of the SIGCHI conference on Human Factors in Computing Systems*, 667–676. Montreal, Canada.

Bourdieu, Pierre. 1984. *Distinction: A Social Critique of the Judgment of Taste*. Cambridge, MA: Harvard University Press.

Brownlie, Julie. 2014. *Ordinary Relationships*. London: Palgrave Macmillan.

Bryson, Bethany. 1996. "'Anything but heavy metal': Symbolic exclusion and musical dislikes." *American Sociological Review* 61:884–900.

Bull, Michael. 2000. *Sounding Out the City: Personal Stereos and the Management of Everyday Life*. Oxford, UK: Berg.

Bull, Michael. 2007. *Sound Moves: iPod Culture and Urban Experience*. London: Routledge.

Bull, Michael. 2012. "iPod culture: The toxic pleasures of audiotopia?" In *The Oxford Handbook of Sound Studies*, edited by Trevor Pinch and Karin Bijsterveld, 526–543. Oxford, UK: Oxford University Press.

Burkit, Ian. 2012. "Emotional reflexivity: Feeling, emotion and imagination in reflexive dialogues," *Sociology* 46(3):458–472.

Chartier Roger. 1994. *The Order of Books: Readers, Authors, and Libraries in Europe between the Fourteenth and Eighteenth Centuries*. Cambridge, UK: Polity Press.

Chen, Shing-Ling S. 1998. "Electronic narcissism: College students' experiences of Walkman listening." *Qualitative Sociology* 21(3):255–276.

Cooke, Mervyn (ed.). 2010. *The Hollywood Film Music Reader*. Oxford, UK: Oxford University Press.

Csordas, Thomas J. 2002. *Body/Meaning/Healing*. New York: Palgrave MacMillan.

DeNora, Tia. 2000. *Music in Everyday Life*. Cambridge, UK: Cambridge University Press.

Duncan, Grant. 2007. "After happiness." *Journal of Political Ideologies* 12(1):85–108.

Dyer, Richard. 1985. "Male gay porn: Coming to terms." *Jump Cut* 30:27–29.

Eisenberg Evan. 2005. *The Recording Angel*. New Haven, CT: Yale University Press.

Erickson, Bonnie H. 1996. "Culture, class and connections." *American Journal of Sociology* 102:217–251.

Featherstone, Mike. 2007. *Consumer Culture and Postmodernism*. London: SAGE.

Foucault, Michel. 1997. *Essential Works of Foucault, 1954–1984 Vol. 1: Ethics, Subjectivity and Truth*. New York: The New Press.

Frith, Simon. 1981. *Sound Effects: Youth, Leisure and the Politics of Rock'n'Roll*. New York: Pantheon.

Frith, Simon. 1984. "Mood music: An inquiry into narrative film music." *Screen* 25(3):78–87.

Garrioch, David. 2003. "Sounds of the city: The soundscape of early modern European towns." *Urban History*, 30(1):5–25.

Gomart, Émilie and Antoine Hennion. 1999. "A sociology of attachment: Music lovers, drug addicts." In *Actor-Network Theory and After*, edited by John Law and John Hassard, 220–247. Oxford, UK and Malden, MA: Blackwell.

Hebdige, Dick. 1979. *Subculture: The Meaning of Style*. London: Methuen.

Holmes, Mary. 2010. "The emotionalization of reflexivity." *Sociology* 44(1):139–154.

Illouz, Eva. 1997. *Consuming the Romantic Utopia: Love and the Cultural Contradictions of Capitalism*. Berkeley, CA: California University Press.

Jagodzinski Cecile M. 1999. *Privacy and Print: Reading and Writing in Seventeenth-Century England*. Charlottesville, VA: University Press of Virginia.

Johnson, James H. 1995. *Listening in Paris*. Berkeley, CA: University of California Press.

Juslin, Patrik N. and Petri Laukka. 2004. "Expression, perception, and induction of musical emotions: A review and a questionnaire study of everyday listening." *Journal of New Music Research* 33(3):217–238.

Kenney, William Howland. 1999. *Recorded Music in American Life*. New York: Oxford University Press.

Kesner, Ladislav. 2006. "The role of cognitive competence in the art museum experience." *Museum Management and Curatorship* 21:4–19.

Kim, Ja-Young and Nicholas J. Belkin. 2002. "Categories of music description and search terms and phrases used by non-music experts." In Proceedings of the 3rd International Conference on Music Information Retrieval. Paris, France, 209–214.

Kimmel, Michael S. 2005. *The Gender of Desire. Essays on Male Sexuality*. New York: State University of New York Press.

Kotchemidova, Christina. 2005. "From good cheer to 'drive-by smiling': A social history of cheerfulness." *Journal of Social History* 39(1): 5–38.

Knobloch, Silvia. 2003. "Mood adjustment via mass communication." *Journal of Communication* 53:233–250.

Knobloch, Silvia and Dolf Zillmann. 2002. "Mood management via the digital jukebox." *Journal of Communication* 52:351–366.

Knobloch-Westerwick, Silvia and Scott Alter. 2006. "Mood adjustment to social situations through mass media use: How men ruminate and women dissipate angry moods." *Human Communication Research* 32:58–73.

Lanza, Joseph. 2004. *Elevator Music: A Surreal History of Muzak Easy-listening and Other Moodsong*. Ann Arbor, MI: University of Michigan Press.

Lerner, Yulia, David Papo, Andrey Zhdanov, Libi Belozersky and Talma Hendler. 2009. "Eyes wide shut: Amygdala mediates eyes-closed effect on emotional experience with music." *PLoS ONE* 4(7): e6230.

Maisonneuve, Sophie. 2001. "Between history and commodity." *Poetics* 29:89–108.

Manovich, Lev. 2001. *The Language of New Media*. Cambridge, MA: MIT Press.

Merleau-Ponty, Maurice. 2002. *Phenomenology of Perception*. London: Routledge.

Mindlin, Galina, Don DuRousseau and Joseph Cardillo. 2012. *Your Playlist Can Change Your Life: 10 Proven Ways Your Favorite Music Can Revolutionize Your Health, Memory, Organization, Alertness and More*. Naperville, IL: Sourcebooks.

Naegele, Daniel 1998. "Object, image, aura." *Harvard Design Magazine* 6:1–6.

Nead, Lynda. 1992. *The Female Nude: Art, Obscenity and Sexuality*. London and New York: Routledge.

Negus, Keith and Patria Román Velázquez. 2002. "Belonging and detachment: Musical experience and the limits of identity." *Poetics* 30:133–145.

Peterson, Richard A. and Roger M. Kern. 1996. "Changing highbrow taste: From snob to omnivore." *American Sociological Review* 61: 900–907.

Pine, B. Joseph and James H Gilmore. 1999. *The Experience Economy: Work Is Theater & Every Business a Stage*. Boston, MA: Harvard Business Press.

Prnjat, Dejana. 2010. "How much can arts education affect the decision-making process when choosing classical or pop music?" A paper presented at the 2nd World Conference on Arts Education. Seoul, May 25–28, 2010.

Reddy, William M. 2001. *The Navigation of Feeling: A Framework for the History of Emotions*. Cambridge, UK: Cambridge University Press.

Rössel, Jörg. 2011. "Cultural capital and the variety of modes of cultural consumption in the opera audience." *The Sociological Quarterly* 52(1):83–103.

Roy, William G. 2004. "'Race records' and 'hillbilly music': Institutional origins of racial categories in the American commercial recording industry." *Poetics* 32: 265–279.

Roy, William G. and Timothy J. Dowd. 2010. "What is sociological about music?" *Annual Review of Sociology* 36:183–203.

Saenger, Paul. 1997. *Space between Words: The Origins of Silent Reading*. Stanford, CA: Stanford University Press.

Schutz, Alfred. 1967. *The Phenomenology of the Social World*. Evanston, IL: Northwestern University Press.

Schwarz,Ori. 2013a. "Bending forward, one step backward: On the sociology of tasting techniques." *Cultural Sociology* 7(4):415–430.

Schwarz Ori. 2013b. "What should nature sound like? Techniques of engagement with nature sites and sonic preferences of Israeli visitors." *Annals of Tourism Research* 42:382–401.

Selfridge-Field, Eleanor. 1997. "Experiments with melody and meter or the effects of music: The Edison-Bingham music research." *The Musical Quarterly* 81(2):291–310.

Simun, Miriam. 2009. "My music, my world: Using the MP3 player to shape experience in London." *New Media & Society* 11(6):921–941.

Smythe, Dallas Walker. 1994. "Communications: Blindspot of Western Marxism." In *Counterclockwise: Perspectives on Communication*, edited by Thomas Guback, 263–291. Boulder, CO: Westview Press.

Spacks, Patricia Meyer. 2003. *Privacy: Concealing the Eighteenth-Century Self*. Chicago, IL: Chicago University Press.

Sterne, Jonathan. 2003. *The Audible Past: Cultural Origins of Sound Reproduction*, Durham, NC: Duke University Press.

Taylor, Charles. 1989. *Sources of the Self: The Making of the Modern Identity*. Cambridge, MA: Harvard University Press.

Warde, Alan, Lydia Martens and Wendy Olsen. 1999. "Consumption and the problem of variety: Cultural omnivorousness, social distinction and dining out." *Sociology* 33(1):105–127.

Wells, Alan. 1990. "Popular music: Emotional use and management." *Journal of Popular Culture* 24:105–117.

Wheeler, Edgar C. 1927. "The mysterious power of music." *Popular Science* January 1927:28–29, 130–131.

Wierzbicki, James. 2009. *Film Music: A History*. Oxford, UK: Routledge.

Williams, Linda. 1995. "Corporealized observers: Visual pornography and the 'carnal density of vision'." In *Fugitive Images: From Photography to Video*, edited by Patrice Petro, 3–41. Bloomington, IN: Indiana University Press.

Willis, Paul. 1978. *Profane Culture*. London: Routledge and Kegan Paul.

Wittmann Reinhard. 1999. "Was there a reading revolution at the end of the eighteenth century?" In *A History of Reading in the West*, edited by Guglielmo Cavallo and Roger Chartier, 284–312. Amherst, MA: University of Massachusetts Press.

Young, Paul J. 2008. *Seducing the Eighteenth-Century French Reader: Reading, Writing, and the Question of Pleasure*. Aldershot, UK: Ashgate.

Zillmann, Dolf. 1988. "Mood management through communication choices." *American Behavioral Scientist* 31:327–340.

Chapter 3

Cinema as an emotional commodity

The horror genre and the commodification of fear

Daniel Gilon

An examination of the American movie industry in recent decades reveals the tremendous success of the horror genre. The genre includes big-budget productions, and its films earn major profits and are made by prestigious directors and actors. In the summer of 1999, for example, horror became a central factor in the US/Canada box office: three of the ten most profitable films were horrors (Abbott 2010: 29, 34–35). This success is extremely surprising, given the characteristics of the American movie industry and the horror genre. The development and success of a cinematic genre after it has been established cannot be taken for granted. The American movie industry is full of examples of very popular genres that have become almost obsolete. Furthermore, the horror genre requires a special explanation, since it contains extreme violence and gore.

Different explanations for the attraction of horror movies and for the genre's success have been proposed. These explanations focus on several aspects, such as the psychological processes which the genre creates in its viewers (e.g. Carroll 2002; Derry 2009; Tudor 1997; Wood 2002), the cultural aspects which the genre represents in each historical moment (e.g. Phillips 2005), and the ways in which the genre enables the construction and performance of gender roles (e.g. Zillmann and Weaver 1996). These explanations supply substantial contributions to the understanding of different aspects of the genre's appeal. However, they tend to neglect the role of the genre as a supplier of various intense emotional experiences. *Furthermore, some of them even aim to explain the arguable paradox of the genre's success, despite the emotional experiences it produces.* For example, Carroll (2002: 33) claims that "even if horror only caused fear, we might feel justified in demanding an explanation of what could motivate people to seek out the genre. But where fear is compounded with repulsion, the ante is, in a manner of speaking, raised". Carroll assumes that the audience is willing to tolerate horrific emotional experiences because the narrative and content of the genre offers cognitive pleasures (Ibid.: 184).

This chapter will offer a simpler and more direct explanation: the genre's success derives from the ability of moviemakers to produce and supply different horrific emotional experiences, horrific emodities in fact, that are oriented towards different audiences and are excluded from one's actions in the "real world". This ability is the result of the combination of two processes: the emotionalization of the American movie industry led by the entrance of market research and the moviemaker's success to commodify the emotion of fear experienced in the "real world" into specific cinematic formulas for producing horrific experiences, by the use of narrative and cinematic tools (e.g. sound, editing, psychological themes). Following a presentation of the creation of the genre, I will describe these processes. Finally, I will show how they have shaped the contemporary horror genre. From this study, we will see how the horror genre became one of Hollywood's *emotion machines* (Tan 1995), creating different horrific emodities.

There are several reasons for the chapter's focus on the horror genre as a case study. Each of these issues will be discussed elaborately in the chapter. Since there is a general agreement in the movie industry that the consumption of a horror film is an emotional experience, it constitutes a solid example of the commodification of emotion. In addition, the fact that it took both time and the involvement of many actors before the industry started to create horror emotions and ultimately to foreground them, exposes the contingency of this process. Finally, the construction of the industry by market research led to the domination of horror movies oriented towards the teenage market. Therefore, the genre is one of the first examples of how market research emotionalized the industry.

In order to explore the development of a commodity in which many actors are involved, the chapter will include the study of several kinds of materials. In addition to reviewing secondary sources dealing with the development of the American movie industry and the American horror genre, I will study interviews and biographies regarding key actors in the production process of selected horror movies; the marketing and production materials of these movies; and reports of market research and academic studies regarding the industry. The mediation of these movies will be studied through the analysis of reviews from industry magazines and daily newspapers.

The first horror movie

In the first decades of the American movie industry, films were often based on pre-existing cultural sources, such as the gothic novel. Although that creation of fictional fearful experiences as part of cultural works can be traced back to as early as ancient Greece, the first clear case of the commodification of fear and horror can be seen in gothic novels. The emotional thrills of these novels could also be found on stage and indeed it was these actors, writers and directors who joined the ranks of the burgeoning movie industry. Early film producers, however, shied away from presenting the kind of graphic horror that could be seen in the theatre, for fear of alienating their audiences: instead, they preferred to rely on psychological effects.

This intention is made explicit in the promotional material for Edison's *Frankenstein* (1910). Based on Mary Shelley's classic gothic novel, the studio magazine is careful to assert that:

To those familiar with Mrs. Shelley's story it will be evident that we have carefully omitted anything which might be any possibility shock [sic] any portion of the audience. In making the film the Edison Co. has carefully tried to eliminate all actual repulsive situations and to concentrate its endeavors upon the mystic and psychological problems that are to be found in this weird tale. Wherever, therefore, the film differs from the original story it is purely with the idea of eliminating what would be repulsive to a moving picture audience.

(The Edison Kinetogram, 15 March 1910)

However, while the studios were clearly hesitant about including horror contents in their movies, the groundwork for horror as a distinct genre was being laid (Worland 2007: 43). Films arising out of the German Expressionist movement, and the impact of the First World War horrors, were major influences on the American movie industry, as can be seen in two new types of movies produced in the 1920s. The 'haunted house comedy' was based on a popular genre from the commercial theatre, which supplied its audience with the emotional experiences of both romance and chills. Second, films like Universal Studios' *The Hunchback of Notre Dame* (1923) were based on classic gothic texts and included a more direct presentation of violence and disgusting acts.

It was from movies like this that the horror genre would emerge, thanks to the input from a combination of creators and reviewers. But it was a slow process. The natural conservatism of the studios meant that Hollywood was not eager to take risks, fearing that gothic horror might prove to be too morbid for conventional taste (Worland 2007: 52). A pioneer in this field was German-born Carl Laemmle who, as head of Universal Studios, made a significant contribution to the development of the genre. As a small studio, Universal tried to get to the audience through a use of diverse contents. As part of this agenda, Universal produced both haunted house comedies and movies based on classic gothic tales.

Universal invested large resources in a psychological oriented adaptation of the gothic tale *The Hunchback of Notre Dame* (1923). Although efforts were made in order to adapt the film to the taste of the general cinema audience (Soister 2012: 284–287), the presentation of violent content and the intensity of the emotional experience were amplified in it. The reviews recognized this move and offered different attitudes regarding its suitability to the audience.

Variety magazine, a weekly tabloid dealing with the industry and aimed at entertainment executives, called *Hunchback* a "Huge mistake":

The Hunchback of Notre Dame is a two hour nightmare … Laemmle's picture is fragile as a film house commodity … It's murderous, hideous and repulsive … misery all of the time, nothing but misery, tiresome, loathsome misery … the audience didn't want the bums, it didn't want the misery, it didn't want the gruesomeness.

(6 September 1923)

The reviews that were oriented to the public expressed more positive attitude towards the emotional tone of the movie. For example, *New York Times*'s review declared that: "It is a drama which will appeal to all those who are interested in fine screen acting, artistic settings and a remarkable handling of crowds, who do not mind a grotesque figure and a grim atmosphere" (3 September 1923). These reviews matched the audience response. The movie was a major success that led Universal to produce a cinematic adaptation of *The Phantom of the Opera* (1925). The reviews responded in a similar way to the *Hunchback*. It is interesting to note that beyond the critical tone of *Variety*'s review, it started to notice (and in fact helped to shape) the creation of a new genre named "horror"; the review opened with the statement that "Universal has turned out another horror" (9 September 1925). The *Phantom* succeeded even more than the *Hunchback* (Soister 2012: 461). Encouraged by this success, along with that of their haunted house comedy *The Cat and the Canary* (1927), Universal produced *Dracula* and *Frankenstein*, both in 1931. The ways that these two films were promoted provides a key insight into the relationship between producers, marketing people and audiences, and here we are first able to discern clearly the creation of horror films specifically as emotional products, albeit still cautiously.

When *Dracula* was in pre-production, the head of the studio, Laemmle, and the film's director could not agree over whether to make it a romance or a thriller. Eventually, after a week's deliberation, they decided to make it both (Spadoni 2003: 144). The film's growing pains didn't end there; scenes that appeared in the script were cut out from the movie since they were considered too frightening (Weaver *et al.* 2007: 30–31). The marketing strategy was confused and conflicted. The film could not be sold as a horror movie – the term "horror" had been first used by *Variety* to describe *Phantom*, but it was not yet an established genre in itself. In the end, it was marketed in a number of ways: as a romantic gothic film, a mystery and even a love story. However, as part of the press book sent to distributors, entitled *Here's How to Sell Dracula*, the studio made it clear that the film would have a strong emotional impact, and that those emotions included horror. The film was an enormous success, critically, commercially and emotionally. According to *Variety*, it evoked "a real horror kick" (quoted in Spadoni 2003: 47). Now Universal energetically set about capitalizing on this success.

With *Frankenstein*, they achieved it. No hesitation surrounded the horror element now – and the film hit the mark. In the preview screening the audience was distraught from the first scene (Jensen 1996). One attendant even recalled that "They gulped and they started to run around the theatre. You never saw such a performance!" (quoted in Ibid.: 22). A day after the preview the theatre manager called Laemmle and said that he had received phone calls in the middle of the night from the previous night's audience who told him that "I can't sleep and I'll be damned if you will" (quoted in Ibid.: 22). Fearing that he had gone too far, Laemmle sought the advice of industry experts. The consensus was to leave the movie alone, since it looked set to be a hit (Ibid.: 22). It was not changed.

The marketing strategy hedged its bets: "To have seen Frankenstein is to wear a badge of courage". *Frankenstein* earned even more than *Dracula*, was voted one of the top films of 1931 by the *New York Times*, and affirmed the genre's popular appeal and commercial potential.

After *Dracula* and *Frankenstein*, the term "horror movie" entered the lexicon of critics and industry commentators. According to Worland (2007: 19), "observers noted the arrival of something new and groped for a commonly accepted name" and they settled on "horror". Once the genre was established, the industry enthusiastically started to produce horror movies that were recognized as producing the emotional experience of horror.

Market research and the emotionalization of the movie industry

The development of the horror genre throughout the years was based on the movie industry's success in producing different emotional experiences for different target audiences. This section will deal with one of the major causes for the construction of the industry as such: the assimilation of market research. As Cochoy (1998) argues regarding the influence of marketing on the economy, it can be argued that the implementation of market research has a double aspect: simultaneously conceptualizing and enacting the movie industry.

In the first decades of the industry, there was no serious research into the market. Producers would judge public response sitting in on public viewings (Ohmer 2006: 2). Based on those personal experiences, they believed they had direct access to audience feelings and could develop over time an almost intuitive sense of what people liked (Ohmer 1991). For example, the founder of Paramount Pictures studio Adolph Zukor, described that in the Nickelodeon he opened in New York at 1904:

> [i]t was my custom to take a seat about six rows from the front ... I spent a good deal of time watching the faces of the audience ... With a little experience I could see, hear and "feel" the reaction to each melodrama and comedy.
> (Zukor and Kramer 1953: 42)

Any systematic attempts to study the audience were thus deemed unnecessary; in any case, the movie industry professed its commitment to provide universal entertainment for an undifferentiated audience. The financial success of the developing leisure industries was dependent on their ability to attract the greatest number of possible customers. In order to do so, these industries needed to be demonstratively inclusive, allowing for the public mixing of genders, classes, ages and ethnic constituencies, pretending to a social homogeneity (Hansen 1990: 53; Jowett 1976: 217).

Following on from this early period, the development of market research in the industry can be divided into three further stages that will be described below.

The 1920s–1930s: from instinct to inquiry by social organization

During the years and following the development of the industry and of marketing in general, different actors within the industry, such as cinema houses and industry publications, started to dip their toes into various types of market research and audience classification techniques (Bakker 2003). The studios aimed to understand the audience taste based on hearing the opinions of the actual viewers and not just the mogul's intuitions. Universal Studios, for example, started from 1922 to publish a weekly advertisement in the magazine *Saturday Evening Post*, asking readers to send letters to the studio in which they would state their favourite stars and answer some questions. In the 1930s, all the major studios had fan mail departments that tabulated the letters by the fan's estimated age, gender and location (Ibid.: 105–106).

Despite these attempts, the main research in that period was conducted by organizations outside the industry. The tremendous success of the industry led to public pressure presented by different social groups concerning the harmful psychological, moral and social influence of the cinema's immense popularity with adolescents and children (Gripsrud 1998: 203; Jarvis 1991: 128). As a result, social science's researchers and social organizations sought to investigate these aspects (Gripsrud 1998: 203).

Not coincidentally, a major part of the research was focused on the emotional impact of movies on the young viewers. The 'American adolescent' had been 'discovered' at the beginning of the twentieth century. Various institutions and businesses identified the passage from childhood to adulthood as a unique phase, and the 'adolescence' was constructed as a distinct class, or – perhaps more significantly – as a distinct market. Stanley Hall, the psychologist credited with the 'discovery' of the American adolescent, defined this stage as highly emotional and as a problematic life stage. In 1904, he wrote that adolescence is period of "storm and stress" (1904, Vol I: Xiii) in which there is a tendency to question and contradict parents. In regards to the emotional aspect, he claimed that "Many of the emotions can almost be said to be born now [in adolescence], and perhaps all are intensified" (1904, Vol II: 21). Dahl and Hariri (2005) argue that Hall's emphasis on the intense emotions and conflicts of puberty is in many ways the hallmark of his legacy. Hall's work quickly exerted a considerable influence in many different directions (Demos and Demos 1969: 635).

Universal Studios was the first to adopt academic research that formulated the cinematic medium as one that creates emotional experiences and have an educational role. In the late 1920s, Universal employed the psychologist Dr WM Marston who took part in experiments at Columbia University that explored the effects on different audience types of particular onscreen episodes which had been specifically designed to evoke particular emotions. As Marston described "we figured out beforehand just what primary emotions we wanted to arouse in the people who watched our pictures and we succeeded in calling forth precisely those emotions we had planned". Writing in the *New York Tribune* (2 January 1929), Marston concluded that movies are "emotion pictures" which have greater educational power that any other force on the emotions of the nation's youth. Therefore, his aim was to "get films to stop juggling the public's emotions and rather to get them to mold the public's emotions into a more pleasurable pattern by offering suitable stories on the screen". Interestingly, in accordance with the common view of conservative social scientists at the time, Marston was strongly opposed to the production of fear in movies. Research in favour of the production of cinematic fear came into use only in the following decades.

The experiments held in Columbia were not the only ones who studied the characteristics of the cinematic experience and its influence. Different social organizations also funded studies in that subject. The most extensive and influential ones were the Payne studies.[1] These studies aimed not just to reveal the characteristics of the medium and its audience but mainly to construct them. The arrangement committee pre-determined that movies were bad and wanted evidence to prove it. Therefore, the head of the committee recruited researchers that were sympathetic to this view (Jarvis 1991: 129; Jowett *et al.* 1996: 7). Even more importantly, when the journalist Henry J. Forman (1934 [1933]) wrote a book that summarized the studies and shaped the collective attitude concerning them, he wanted to show the dramatic and harmful effect of movies. Therefore, he tended to select only the features of the studies that support these notions (Jarvis 1991: 132; Jowett *et al.* 1996: 95). Not surprisingly, the Payne studies revealed that movies have a crucial influence on the moral, psych and social behaviour of the nation, especially on the nation's youth.

As part of this discovery, these studies had an important role in shaping the view that the cinematic experience is an emotional one that is extremely popular in the youth audience. When Forman summarized the results of the studies, he declared that the percentage of minors in the cinematic audience is larger than their percentage in the total population and that "the movie population of minors includes virtually the children of the entire nation" (Forman 1934 [1933]: 274). Two studies in particular shaped the view that the cinematic experience is emotional in nature, that it can be measured and that the youngsters react to it with the highest emotional intensity. Blumer (1933), a Chicago School sociologist conducted a research that was based on motion picture 'biographies'. He concluded his research by arguing that "It seems clear that the forte of motion pictures is in their emotional effect . . . their appeal and their success reside ultimately in the emotional agitation which they induce" (Ibid.: 198). Another Payne study added evidences that helped to construct the effect of movies as emotional ones and showed that this effect can be measured in a quantitative way. The researchers in this study used an instrument called a psycho-galvanometer, which arguably could measure quantitatively the intensity of the emotional response to different cinematic scenes through the measure of bodily reactions. As described by Forman (1934 [1933]: 97), the study discovered that the emotional reactions of children and adolescents are much stronger than those of adults.

The Payne studies and others similar in nature had a profound effect on the movie industry (Jowett 1976: 226). The direct impact was increasing the censorship of movies. In addition, the studies and the discussions around them influenced the industry's perceptions of its main characteristics. However, it was still research mainly obtained outside the industry. The full construction of the industry as one that produced emotional experiences for emotional audiences happened in the following decades as the result of the massive entrance of market research as an integral part of the industry.

The 1940s–1960s: the emotionaliztion of the industry by the entrance of systematic research

The 1940s saw the onset of a crucial transition in Hollywood's relationship with market research. Different social, legal and technological changes made the audiences shrink rapidly and this led to the entrance of market research to the industry itself as a means of minimizing risk. According to Ohmer (2006), what started in the 1940s revolutionized the industry within a couple of decades. Key to this transition was the pioneer of polls and surveys, George Gallup. In 1940, he founded the Audience Research Institute (ARI), which adapted the techniques he used in advertising and political polling to the study of film audiences. The ARI's studies represent the first full-scale effort at empirical market research in Hollywood (Ibid.: 4). Market researchers redefined the industry's problems in their own language and thus reframed the audience and the movie experience. I will now describe these results and their influence on the horror genre.

The spectator as a teenager emotional subject

Following the earlier social studies' focus on the youth as the main audience, Gallup supplied the first empirical evidence of the importance of teenagers to the commercial success of a movie. He did so in his first major audience survey in 1940, which included a preponderance of young people in its sample (Ibid.: 107–108). However, this research went largely unnoticed until more than a year later, when Gallup was conducting studies for RKO Pictures (Ibid.: 114). David Ogilvy, Gallup's assistant director and account manager for RKO, made much of this insight: he thought that the fact that 34 per cent of cinema tickets were purchased by people under 20 years old was one of the ARI's most important discoveries; claiming he was merely "reporting the facts", Ogilvy relished the opportunity to make sweeping generalizations about American filmgoers (Ibid.: 112). He continually stressed the importance of teenagers in his reports to RKO, urging the studio to develop and promote films aimed at that market (Ibid.: 132). For example, in Gallup's February 1941 report to RKO, it was pointed out that while 52 per cent of filmgoers were under 25, only about 20 per cent of RKO stars were in that age group, and RKO was advised to develop young stars who matched this profile (Bakker 2003: 118). According to Doherty (2002), by the end of the 1950s, Hollywood had grasped that the teenage market was a rich seam to mine, and adopted teenagers as their ultimate audience.

An important case study of the market-oriented approach to film-making is provided by American International Pictures (AIP), an independent film studio formed in 1954 by James H. Nicholson and Samuel Z. Arkoff. AIP used market research data to establish the most profitable formulas for moviemaking and exploited these to drive its productions (Booker 2011: 22); for more than 20 years it determined the tastes of successive generations of teenagers in its formulaic movies (Heffernan 2004: 68). It was AIP who developed the "Peter Pan Syndrome" strategy, a syllogism that works as follows:

> A younger child will watch anything an older child will watch; An older child will not watch anything a younger child will watch; A girl will watch anything a boy will watch; A boy will not watch anything a girl will watch; therefore to catch your greatest audience you zero in on the 19-year old male.
>
> (quoted in Doherty 2002: 128)

Given the earlier framing of adolescents as 'problematic' emotional subjects, it is no surprise that when the industry constructed the teenage cinematic audience, it strongly emphasized these aspects. The first creators of 'Teenpics' in the 1950s were deeply influenced by the perception of teenagers as emotional subjects that rebel against their parents. As a consequence, horror movies, along with science fiction and Rock'n'Roll movies, dominated the Teenpics market. These movies became more sensational, deliberately attracting teenagers and deterring adults. Heffernan (2004: 68–69) claims that the deliberate alienation of the older audience was a crucial factor in the aesthetic changes in horror movies in the 1950s and 1960s. Increasingly, horror films began to stretch the limits of acceptable gore and violence, expanding the Cinema of Attractions at the expense of the Cinema of Narrative.

Measuring the experience

As we have seen, research held as part of the Payne studies enabled the measurement of the intensity of emotional responses to films of different age groups. The entrance of market research into the industry promoted this ability and made producing a movie into a quantifiable process. Starting with Gallup's experiments in the 1940s, studios could break down movies into different factors which could be scientifically designed, and then find the exact features of movies which had an emotional effect on viewers (Ohmer 2006: 218). The most vivid demonstration of measuring the audience experience in that period was the introduction to preview screenings of the Hopkins Televote machine, a handheld dial allowing viewers to respond to the action onscreen by selecting "very dull", "dull", "neutral", "like" or "like very much". Producers could then view a bar graph giving collated audience responses to each moment of the film (Ibid.: 221). This technology was subsequently developed to zoom in on the reactions of specific demographic groups (Ibid.: 228). It should be noted, however, that while this type of research was available from the 1940s, there are no documented instances of its use for horror movies until much later, presumably because the costs of using such technology were prohibitive in what was still a low-budget genre.

Marketing

During the 1940s, the ARI branched out into the marketing aspects of moviemaking and began to offer total management services for films (Ibid.: 217); as a result, it evolved into more of an advertising agency, as it struck upon the insight that the success of a movie depended not just upon the quality of the movie itself but also upon the publicity surrounding it (Ibid.: 222). The boundary between a movie and its marketing started to blur, and the marketing of a movie began to take precedence over its creative development.

The increasing importance of advertisements contributed to the emotionalization of the industry, since advertising emphasized and conceptualized the emotional experience of movies at the same time. According to Heffernan (2004: 64–66), it was the combination of the need to attract the adolescent audience with the perception that its advertising techniques were outdated that led in the 1950s to the growth of sensationalist advertising which preceded a movie's casting and even script-writing. This developed by the end of the decade into theatres and trade journalists calling on movie producers to exploit the insights of clinical psychology into advertising in order to attract the movie-going public. Of particular interest was the field of Motivation Analysis, which deployed the insights of depth psychology to uncover the unconscious desires behind consumption habits and to design advertising campaigns which tapped into these desires. As Heffernan points out, "In 1956, the Theater Owners of America hired promotional consultant Claude Mundo as an administrative assistant to the organization. At the owner's annual meeting in Los Angeles, Mundo asserted that 'mental manipulation is what the industry's showmen need'" (Ibid.: 69).

The centrality of emotions to the horror genre – in the movies themselves, as well as in the sensationalist advertising which accompanies them – is summed up by this comment from Arkoff, the manager of AIP, who said to *Time* magazine in 1958:

> I always think of the title first. The story comes last. After the title come the advertising ideas – the gimmick, the illustrations, for these are what get the kids into the theater. Then comes the story – and every drop of blood and graveyard shudder must be as advertised.
>
> (Quoted in Ibid.: 70)

Arkoff is effectively describing the deliberate creation of a consumption process in which the advertisement highlights the emotional appeal of a movie, which is then consummated by the movie itself. This is significantly different from the traditional understanding of the consumption pattern as a cyclical and misleading process (Campbell 1987: 496–500). Arkoff's model is more sophisticated, because in his process the particular emotion is constructed for the consumer by the advertising, and then actually and satisfyingly fulfilled in the consumption of the movie, giving the consumer an authentic sense of emotional fulfilment (Illouz, conclusion to this volume).

The 1970s–2010s: the specification and development of the cinematic emotional experiences

Over the years, the incentive has grown for different actors within the industry to improve the quality of its measurement of audience characteristics and of the cinematic experience, and their ability to do so has grown with it. Market research companies have become an integral part of the industry at all stages of the production of a movie. As a consequence, it has become possible for the industry to produce different emotional experiences, targeted at specific types of audience.

First, filmmakers have increasingly moved towards creating particular emotional experiences tailored towards specific target audiences. While teenagers have always maintained their status as the main audience for new movies, studios have endeavoured to divide teenagers into smaller, more specific groups, and to make movies for other target audiences as well (Ohmer 2006: 227).

It is not the studios alone who have helped to match the emotional experience to its target audience. Following public pressure, The Motion Picture Association of America introduced its Production Code in 1930, which required signatory studios to adhere to a set of "general principles" to ensure that all movies were "appropriate"; then, in 1968, abandoned this code for a Rating System according to which potential audience members could choose for themselves what kind of content is appropriate for them or their children. This ratings system has evolved over the years: categories have changed; they have increased in number; and written justifications for the rating have been added. As a result, cinemagoers are supplied with a description of the kind of content featured in the film and the level of its intensity. Therefore, in addition to their direct influence on the audience's type, the rating and the description also acts as mediators for the type and intensity of the emotional experiences predicted in the movie.

There are a number of examples of filmmakers reshooting or re-editing a movie in order to receive a rating which better suits its target audience. When the horror movie *Scream* (1996) received an NC-17 rating – meaning that no-one under 17 could see the film in a cinema – its financial backers forced the director to make changes so that the film could be reclassified as R rated. This would allow youngsters to watch the film if accompanied by an adult. Examples of changes include cutting out a long shot of a murder victim with his guts spilling out and replacing it with a close-up of the victim's face; and doubling the speed of the camera movement as it zooms into the face of a corpse hanging from a tree.[2] In this case, and others besides, the filmmakers have used cinematic tools and techniques deliberately to manipulate the type and intensity of the emotional experience of horror content with the explicit purpose of better reaching their target audience.

Second, recent decades have seen increased use of advanced research tools, based on cutting-edge science, in order to shape the emotional cinematic experience. An interesting type of research in this field aims to read an audience's subconscious emotional responses, as reflected by different psycho-neurological measures, and to shape a movie accordingly. For example, the company Innerscope offers studios the use of neurosciences tools in order to quantify the subconscious emotional engagement of viewers with movie trailers.[3] Innerscope claims that with this technique it can accurately predict the financial success of a movie. If a trailer fails to reach the emotional engagement level of 65, the movie is very likely to generate less than $10 million in revenue in its opening weekend; a trailer that scores above 80 is very likely to earn $20 million during the first weekend (Randall 2013). What is more, according to Innerscope's CEO, this procedure can also help tweak movie trailers in order to turn up the emotional engagement (Ibid.).

Big Hollywood studios are using this type of research, and leading directors have praised it. But it is not limited just to trailers. For example, fMRI studies, performed by the company MindSign, in which the emotional reactions to cinematic scenes are examined through the study of neural responses, have been used in order to heighten the experience of horror for viewers.[4] In an article that describes the use of this method for the creation of the horror movie *Pop Skull* (2007), the movie's director and the president of MindSign both argue that "If an fMRI scan shows activity in the amygdala, there's reason to infer that the person is scared. Scan enough brains and average the results and you could learn which buttons to push to increase the amygdala's response" (Kotler 2010). The results of the early test of the movie were surprising: "A shot of a hand creeping along a wall incited a greater amygdala response than a scene involving the villain jumping out of the bushes – the opposite of what standard moviemaking rules would predict" (quoted in Ibid.).

Creating the experiences

Market research is, of course, only one of the tools that filmmakers use in order to create powerful emotions of horror in their audiences. Another way is the use of narrative and cinematic tools and the establishment of formulas for the creation of different emotions based on these tools. In this section I will demonstrate these procedures by examining the use of music and sound to heighten the cinematic effects of horror movies. In addition, I will demonstrate the establishment of a formula for the creation of specific horrific emotional experience.

Music and sound

Music and sound have played a major part in the creation of emotions in cinema since the silent film era and of course after their introduction into movies in the late 1920s. As Schwarz claims (this volume) "The role of film music ever since the silent film era is to fix the emotional meaning of an often polysemic visual narrative". In the same tone, film theorist Caryl Flinn (1992) claims that from the early years of the medium, film music "was repeatedly and systematically used to enhance emotional moments in the story line [and] to establish moods" (Ibid.: 12, quoted in Hayward 2009: 6).

While music and sound are important to the emotional impact of any movie, this is especially the case for horror: music's "capacity to create tension and shock supplementary to narrative and visual design is a key element in the horror genre" (Hayward 2009: 2). Lerner (2010a: iix) claims that "of all the cinematic genres, horror gives music a heightened responsibility for triggering feelings of horror, fear, and rage". I shall argue here that the process in which different music and sound effects were created and added to the genre's repertoire of emotion production techniques is a key element in the commodification of emotions in horror movies. In what follows, I will investigate the use of music and sound in the early days of the genre and then present the case of *Psycho* (1960) as a key stage in the story of music in horror.

The roots of music in horror films can be found in its theatrical predecessors. Lerner argues that words and music in combination to create atmosphere can be traced to the beginning of the nineteenth century, and that "film music absorbed some of the practices of aesthetic modernism from the concert hall, and that in particular the genre of the horror film turned to unresolved dissonance, atonality, and timbral experimentation as part of its characteristic stylistic qualities" (Ibid.: ix). Music and sound, then, were used from the very beginning to create an atmosphere of horror, but at first this was an unintentional byproduct: according to Spadoni (2003), the introduction of sound to movies created an uncanny, disturbing experience, making the characters seem ghostly, somewhere between alive and dead. This was of course a problem for most movies, but for horror it was a perfect fit.

A pioneer in this field is Rouben Mamoulian, director of Paramount's *Dr Jekyll and Mr Hyde* (1931). In the scene where Jekyll breaks up with the female lead, Mamoulian added background music without showing an onscreen character playing it, a ground-breaking technique in cinema at that time. This was, he says, a conscious decision, made in order to add ironic impact to the scene: "the music goes against the mood which, of course, makes the despair much more poignant" (quoted in Lerner 2010b: 62). Another technique he used to heighten the tension from one scene to the next was to repeat the melody in a higher key.

According to Greber (2004), the use of sound in combination with visual effects allowed the audience to experience Jekyll's transformation into Hyde in a more visceral way than ever before. Mamoulian gives a fascinating account of the process of creating the unique sound for this scene:

> I thought the only way to match the event and create this incredible reality would be to concoct a mélange of sounds that do not exist in nature that a human ear cannot hear … But no matter what we used, it always sounded like what it was – a drum. Finally in exasperation I got this wonderful idea. I ran up and down the stairway for a few minutes, and then I put a microphone to my heart and said, "Record it." And that's what is used as the basic rhythm in the scene – the thumping noise which is like no drum on earth because it's the heartbeat, my own heartbeat.
>
> (Quoted in Lerner 2010b: 70)

Over the years, composers and sound designers have become more sophisticated in their use of music and sound effects to create particular emotional effects in the audience. A landmark moment is the music for the famous shower scene in Alfred Hitchcock's *Psycho*, and this example demonstrates how a musical formula for the creation of an emotional response was generated.

Hitchcock initially wanted no musical accompaniment to the shower scene, preferring to highlight the diegetic sounds of the scene itself. The composer of the movie, Bernard Herrmann, has told of his dissatisfaction after Hitchcock showed him an initial cut of the movie, and he suggested that Hitchcock take a few days off while he worked on the score; Hitchcock agreed, but insisted that no music should be added to the shower scene. It was at this point that Herrmann composed the film's iconic musical cue, "The Murder", with its famous shrieking violins. Hitchcock returned to review his work. Herrmann takes up the story:

> We dubbed the composite without any musical effects behind the murder scene, and let him watch it. Then I said, "I really do have something composed for it, and now that you've seen it your way, let's try mine." We played him my version with the music. He said, "Of course, that's the one we'll use." I said, "But you requested that we not add any music." "Improper suggestion, my boy, improper suggestion," he replied.
>
> (Quoted in Wierzbicki 2009: 18–19)

Herrmann notes that it was during his viewing of the rough cut of *Psycho* that it occurred to him to use only string instruments for the score of the movie (Wierzbicki 2009: 19), although Smith (1991: 236) adds that this was also motivated in part by the movie's low budget. While Herrmann's choice of string instruments for creating emotional effects has excellent musical pedigree – and Rothman (1982: 298, quoted in Wierzbicki 2009: 16) notes that "much of the shattering impact" of the very start of the murder scene derives from the "sudden high-pitched shriek of violins" – Herrmann was in fact making film history. This was the first time string instruments had been used on their own to match the texture of the cinematography (Smith 1991: 237–239). According to noted film composer Fred Steiner (1974: 31–32, quoted in Smith 1991: 237):

Herrmann's selection of a string orchestra deprived him of many tried and true musical formulas and effects which, until that time, had been considered essential for suspense-horror films: cymbal rolls, timpani throbs, muted horn stings, shrieking clarinets, ominous trombones, and dozens of other staples in Hollywood's bag of chilly, scary musical tricks.

To which Fenimore (2010) adds:

The use of strings to perform the entire score collapses the timbral canvas from the classical Hollywood style ... the "shower scene" provides the most prominent display of emotions in the film and the scoring matches the coarse tearing of the narrative trajectory. Herrmann pulls far outside the expectation of classic Hollywood film scoring so that he can directly assault the audience.

(Ibid: 85–88)

Herrmann's music for *Psycho* entered the repertoire of tools used by horror films to create emotional impact, as can be heard in countless subsequent slasher flicks. And as well-known as the original model is, its derivatives can still be remarkably effective, since they almost invariably trigger a "startle" reflex (Wierzbicki 2009: 16). An example of this can be observed in the movie *Halloween* (1978), one of the most successful horror films in history. Hayward (2009: 1–2) claims that the movie's success can be attributed to its ability to update elements from *Psycho* for a contemporary audience, and highlights in particular the importance of its soundtrack. Acknowledging the major influence of Herrmann's use of string instruments in *Psycho*, John Carpenter, who directed *Halloween* as well as writing the screenplay and soundtrack, said:

Hermann's ability to create an imposing, powerful score with limited orchestra means, using the basic sound of a particular instrument, high strings or low bass, was impressive. His score for Psycho, the film that inspired Halloween, was primarily all string instruments.

(Carpenter 2016)

This influence can be seen in one of the main 'musical tools' deployed in *Halloween*: stingers. According to Carpenter, stingers "emphasiz[e] the visual surprise, [and] are otherwise known as 'the cattle prod': short, percussive sounds placed at opportune moments to startle the audience" (Ibid.). The sound designer of *Halloween* characterized stingers as the "ultimate horror sound", and identified them as standard musical effects:

[a] lot of the time we'll score the show and then I'll make him [Carpenter] what's called a grab bag of stingers, just all these horrible sounds with sharp attacks, that go "eeaaahhh", and then he can go and cut those in at just the moments he needs to sweeten the score.

(Quoted in Hayward 2009: 2)

It can be argued that stingers are directly descended from the string instrumentation used in *Psycho*. Hayward concludes that *"Halloween* utilized, inflected and – perhaps most significantly – refreshed a set of pre-existent traditions and referents" (Ibid.: 2–3). Following *Halloween*'s success, new musical tools entered the horror genre's repertoire.

It can therefore be seen from the cases of both *Psycho* and *Halloween* that their successes in creating a musical tool, which can be successfully deployed to reliably intensify the horrific experience of a movie, have contributed to the repertoire available to creators of horror movies, who can refine and manipulate them to create different kinds of horrific sensations in their audiences.

The creation of formula for a new emotional experience

So far, I have demonstrated the use of distinct cinematic tools used discretely. Now we shall focus on an example from the movie *Cat People* (1942) in order to examine the creation of a specific horrific emotional experience achieved through the combination of different narrative and cinematic tools.

Cat People is credited with being the first movie to feature the startle effect, described here by the editor of the movie, who reveals how cinematic manipulations (sound, lighting, editing and narrative) were used in order to create it:

> In each of these films we had what we called the "bus", an editing device I had invented by accident, or possibly by design, on *Cat People*, that was calculated to terrify people and make them jump out of their seats. It derived from a sequence in *Cat People* in which a girl was walking through the transverse in New York's Central Park, imagining that she was being followed … Looking over her right shoulder in terror, this girl backed away from the mysterious sound … From the other side of the park a bus came by, and I put a big, solid sound of air-brakes on it, cutting it in at the decisive moment so that it knocked viewers out of their seats. This became the "bus", and we used the same principle in every film.
>
> (Quoted in Newman 1999: 42)

His description shows the creation of a formula for producing a specific cinematic emotion. After the formula had been created, it could be used repeatedly in different variations.

Emotional specification: contemporary horror genre

This section deals with the consequences of the processes described in the previous sections. It will present the contemporary repertoire of emotional cinematic experiences in horror and the results of emotional specification in the horror genre.

In the early years of the genre, the horror experience that it produced was general and aimed at mass audiences. The combination of the results of market research in the industry and the assimilation of different cinematic and narrative tools into the moviemaking process generated increased levels of specification and intensification of the emotion of horror. Market research created the cinematic experience as emotional, designed for an emotional audience; in addition, measuring amorphous cinematic experiences and their division into distinguished characteristics enabled the transformation of emotional experiences, created by various cinematic and narrative tools, into emotional formulas which could be managed, reviewed, enhanced and reproduced. Over the years, the general emotion of horror evolved into more specific and defined emotional experiences and the emotional repertoire of horror movies became more diverse.

Hanich (2010) explores the cinematic emotions in horror films and thrillers and describes five main emotions ("cinematic fears") which are produced and experienced in them: direct horror, suggested horror, cinematic shock, cinematic dread and cinematic terror. In addition to these cinematic fears, the genre contains other emotions, for example disgust (Hanich 2009), suspense (Carroll 1990) and the uncanny (Hanich 2010). While movies can contain several of these emotions, they can also focus only on one of them. The ability of moviemakers to "play" with the type, intensity and frequency of the horror experience, and with other related characteristics such as the movie's genre, its rating and its marketing, enables them to match the movie to different target audiences. Consequently, the genre has evolved in the following ways.

Over time (mainly since the 1970s) the horror genre has branched out into co-existing subgenres, while each subgenre is meant to produce a different emotional experience. In the 1990s, three subgenres dominated: self-referential teenage 'slashers'; psychological horror; and action-led creature feature. In the 2000s, three other subgenres dominated: remakes of Japanese horror movies largely dealing with demon possession and haunted houses; remakes of American horror classics; and gruesome torture films (Hanich 2010). Although every decade was dominated by different subgenres, the others did not simply disappear. A successful subgenre keeps generating movies.

The division does not end in subgenres. Each subgenre can be divided into movies which create a specific combination of emotional experiences. The different type and intensity of the horrific emotional experience (and other related characteristics) enables not just the production of an endless amount of different horrific emodities, but also the tracking of different audiences. For example, the creation of horror movies with recurring powerful emotional experiences of fear and disgust makes them oriented mainly towards teenage boys. Reducing the amount of gore and including strong female characters attracts female audiences (Cunningham 2013).

A related and corresponding process to the specification of the genre was its gradual infiltrate to the mainstream film industry. Despite the success of the genre in its early years, horror remained firmly rooted in the low-budget sector. The popularity of *Night of the Living Dead* (1968) and *The Exorcist* (1973) made gruesome horror respectable. By the 1980s, horror had moved up the genre ladder to the highest budget levels, and more prestigious directors were creating horror movies (Bordwell 2006: 53), and this trend continued into the 1990s after the massive success of *The Silence of the Lambs* (1991). Since then, horror has become one of the most profitable genres, with movies earning profits often exceeding $100 million (Abbott 2010: 29, 34–35).

Abbott (2010) offers an examination of different high-budget horror movies since the 1990's and reveals how the emotional experiences of these movies (and other related characteristics) are produced and marketed, so that they suit the largest possible audience. Columbia, the studio which produced *Bram Stoker's Dracula* (1992), perceived the story as a classic whose appeal could extend well beyond the traditional audience for horror; therefore, the movie was deliberately produced and marketed for as wide an adult viewership as possible, in particular a strong female audience (Ibid.: 29–31). The studio employed a multi-faceted approach. An acclaimed director (Francis Ford Coppola) directed the film, and the cast included both actors who were popular with young audiences and older actors who combined sex appeal and the respectability of classical acting. In addition, the promotional material for the movie consistently emphasized the movie's romantic storyline in addition to the well-known horror aspect of the story. The film was very successful and was followed by adaptations of other classic horror narratives such as *Frankenstein* (1994), *The Wolf* (1994) and *Interview with the Vampire* (1994). As with Dracula, the studios which produced these movies sought to distance them from the specificity of the horror genre in order to draw in larger audiences.

Another way to address large audiences is to create horror emotions in a milder tone as part of similar genres like mystery, crime, science fiction, romantic fantasy made for teenage audiences, and especially thrillers. Since the late 1980s, the thriller has become increasingly associated with various forms of fear, to the point at which what is described today as a thriller has come to include aesthetic elements formerly associated only with horror movies. However, as the distinction between horror and thriller has blurred, "thriller" still implies a milder form of emotional involvement: less violence, fewer shocking moments and more moments of relief (Hanich 2010: 32–34). These differences enable producers to create and market movies for different specific audiences, thus increasing revenue.

In order to attract a broader audience, big-budget horrors and movies from similar genres usually decrease the intensity of the horrific experiences and add different non-horror emotional experiences. However, this is not the case with all big-budget horror movies. For example, the scriptwriter of *Blade 2* (2002) claimed that the aim of the sequel was to play up the horror angle. To achieve this, the studio hired the Mexican horror filmmaker Guillermo Del Toro who confirmed that he "was attracted to the idea of making vampires scary again" (quoted in Abbott 2010: 39). Furthermore, some of the small and medium budget contemporary horror subgenres, such as adaptations of Japanese horror movies and gruesome torture films, contain hardcore direct horror and gory elements. These movies are produced and marketed very clearly at the teenage audience; but despite this limited potential audience they can still be very successful.

Conclusion

Considering the 'paradox of horror' (Carroll 1990: 159), the development of the horror genre cannot be taken for granted. This chapter aims to explain this development by arguing that the ongoing production, management and marketing of emotional experiences, even ones that are traditionally perceived as unpleasant, can make them desirable to different kinds of audiences. These emotional experiences can be consumed in a hedonistic way, since as part of the cinematic experience they do not require an immediate reaction in the "real world".

Illouz argues that the simultaneous intensification of economic rationality and the emotional nature of life in the recent decades has resulted from the transformation of emotions into commodities (emodities; Introduction to this volume). The present chapter demonstrates this process by revealing the connection between rationality and emotions in one of the largest experience industries in the world. Three interesting conclusions can be made, based on processes described in the chapter.

The chapter demonstrates the way in which processes of measuring cinematic experiences, and the creation of models for understanding the cinematic market, actually shaped the market and the values of cinematic products. Ohmer (2006: 229) set the foundations for this study by describing the entry of Gallup's market research into the movie industry as the first full-scale effort to translate "the complexity of our desires into quantitative forms". The present chapter aims to take Ohmer's work one step further by claiming that this development was a major factor in the emotionalization of the industry.

The movie industry is not the only industry to have undergone a process of emotionalization. There are studies that deal with the emotionalization of industries such as fashion (Strähle 2015), broadcast news (Pantti 2010), journalism (Franklin 1997), tourism (Benger Alaluf, Chapter 1 this volume) and music (Schwarz, Chapter 2 this volume). As in the case of the current chapter, these studies are based on the assumption that the emotionalization process includes the framing of the emotional experiences as a central and explicit component of the products that are produced and managed as such, and the notion of consumers as subjects who aim for emotional experiences. In addition to this type of emotionalization, Holmes (2010) deals with the emotionalization process that individuals undergo, in which they increasingly draw on emotions in assessing themselves and their lives. Therefore, emotions become central to subjectivity. Since the industries described above do not just perceive the consumer but also construct him/her as an emotional agent (Illouz and Benger 2015), we can ask whether the emotionalization process that individuals undergo is always part of a process of commercialization. In accordance with Illouz's stances (in the conclusion to this volume) that "capitalism has shaped subjectivity itself" and that "emotions are *not* interior or psychological", it appears that today we cannot separate these two processes. In the conclusion chapter, Illouz offers strategies for critical writing that suit this situation.

Studying the influence of market research on the industry promotes the understanding of the *experience economy* (Pine and Gilmore 1999). The role that marketing plays in adding an experiential dimension to goods and services has been broadly discussed in the past (e.g. Lury 2004; Vargo and Lusch 2004). However, the construction of experiences by market research needs further definition and elaboration. The present study shows how market research enabled the entrance of tangible elements into the production of experiences, and through this made aesthetic services become commodities. It can be claimed that in addition to the mechanical ability of mass production of aesthetic services/experiences (Benjamin 2008 [1936]), market research enhanced the experience industries' ability to create experiences as commodities with defined characteristics and audiences.

This chapter shows the social production of emotions. Empirical and theoretical knowledge regarding the definition of emotions and the ability to manipulate them, together with knowledge gained from processes of trial and error, were adopted by the film industry and enabled it to expand its repertoire of emotional products (emodities). By deploying its knowledge of emotions, the movie industry constructs them according to this knowledge (Illouz *et al.* 2014: 237–240). Additionally, this type of production enables the industry to produce emotional experiences that are based on the attitude of the viewer towards characters and narrative developments (e.g. suspense), thereby expanding the cultural repertoire of emotions.

Despite the chapter's focus on the horror genre, it seems reasonable to assume that processes that are similar to the development of the horror genre occurred in other emotional genres: suspense, thrillers, drama, action, comedy, feel-good movies and tear jerkers. As a matter of fact, these emotional genres have developed to such an extent that it can be argued that today they constitute the entire American movie industry, and that films can indeed be correctly defined as *emotion machines* (Tan 1995) or as a machine for cinematic emodities.

Notes

1 A series of studies that were conducted by academic researchers, sponsored by the Payne fund, and published between 1933 and 1935.
2 The changes between the versions are described in the following site: "Scream (Comparison: R-Rated – Unrated Director's Cut) – Movie-Censorship.com." Retrieved March 18, 2014 (www.movie-censorship.com/report.php?ID=256325).
3 Nielsen bought Innerscope in 2015 so now it is a Nielsen company (http://innerscoperesearch.com/).
4 MindSign was active between 2008 and 2013.

Bibliography

Abbott, Stacey. 2010. "High concept thrills and chills: The Horror blockbuster." In *Horror Zone: The Cultural Experience of Contemporary Horror Cinema*, edited by Ian Conrich, 27–45. New York: Palgrave Macmillan.

Bakker, Gerben. 2003. "Building knowledge about the consumer: The emergence of market research in the motion picture industry." *Business History* 45(1):101–127.

Benjamin, Walter. 2008 [1936]. *The Work of Art in the Age of Mechanical Reproduction* (trans. J. A. Underwood). London: Penguin Books.

Blumer, Herbert. 1933. *Movies and Conduct*. Vol. 4. New York: Macmillan.

Booker, Keith M. 2011. *Historical Dictionary of American Cinema*. Lanham, MD: Scarecrow Press.

Bordwell, David. 2006. *The Way Hollywood Tells It: Story and Style in Modern Movies*. Berkeley, CA: University of California Press.

Campbell, Colin 1987. *The Romantic Ethic and the Spirit of Modern Consumerism*. New York: Blackwell.

Carpenter, John. 2016. "Halloween soundtrack." The official John Carpenter. Retrieved May 1, 2016 (www.theofficialjohncarpenter.com/halloween-soundtrack/).

Carroll, Noël. 1990. *The Philosophy of Horror, or, Paradoxes of the Heart*. New York: Routledge.

Carroll, Noël. 2002. "Why horror?" In *Horror, the Film Reader*, edited by Mark Jancovich, 33–46. London: Routledge.

Cochoy, Franck. 1998. "Another discipline for the market economy: Marketing as performative knowledge and know-how for capitalism." In *The Laws of the Markets*, edited by Michel Callon, 194–221. Oxford, UK: Blackwell.

Cunningham Todd. 2013. "Box office: How horror films like 'the conjuring' win by scaring up young women (video)." TheWrap. Retrieved May 3, 2016 (www.thewrap.com/movies/article/box-office-how-horror-films-conjuring-win-scaring-young-women-104901).

Dahl, Ronald E. and Ahmad R. Hariri. 2005. "Lessons from G. Stanley Hall: Connecting new research in biological sciences to the study of adolescent development." *Journal of Research on Adolescence* 15(4):367–382.

Demos, John and Virginia Demos. 1969. "Adolescence in historical perspective." *Journal of Marriage and the Family* (1969):632–638.

Derry, Charles. 2009. *Dark Dreams 2.0: A Psychological History of the Modern Horror Film from the 1950s to the 21st Century*. Jefferson, NC: McFarland & Company, Inc., Publishers.

Doherty, Thomas. 2002. *Teenagers and Teenpics: The Juvenilization of American Movies in the 1950s*. Philadelphia, PA: Temple University Press.

Fenimore, Ross, J. 2010. "Voices that lie within: The heard and unheard in *Psycho*." In *Music in the Horror Film: Listening to Fear*, edited by Neil Lerner, 80–97. New York: Routledge.

Flinn, Caryl. 1992. *Strains of Utopia: Gender, Nostalgia and Hollywood Film Music*. Princeton, NJ: Princeton University Press.

Forman, Henry James J. 1934 [1933]. *Our Movie Made Children*. New York: Macmillan.

Franklin, Bob. 1997. *Newszak and News Media*. London: Arnold.

Greber, Erika. 2004. "Mediendopplegänngerien: Dr. Jekyll and Mr. Hyde verwandeln sich in Film." *Poetica* 36(3/4):429–452.

Gripsrud, Jostein. 1998. "Film audiences." In *The Oxford Guide to Film Studies*, edited by John Hill and Pamela C. Gibson, 202–211. New York: Oxford University Press.

Hall, Stanley H. 1904. *Adolescence: Its Psychology and Its Relations to Physiology, Anthropology, Sociology, Sex, Crime, and Religion and Education* (Vols. I & II) New York: D. Appleton and Company.

Hanich, Julian. 2009. "Dis/liking disgust: The revulsion experience at the movies." *New Review of Film and Television Studies* 7(3):293–309.

Hanich, Julian. 2010. *Cinematic Emotion in Horror Films and Thrillers: The Aesthetic Paradox of Pleasurable Fear*. New York: Taylor & Francis.

Hansen, M. 1990. "Adventures of Goldilocks: Spectatorship, consumerism and public life." *Camera Obscura: Feminism, Culture, and Media Studies* 8(1 22):50–72.

Hayward, Philip. 2009. "Introduction: Scoring the Edge." In *Terror Tracks: Music, Sound and Horror Cinema*, edited by Philip Hayward, 1–13. London: Equinox Publishing.

Heffernan, Kevin. 2004. *Ghouls, Gimmicks and Gold: Horror Films and the American Movie Business, 1953–1968*. Durham, NC: Duke University Press.

Holmes, Mary. 2010. "The emotionalization of reflexivity." *Sociology* 44(1):139–154.

Illouz, Eva and Yaara Benger. 2015. "Emotions and consumption." In *The Wiley Blackwell Encyclopedia of Consumption and Consumer Studies*, edited by Daniel Cook and J. Michael Ryan, 263–268. London: John Wiley & Sons.

Illouz, Eva, Daniel Gilon and Mattan Shachak. 2014. "Emotions and cultural theory." In *Handbook of the Sociology of Emotions: Volume II*, edited by Jan E. Stets and Jonathan H. Turner, 221–244. Dordrecht, The Netherlands: Springer.

Jarvis, Arthur R. 1991. "The Payne fund reports: A discussion of their content, public reaction, and affect on the motion picture industry, 1930–1940." *The Journal of Popular Culture* 25(2):127–140.

Jensen, Paul M. 1996. *The Men Who Made the Monsters*. Boston, MA: Twayne Publishers.

Jowett, Garth. S. 1976. *Film: The Democratic Art*. London: Little, Brown and Company.

Jowett, Garth S., Ian C. Jarvie and Kathryn H. Fuller. 1996. *Children and the Movies: Media Influence and the Payne Fund Controversy*. Cambridge, UK: Cambridge University Press.

Kotler, Steven. 2010. "Hollywood science: Reading your mind to make horror movies even scarier." *Popular Science*. Retrieved March 18, 2014 (www.popsci.com/science/article/2010–05/hollywood-science-how-your-brain-reacts-horror-movies).

Lerner, Neil. 2010a. "Preface: Listening to fear/listening with fear." In *Music in the Horror Film: Listening to Fear*, edited by Neil Lerner, viii–xi. New York: Routledge.

Lerner, Neil. 2010b. "The strange case of Rouben Mamoulian's sound stew: The uncanny soundtrack in Dr. Jekyll and Mr. Hyde (1931)." In *Music in the Horror Film: Listening to fear*, edited by Neil Lerner, 55–79. New York: Routledge.

Lury, Celia. 2004. *Brands: The Logos of the Global Economy*. New York: Taylor & Francis.

Newman, Kim. 1999. *Cat People*. London: British Film Institute.

Ohmer, Susan. 1991. "Measuring desire: George Gallup and audience research in Hollywood." *Journal of Film and Video* 43(1/2):3–28.

Ohmer, Susan. 2006. *George Gallup in Hollywood*. New York: Columbia University Press.

Pantti, Mervi. 2010. "The value of emotion: An examination of television journalists' notions on emotionality." *European Journal of Communication* 25(2):168–181.

Phillips, Kendall R. 2005. *Projected Fears: Horror Films and American Culture*. London: Greenwood Publishing Group.

Pine, B. Joseph and James H Gilmore. 1999. *The Experience Economy: Work Is Theater & Every Business a Stage*. Boston, MA: Harvard Business Press.

Randall, Kevin. 2013. "How your brain can predict blockbusters." *Fast Company, March 1.* Retrieved January 24, 2016 (www.fastcompany.com/3006186/how-your-brain-can-predict-blockbusters).

Smith, Steven C. 1991. *A Heart at Fire's Center: The Life and Music of Bernard Herrmann.* Berkeley, CA: University of California Press.

Soister, John T. 2012. *American Silent Horror, Science Fiction and Fantasy Feature Films, 1913–1929.* Jefferson, NC: McFarland & Company, Incorporated Publishers.

Spadoni, Robert. 2003. *Uncanny Bodies: The Coming of Sound Film and the Origins of the Horror Genre.* Berkeley, CA: University of California Press.

Steiner, Fred. 1974. "Herrmann's 'black-and-white' music for Hitchcock's 'Psycho'." *Filmmusic Notebook* Fall(1):28–36.

Strähle, Jochen, (ed.). 2015. *Emotionalizing Fashion Retail.* Norderstedt, Germany: BoD–Books on Demand.

Tan, Ed. S. 1995. *Emotion and the Structure of Narrative Film: Film as an Emotion Machine.* Mahwah, NJ: Lawrence Erlbaum Associates.

Tudor, Andrew. 1997. "Why horror? The peculiar pleasures of a popular genre." *Cultural Studies* 11(3):443–463.

Vargo, Stephen L. and Robert F. Lusch. 2004. "Evolving to a new dominant logic for marketing." *Journal of Marketing* 68(1):1–17.

Weaver, Tom, Michael Brunas and John Brunas. 2007. *Universal Horrors: The Studio's Classic Films, 1931–1946.* Jefferson, NC: McFarland & Company, Incorporated Publishers.

Wierzbicki, James. 2009. "Psycho-analysis: Form and function in Bernard Herrmann's music for Hitchcock's masterpiece." In *Terror Tracks: Music, Sound and Horror Cinema,* edited by Philip Hayward, 14–46. London: Equinox Publishing.

Wood, Robin. 2002. "The American nightmare: Horror in the 70s." In *Horror, the Film Reader,* edited by Mark Jancovich, 25–32. London: Routledge.

Worland, Rick. 2007. *The Horror Film: An Introduction.* Hoboken, NJ: Wiley-Blackwell.

Zillmann, Dolf and James B. Weaver. 1996. "Gender-socialization theory of reactions to horror." In *Horror Films: Current Research on Audience Preferences and Reactions,* edited by James B. Weaver and Ron Tamborini, 81–102. Mahwah, NJ: Lawrence Erlbaum Associates.

Zukor Adolph, with Kramer Dale. 1953. *The Public Is Never Wrong: The Autobiography.* New York: Putnam.

Chapter 4

Sex cards in Tel Aviv

Mood work, recreational sexuality and urban atmospheres

Dana Kaplan

This chapter is about business card sized sex cards that advertise heterosexual prostitution in Tel Aviv and the creative urban atmosphere they help to create. The sex cards, depicting erotic images of half-naked women, are either attached to parked cars' windshields, or scattered on sidewalks. Sex cards were first seen in the city's streets some fifteen years ago, when prostitution had been relocated indoors and became less visible than before. This spatial shift has increased the dependence of the sex industry on advertising, and the cards were thus a promotional media and part of the urbanscape. This chapter, however, is not about the sex industry as such. Rather, I seek to explain how objects that originate from and signify the world of prostitution become a "quality" that animates the urbanscape and potentially contributes to its seductive atmosphere and creative appeal. In short, I ask what kind of affectivity the sex cards afford, and how.

My initial assumption is that the cards' remarkable visibility help in sexualizing the city. Historically, there is nothing new in the significance of sex-related businesses to the economic, cultural, and political life of cities. However, what *is* perhaps new in the neoliberal present is the positive role sexualization plays in urban regeneration projects and branding policies for "creative" cities. Such branding efforts are "oriented towards middle-class sensibilities and modes of comportment" (Hubbard 2016: 315). Under neoliberalism, Löfgren (2003: 244) argues, "a cultural heritage becomes a brand . . . a city is turned into an event, a commodity into an experience [and] a way of life into a style". Urban lived experiences eventually yield economic outcomes (Löfgren 2014; Mould 2014; Silver and Clark 2015). As the neoliberal city turns into the gentrifiable emodity that Löfgren and others describe, sexual diversity is increasingly used to signal normalized, "cool" and fundamentally middle-classed urban scenes, experiences, and atmospheres (McGuigan 2016: 143).

The sexualization of cities according to middle-class sensibilities is realized through various zoning and clustering tactics that separate gay-friendly, hip, and consumerist "cool" spaces, from sexually "perverse" spaces of paid sex (Berlant and Warner 1998; Hubbard 2016: 317–318).[1] Focusing on clustered spaces of prostitution, Hubbard identifies a "distinctive choreography of many red-light districts, typified by particular rhythms of inhabitation, tactical ways of looking and being, and the creation of sights and sounds that might be viewed as 'out of place' elsewhere in increasingly sanitized cities" (Hubbard 2016: 313). Alongside such clustering policies, a new technique to take prostitution off the streets has recently been on the rise. Increasingly, "adult-businesses" are made *invisible* by dispersing them across the urbanscape (Hubbard 2016: 316; also Berlant and Warner 1998: 551–552, 562). Both the clustering and dispersing policies share the same sanitizing logic whereby, in order for the city to "feel" civilized and properly middle-class, its zones of vice must be hidden and contained. However, the cards defy the distinction between civility and vice by making prostitution highly visible. This chapter illuminates the affective "body/ space entanglement" associated with the sex cards (Amin 2015). It asks: what is the "affective atmosphere" the cards afford in their constant and expansive urban presence (Anderson 2009, 2014)?

Theoretically, this chapter is influenced by the application of the affective turn to urban studies. A central focus of this scholarship is urban atmospheres and to "non-discursive dimensions of affects, moods and sensibilities" as they unfold in urban contexts (Löfgren 2014: 256). Following Löfgren and other urban scholars, I perceive atmospheres as resources for the production of the creative city-emodity. Atmospheres can be defined as those affective-sensory qualities that enclose people, things, and environments together, if momentarily (Anderson 2014: 149). Atmospheres and the moods they bear, give coherence to everyday, fleeting instances of sociability that are not yet anchored in socially fixed and attainable emotions, discourses, and identities (Anderson 2009, 2014; Böhme 2003). In this context, I am less inclined to study the sex cards merely as public representations of hegemonic discourses on heterosexuality, gendered bodies and prostitution. Instead, I look at their material, spatial, and atmospheric qualities and the *general mood work* these qualities may induce among the individuals who happen to encounter them. Carlson and Stewart (2014: 114) define mood work as "a labour of living" that "marshals bodies, objects, technologies, sensations and flights of fancy into forms of partial coherence". Mood work thus refers to sociability that does not center around explicit identity categories or other, already articulated socio-cultural discourses. The concept of mood work emphasizes two elements that are specifically important for my analysis. First is the notion of a shared affect that is not necessarily concerted and synchronically felt. Mood work as I perceive it refers to affects that people might experience the same way, albeit not collectively. Essentially, this suggests that mood work neither presupposes groups or collective identities, nor forms them. Second, I propose that even an ephemeral mood work can crystalize into a more coherent, stable atmosphere that may gradually be associated with the city-emodity and potentially add character to its brand.

In what follows, I first unfold my theoretical and methodological approach, developing the concepts of *atmospheres* and *recreational sexuality*, both of which are crucial for understanding the sex cards phenomenon. The next empirical section examines the affective affordances of the sex cards phenomenon. Based on this analysis, I argue that the sex cards transpose prostitution "out of its place" of vice and into middle-class neighborhoods, facilitating a spillage of abjection from one zone to another and into the city at large. Finally, I propose that this affective sexualization of space, an affective atmosphere I dub *intense indifference*, helps reproduce the city as a cool emodity. I conclude by linking mood work and sexy urban atmospheres to a contemporary affective modality of neoliberal aesthetic capitalism (Illouz, Introduction to this volume). This chapter thus raises two theoretical claims: first, that even unglamorous, abject qualities of the sex trade can be displaced and become part of the broader processes of urban branding; and second, that urban branding may be achieved implicitly, through the affective investment or mood work of dispersed passersby.

Theoretical and methodological approach

The chapter starts from the assumption that cities inhabit scenes of "collectivization" (Blum 2003; Silver and Clark 2015). By this I do not refer to bottom-up, participatory, activist, and other collaborative or highly engaged practices of place making (e.g., Blum 2003). Rather, I accentuate unfixed and destabilized urban atmospheres that are felt by individuals who are loosely connect to each other. I refer to the ways in which subjects and artifacts, amenities, and surroundings, potentially interact as part of a shared – yet not synchronized or conscious – mood work. As Ash Amin (2015: 244) puts it, "sociality arises in the embodied experience of an environment in which thinking and feeling are shaped by the interaction between sentient bodies, technologies, and environments". It is this affective interaction between the city's inhabitants and their environments that creates scenes and atmospheres.

The ensuing analysis of the sex cards joins a nascent "haptic cultural sociology" (Green *et al.*, 2010; Kingsbury 2011; Paterson 2009; Roadway 1994; Thrift 2008). This line of research espouses a "material aesthetics" of everyday life, particularly in urban settings (Masterson-Algar and Vilaseca 2015). It accounts for "the mediating role of products – the ways they co-shape the sensorial contact between humans and their world" (Verbeek 2010: 12). Shifting focus to the material aesthetics of things does not mean that the cards, as in our case, do not carry socio-cultural meanings or that people do not decode these meanings. It is simply to argue that non-discursive qualities of sexualized spaces and scenes (for example) are as important as the discursive ones. Like Olsen (2003: 100), I believe that instead of simply assuming that "everything is language, action, mind and human bodies", we must pay more attention to its sensory and affective dimensions of social life (Carlson and Stewart 2014; Fox 2015).

As the various contributors of this book demonstrate, affectivity is not outside of capitalist relations. Nigel Thrift (2004a: 87–88) sees social life as an ongoing process of becoming, defined as "the capacities of affecting and being affected".

He also argues that this form of sociality, which he calls "summoning life" is what defines the present (Thrift 2004a: 88). Moreover, "summoning life", or "the labour of living" (Carlson and Stewart 2014) has been coopted into capitalist production itself. In this process everyday life – including singular tastes, social differences and the "stuff" of social relations – can potentially produce value (Jansson 2002). Based on postmodernist scholarship, Böhme (2003: 73) similarly argues that capitalism now extracts value from an excess of signs, affects, spectacles, and desires and "needs which, far from being allayed by their satisfaction, are only intensified". This new value regime, which Böhme terms "staging value", marks:

> [a] remarkable change in how bio-power is produced and welded. It aims to produce expressive rather than docile bodies, active yet passive bodies that have been taught to act in the moment, thereby producing added value for business and the state.
>
> (Thrift 2004a: 95)

As I explain in the next section, sex and sexuality have become key resources of staging value.

Scholars who study the dominance of immaterial and affective labor in contemporary capitalism assume that productive work is no longer bound to the traditional workplace but has expanded to include life itself (Brook 2013; Fox 2015; Hardt and Negri 2000; Kennedy 2010; Tsogas 2012). According to this perspective, the value of many experience-based emodities stems from the affects invested in them through labor that is increasingly performed outside of the traditional workplace. From a Marxian perspective productive work counts as any "act that involves the direct production of potentials for doing and being" (Anderson 2012: 33), much like those capacities to affect and being affected mentioned earlier. Thus, according to Tsogas (2012: 391), "commodities in cognitive capitalism are born affective, desirable, sexy and made-to-sell and do not become so later". Tsogas goes on to claim that compared to industrial capitalism, in cognitive capitalism commodities become biopolitical in that they are premised on "exceptional and numerous cognitive qualities . . . the sex appeal, the ability to generate desire, evoke feelings, complement the identity of an individual, become a visual display of individuality, status, even mood and so many others" (Tsogas 2012: 391).

However, most studies of immaterial labor are still focused on the social value and the affective qualities of various end-products that are produced, moreover, within traditional workplace relations and organizations (Brook 2013; Tsogas 2012; Warhurst and Nickson 2009). The scholarship does acknowledge that immaterial workers infuse commodities with "sexy interpretations, creative cues and general ambience" by using their physical, cognitive, and affective labor power (Thrift 2004a: 92; Tsogas 2012). Still, the more random and less organized forms of labor remain understudied. Thus, while "summoning life" as a capitalist strategy is a widely discussed topic, most studies in this area continue to focus on well-defined points of production or consumption and to differentiate between spheres of work and non-work. Differently put, while "the measure of wealth is no longer surplus labour (creating value) but rather the increase in disposable labour time" in which individuals can develop their physical, cognitive, and affective skills (Kennedy 2010: 835), labor processes are still understood as "constituted by human beings consciously activating their labour power to produce use-values by engaging with the natural world" (Brook 2013: 338). Furthermore, studies of non-work time and the (re)-production of social life through emotions are not that helpful either, because such studies tend to emphasize collective forms of public feeling (Carlson and Stewart 2014; Fox 2015). Consequently, we are still very much in the dark when it comes to understanding how shared yet unsynchronized affects, or general mood work may help produce value.

If we take seriously the idea that the labor of living is inside capitalist relations (Hardt and Negri 2000), then we must also acknowledge that non-waged mood work can create value for capital even when it is neither a conscious effort nor a concerted, collective effervescence but a fluid, longitudinal, and aggregative shared feeling. I would therefore argue that urban atmospheres are created through the general mood work of being in the city. And, moreover, that the sex cards, being part of the current "recreational" phase of sexuality, help create a sexually charged urban atmosphere through what I dub *intense indifferent* affects.[2] In this way, the sex cards and the mood work they generate are conducive to the workings of neoliberal capitalism.

Recreational sexuality and neoliberal antinomies

By "recreational sexuality" I mean a tendency towards sexual experientialism, creativity, and entrepreneurialism that is closely aligned with neoliberal capitalism (Attwood and Smith 2013; Bernstein 2007; Kaplan 2011, 2017; Maddison 2013). According to this understanding, recreational sexuality produces both capital *and* the subjectivities and social relations which facilitate, advance, and legitimize neoliberal capitalism (Agathangelou 2004: 5). A central theme of the scholarship on recreational sexuality in neoliberalism is sexual agency or lack thereof (for example, Gill and Scharff 2011). This theme runs not just in the feminist scholarship, but is also prevalent in queer and post-structuralist studies of current sexualities. Such works tend to circle around emancipatory agendas, parsed as "sexual agency", "empowerment" or "transgression" (Dean 2012; Woltersdorff 2011). However, while many studies to date have focused on the political economy of the global sex industry and the cultural discourses which have amplified, disseminated, and ultimately mainstreamed recreational sexuality, less attention has been paid to the everyday aesthetic and material qualities of recreational sexuality.

Most studies on recreational sexuality have analyzed either the "upper", glamorous, fun, and consumerist sex culture (e.g. BDSM fashion, sex toy parties), or the "lower", clearly exploitative circuits of sex in global capitalism (Agathangelou 2004). Specific areas of interest for the "lower" ranks are pornography, human trafficking, prostitution, and sex tourism (Agathangelou 2004; Bernstein and Shih 2014; Binnie 2004; Gamson and Moon 2004: 52–53; Kotiswaran 2010; Parker and Easton 1998). Unsurprisingly, whereas the tenets of the "lower" ranks of recreational sexuality emphasize lack of options, constrained choices as well as exploitation and risk, the "upper" ranks of recreational sexuality pivot upon freedom, agency, self-realization, and choice.

Studies on the "upper", glamorous side of recreational sexuality usually assume *the sexualization of culture* thesis. According to the *sexualization of culture* thesis, sex has become more visible in the public sphere, through consumer and popular cultures (Kaplan 2011). Sex not only sells other commodities but is also a lifestyle commodity in itself that satisfies varied tastes and forges individual self-identities (Arvidsson 2007; Attwood and Smith 2013; Maddison 2013; Mazzarella 2001; Mears 2015; Piller 2010). We have come to identify this form of individualism with the figure of the empowered consumer-citizens and the historically specific structure called "consumer culture" (Illouz 1997, 2009; Maddison 2013: 106–107). As noted above, neoliberal capitalism pushes forward this logic, as life itself (e.g. sexual relations, consumed lifestyle commodities, subjectivities) become forms of labor. Neoliberalism renders subjects as autonomous and valuable (or not), based on their differential capacities "to affect and be affected" – to produce and handle heightened affective energies (which is not necessarily the same as "positive emotions", see later) – and then translate these affects into self-appreciation (Hearn 2008; Kaplan 2011; Tyler 2011; for the emotional strains of consumer culture, see Hayward 2004: 7; Illouz 2009). This structure of feeling is part of a current "aesthetic" economy, whereby (staging) value is produced by inducing and tending to strong reactions and desires. Again, the labor of living branches out from workplace – to almost everything we do in our personal lives. This includes sexuality. Recreational sexuality is part of this social reality in which life in its entirety is harnessed into producing capitalist value (Arvidsson 2007; Böhme 2003: 72; Brook 2013; Hardt and Negri 2000; Kennedy 2010; Preciado 2013; Tsogas 2012). By being (or feeling) sexually recreational, neoliberal subjects not only consume sexual commodities but also associate themselves with the empowered, glamorous world of those who have the power to affect and be affected.

In this regard, it is easy to see that the affective labour associated with recreational sexuality creates value. This calls for a closer look at the everyday aesthetic, material, and atmospheric affordances of recreational sexuality. The next empirical section provides such an analysis. As will be shown, it finds that the twofold character of recreational sexuality described earlier – the "lower", exploitive side and the "upper", empowered side – blends at the level of everyday life and in actual places.

An atmospheric analysis of sex cards in Tel Aviv

Cards in the city

Walking in Tel Aviv, even in the upscale streets of the city, one cannot avoid the plethora of business card like ads advertising sex services. These sex ads are usually affixed to parked cars, where they are later thrown onto the sidewalks, kept, or collected – which is what I have been doing for the last couple of years, in the interests of scholarly research. With the help of devoted friends and colleagues, I am now the proud owner of a collection of more than 200 different colour-printed cards.

From the subjects' point of view, this might be a case in which sex-related incivilities are imposed on the civil public realm of Tel Aviv residential areas (Bannister *et al.* 2006: 857). Indeed, while prostitution is accepted in Israel as a fact of life and is not a criminal act,[3] it would still be wrong to assume that commercial sex is unproblematic.[4] In fact, during the 1990s and with the collapse of the former USSR and rising rates of trafficking, prostitution has become a pertinent social problem, even though prostitution was on the rise even before that time, and especially since the mid 1970s (Cnaan 1982). According to official data from the mid 2000s – when the state enhanced its anti-trafficking operations, police "closed down as many as 300 brothels" in Tel Aviv (Bensinger 2007: 284). This speaks to a certain normalization of sex work in the urbanscape (Levenkron 2006). There are indications that the number of sex venues in Tel Aviv has risen since the mid 2000s, and that working hours in the venues have expanded to daytime as well (Lee 2012). Thus, whereas urban sexscapes have generally become less visible because the sex industry has moved indoors and into residential areas, the felt presence of commercial sex seems to have increased. Prostitution is no longer restricted to the night time economy and "red-light" clusters.

Significantly, the public forms of marketing for sex businesses are always shaped by local circumstances and regimes of regulations (Prior and Gorman-Murray 2014: 109). Piller (2010) thus describes the sexualization of public spaces in Basel and the ways the high visibility of the sex industry and its signage contribute to the marking of the city as mobile and cosmopolitan. In most cities, however, "planning authorities have tended to tacitly accept commercial sex premises as legitimate businesses but use planning and zoning policies to relegate them to marginal locations and control the design (internal and external) and signage" (Steinmetz and Maginn 2015: 129). The urban sex industry is usually heavily regulated in terms of proximity to residential functions and policies tend to restrict the visibility of public signage of the sex industry (Prior and Gorman-Murray 2014: 110).

In Israel, the law penalizes the publication of prostitution services and the displaying of offensive publications on billboards.[5] This has considerably contributed to the rise of the sex cards and shaped their dispersion and design in specific ways. In fact, and as will be shown below, in their semi-private emplacements, barely-legal imagery and vague wordings, the cards embody the "paradox of illegal legality", whereby illegal prostitution-related acts are given a legal or regulative and procedural veneer and publicized in law-abiding ways (Hubbard 2016; Venger 2014).

The cards are not pornographic in themselves, but market indoor sex services taking place at "massage parlors", "discreet apartments" and strip clubs. Vered Lee (2012) quotes a spokesman for the Tel Aviv Municipality explaining why there are so many brothels in Tel Aviv that operate without interference:

> [u]nder the Business Licensing Law, brothels and escort parlors are not businesses which require a license and they do not undergo a licensing process, because they are illegal. Enforcement in their case is carried out solely by the Israel Police and does not fall within the purview of local government.

But while it is illegal to both "hold, manage, or lease" a place for the purpose of prostitution[6] and to publicize prostitution, police enforcement is rather weak and inconsistent and has raised some serious problems. One major problem has been separating the real offenders (criminals who own and run these businesses) from the women who are (legally) in prostitution (see Knesset Protocol 16.3.2011). As I shall explain later, the cards' "in-between" quality, as ubiquitous semi-private objects placed in the public sphere, presents another difficulty. As the municipality's spokesperson cited above explained, "offering sex services is an offence which can only be enforced by the police. However, the Tel Aviv Municipality regularly penalizes [illegal] ads presented in places that are *not vehicles*" (Lee 2012, emphasis added).[7]

It is also illegal to publicize pornographic materials[8] and for this reason the cards do not show explicit nudity. Some cards include "no sex" captions, which, paradoxically, is the clearest sign of the card's association with the sex trade. Most cards do not give any details as to the specific nature of the service offered, but whatever they are, they are always heterosexual and rarely extreme or kinky. Also, and unlike the similar phenomenon of sex ads in London (Hubbard 2002; Pile 2000), a police official said in an interview I conducted with him that hardly any civilian complaints are ever made against the cards (cf. Hubbard 2002: 354). While some grass-root initiatives suggest that city dwellers are not impartial to the issue,[9] it would seem that in their everyday life, residents and visitors alike have grown to accept the reality of sex cards.

There are other cities in Israel in which sex work cards are as visible and ubiquitous, most notably Eilat, a popular tourist resort. The reason I focus on Tel Aviv is because it has acquired a certain mythical quality (Azaryahu 2007). Tel Aviv oscillates between three particular mythologies: "the First Hebrew City, a showcase of national revival and Zionist argument", the modernist "White City" of Bauhaus structures, and "the Nonstop City, a unique urban experience and a cultural statement" (Azaryahu 2007: 5). In their ubiquity and low-tech quality, the sex cards interact with each of the three myths, but especially with the branding of Tel Aviv as an experiential, sexy city.

In what follows I first examine the visual images carried by the sex cards, asking what kinds of cultural codes of sex and gender they convey. This is not because I take cultural representations and visual images as preceding other, material-aesthetic forms of analysis. On the contrary, while images do "play a significant role in shaping and contesting the meaning of place and space" (Latham and McCormack 2009: 252), semiotic interpretive procedures are hardly reconcilable with the atmospheric approach I employ here. This does not mean, however, that we need to disregarded images altogether. Instead, I regard visuals as more than ideologically charged, representational content. In this perspective, "images are also blocks of sensation with an affective intensity: they make sense not just because we take time to figure out what they signify, but also because their pre-signifying affective materiality is felt in bodies" (Latham and McCormack 2009: 253).

In this regard, the sex cards, what is printed on them and the material qualities of these makeshift pieces of paper are part of the "'everyday ecologies' – the unstable, never quite concrete 'stuff' of the city" (Latham and McCormack 2009: 254). Hence, I am more interested in the affective aggregation of the somewhat replicable, highly recognizable, mainstream-yet-racy image-bank photos of half-naked white women (for a similar strategy, see West, Chapter 5 this volume). This visual analysis accounts for the most recurring and iconic images as well as some of the more exceptional ones. After accounting for the imagery on the cards, I discuss the spatial organization of the cards themselves across the urban space.

Visual imagery

Overall, the images are rather tame (Hubbard 2002): there are no naked bodies or explicit body parts or sexual acts. Since the cards advertise only heterosex, there are no representations of men, and when more than one woman appears they are not touching each other. One of the most widely circulated cards carries a typical image of an attractive, skinny, sluttish, full-busted, and sexually available young woman. She is wearing seductive lingerie, directly gazing at us in an inviting, non-intimidating way, in a typical "glamour modeling" pose (as the current erotic media industry is euphemistically called). In Israeli culture, she would pass as ethnically unmarked, given her complexion and Mediterranean features. Some images presume to be "authentic", some even of "real Israeli girls". Authenticity is indicated by a pixelated face and a caption reading "actual picture". However, most cards represent highly ethnicized images of Slavic-looking, blond women, also wearing lacy lingerie, posing in an erotic way, and exposing their thong-clad behinds. This particular type of "Slavic" femininity unmistakably carries a symbolic weight in the contemporary global political economy of sex. Images of Eastern European women embody sexual Otherness and hence promiscuity (Piller 2010). This is particularly true in Israel, which was a major trafficking hub until the mid 2000s. Fewer cards display black women or Israeli-looking women (i.e. not Slavic/Asian/black/Latin).

Text is important, too, in rendering the cards sexual. Accompanying texts tend to be suggestive: "in my house everything is permitted", "come and make your dreams come true", "with me, you won't hear no", "sexy spa – quality massage by high standard models + parking", "Sandy's clinic – you are welcome to play around in a magical atmosphere", and, possibly my all-time favorite, which directly address the religious market-share: "with the help of God,[10] Fridays until the Sabbath commences, a luxurious place, Friday night, from young professional women, all types of massage, until very late at night".

Importantly, while some cards incorporate English text, they do not exhibit what Piller (2010) describes as "multilingual proficiency" as a marker of high class in order to appeal to higher-class business travellers. In fact, many texts present poor Hebrew proficiency as well. Curiously, however, some of the cards do seem to aim for clients with high cultural capital. These much rarer cards may depict, for example, a Charlie Chaplin's *Tramp* image on one side, and a "discreet girl next door beauty" (as the Hebrew caption reads) on the other. Another exceptional image I found was of Jessica Rabbit, the cartoon figure from the 1988 Disney/Touchstone film *Who Framed Roger Rabbit*. This card not only hails cinema connoisseurs but also those potential clients who are put off by the mass-produced erotic images of most cards.

To summarize, the cards represent universally sexy images of attractive, lean women, mostly taken from image banks. As many of the cards imitate the style of a modeling "book", it seems that sex work is represented as a clean, normal, and healthy service. In the next section, I suggest that the particular affectivity of the cards, which I describe as an *intense indifference*, relates more to their spatial affordances than to their iconic content.

Spatial and physical properties

In line with the bounded legality of prostitution in Israel, there is no designated red-light district in Tel Aviv. Places of commercial sex are scattered around the center (which mixes business, entertainment, and residential functions) in regular buildings and rented apartments. Even if sex places are obscured and hidden from the untrained eye, the cards themselves are contained within the city's fabric of the everyday. According to the police official I interviewed (and mentioned earlier), most cards are distributed in the city center and are less likely to be found in the southern, underprivileged parts of the city, where undocumented migrant workers, refugees and Arab residents dwell. This geography is rather different from Piller's (2010) analysis of the signification of Basel as a cosmopolitan zone of commercial sex. In Tel Aviv, the cards help produce a *local* sexual atmosphere.

I want to focus on five spatial and physical properties of the cards in particular, which, I would argue, coalesce to create intense *indifference*, or, conversely – *a muted, or withheld feeling of abjection*. The first of these physical properties is the small *size* of the cards. The cards are designed as business cards. Their pocket size makes them easy objects to distribute, to stow for later use, or dispose of.

Recently, distributers of cards (very often teens on bikes) have started dispensing packs of cards directly onto the sidewalks. The smallness of the cards enables this.

Another significant physical dimension of the cards is their *visuality*, defined as "specific ways of seeing and being seen" (Szerszynski and Urry 2006: 118). Influenced by Henri Lefebvre, geographers divide cities into larger scales and smaller, street-level scales (see Thrift 2004b for a review). The cards are rooted at street level, below the eyeline. We do not look at them from afar, but from above. This is in contrast to the city's large-scale, unapproachable texture of modern, glass-plated skyscrapers, glamorous fashion billboards, or ubiquitous large screen displays, and other remote structures which we submissively look *up* at from our street position. Passersby might only glimpse (down or up) at both large- and small-scale urban objects, or step on them. However, once tacked to one's own car, it becomes harder to ignore the cards. Either way, the physical closeness between the cards and city dwellers make them hard objects to ignore.

A third physical property of the cards is their *rawness*, their low-tech quality. Even if the sex cards emulate business cards, they still do not belong to the fast and sleek world of business pitches, strategic marketing teams, and high consumerism. The sex cards are "of the street", and do not belong to hygienic, air-conditioned, perfumed shopping malls. Neither are they virtual cybersex images or privately owned mobile devices loaded with "people-nearby sex applications" (Weiss and Samenow 2010). As opposed to such personal mobile media and large, immobile screen devices, the artifactual cards remain outside the glamorous realm of new, interesting, spectacular, and cosmopolitan media-space (Arvidsson 2007; Couldry and McCarthy 2004). This conventional print-based media recruitment technique stands in sharp contrast to newer, more private, digital and personalized ways of recruiting clients and participants to sex activities (e.g., Kolar and Atchison 2013). The natural habitat of the card is the cracked and dirty sidewalk or the dusty car. They are raw, however, not only because they reside in the street but also because of their straightforward design and mass-produced images (see West, Chapter 5 this volume), and because they usually sell the least upscale type of sex services.

A fourth property is what I call *mobility*. The cards exemplify what Büscher *et al.* (2010: 5) typify as "the physical movement" of objects and subjects entailed by capitalist production and consumption. This includes the movement "of objects to producers, consumers and retailers, the sending and receiving of presents and souvenirs, as well as the assembly and (re)configuration of people, objects and spaces as part of dwelling and place-making" (Büscher *et al.* 2010: 5). The cards are inseparable from the city's economy. Their aim is to help recruit and mobilize customers to not-too-remote sex services. More broadly, the cards are one route through which sex work is contained in the city's everyday life, and enhances its erotic image. This kind of mobility raises the issue of sex tourism. Tel Aviv is undergoing a rebranding as a cosmopolitan and cool city to visit. While being a gay-friendly city, it is not a favorite sex tourism destination for heterosexuals. Unlike transnational hubs (like Basel and London) where sex work is advertised in transitory, "travel", "non-spaces" such as airports, transportation, and billboards, in Tel Aviv sex cards advertise nearby sex joints for locals and, as noted above, this is the reason why the cards are distributed in residential areas. Nevertheless, the cards can be seen as inducing what Büscher *et al*. (2010: 20) deem "the imaginative travel, effected through talk, but also the images of places and peoples appearing on and moving across multiple print and visual media". As with any other marketing media, the cards open up an imaginative space of affects. In this respect, even the most normative city dwellers and pedestrians might develop sexual, desirous feelings upon encountering a card.

Fifth, as objects, the cards are *temporarily stationary*: after being distributed they end up being tossed into garbage cans, onto sidewalks, or secreted into one's pocket. Once more, the cards reveal their "low-tech" nature. In the not-too-distant past, business cards were related to the city's rushed pace of capital and business. Nowadays they seem to be downgrading to the city's shady sex economy. A good example, the calling cards "found a new home: the telephone boxes of central London have become the advertising hoardings of sex workers" (Hubbard 2002; Pile 2000: 29–30).

Finally, the sex cards dramatically raise the issue of *private and public* boundaries, and exemplify how these boundaries are flexible, blurred, and disturbed (for reviews, see Allon 2004: 263–266; Gal 2002; Thompson 2011). As communicative media, the scattered sex cards can be seen as violating one's privacy. This is because they are physically attached to privately owned cars (tellingly, until the 1990s, the slang word in Hebrew for 'car' translates into English as 'private'). A car is a private enclave, "a mobile privatization" (Allon 2004) which extends one's home and stores some personal belongings in the public domain. This is expressed in the words of the Tel Aviv Municipality spokesperson who says that the city penalizes the placement of cards in public spaces – as long as they are not on cars. Furthermore, that cards are an extension of self has become even more true with "the changing nature of driving" in which cars technologically adjust themselves perfectly to their drivers (Thrift 2008: 48–52). Since cars in Tel Aviv are parked on the streets, when car owners encounter the sex ads they must respond to them. Like junk mail, and unlike non-personalized types of marketing and mass-media contents (such as outdoor advertising, shop window displays, or the constant glare of TV ads) which we have learned to ignore, the sex ads necessarily attract our attention and stimulate some affects. Should we leave the card in place, acknowledging that it is someone's source of income? Responsibly tear it up and throw it away to prevent its further use? Or practice feminist activism and walk down the block and collect all the cards?

Discussion: intense indifference and value under neoliberalism

Many scholars have investigated the carefully designed and manipulated glamorous images of recreational sexuality circulating in the mass media. These researchers ask how popular representations of sex and sexuality may influence people's sex-related understandings and behaviors. But in this chapter I have sought to examine the lower and unglamorous side of recreational sexuality, by focusing on the ephemeral mood work the low-tech cards afford. This analysis teases out, if only in a preliminary way, a common critical stance in cultural studies which looks for "fissures" and transgressive potentialities. Unlike most theories of the everyday, my critical approach does not conceive of the fleeting, the sensory, and the affective as a priori more emancipatory than the fixed and discursive. Instead, I would argue that the content, spatial organization, and material qualities of the cards do afford an affective response; they do form an atmosphere or "affective intensity" (Arvidsson 2013: 377). But the intensity of this affectivity does not seem to be very strong.

As already mentioned, not many people are emotionally or politically engaged with the cards. As a constant reminder of prostitution, we could expect the cards to stir strong emotions such as rage, hopelessness, disgust, lust, etc. (unlike the sterile "natural-like" resorts in Benger Alaluf, Chapter 1 this volume). Such strong *negative* emotions contrast with other types of sexually related strong emotions such as fun, pleasure, or empowerment that are unusually associated with the upper, glamorous side of recreational sexuality. On this side of recreational sexuality, sex signifies "intense experiences", and "intense experiences" signify sex (Jancovich 2006: 75). Marxist-feminist theorist Anna Agathangelou (2004: 4–6) explains this from a global political economy perspective. She notes that aspiring middle-class subjects fantasize themselves as "sexual bourgeoisie" (p. 4), whose sense of freedom and entitlement is associated with being sexually recreational, the feeling of having the capacity to affect and being affected.

Going back to the cards, there is no doubt that many people feel passionately towards them and the exploitive reality they represent. However, most passersby accept the cards as part of their everyday lives and the texture of the city, and are not intensely affected by them (cf. Hubbard 2002). They encounter the cards separately, individually, and in a non-synchronized way, not as a collectively organized crowd, and not even as a public or a multitude with some shared sense of a common goal or identity. Unlike online networked publics that gather around a coherent thing, even if only temporarily, what unites those who encounter the cards is a shared indifference toward them and what they advertise. Together with the cards' inbuilt abject-yet-mundane quality, the result is a rather muted affective reaction. But how does a mood work of *intense indifference* correspond to contemporary neoliberal capitalism? How, in other words, does this very loose arrangement of indifferent, non-integrated, disorganized, unmeasurable mass of non-publics, actually help create the city-emodity and its intangible value as sexy and creative?

We are used to thinking of sexually related issues as emotionally intense. Above I noted the strong emotions that can be associated with it, whether negative or positive. However, what this case seems to suggest is that recreational sexuality can be thought of as a *relational* system of affects. The upper end is comprised of positive strong emotions that indicate one's capacity to affect and being affected. On the other end, we can find those less intense emotions. By immersing in the urban atmospheres through their mood work, passersby face the "lower" echelons of the sex industry, those still slightly abject, smutty enclaves of exploitive sex. In a consumerist cultural environment which glamorizes sex, the cards market a far less glamorous kind of sex. With their mass-produced eroticism, poor language, and less than sophisticated design, sex cards cannot escape the street level. Those same abject qualities result in a mood work of indifference.

Berlant (2004: 9–11) suggests that coldness, or withholding, or a refusal to engage with an upsetting situation, like that of the cards and the exploitive sexuality they publicize, is the other side of compassion. Hence, compassion and lack of engagement are not opposites but indications of who is worthy of our pain, our attention, and our taking responsibility – and who is not. I would therefore argue that unlike "the transformational purchase" brought about by intense emotions about specific problems (such as prostitution), the atmospheric presence of the cards allows us to basically ignore or detach ourselves from the exploitive reality of sex work, disavowing the suffering of others. The cards foster a mood work of non-engagement, and this may actually help diluting the negative elements the cards represent, while keeping, still, their sexiness "in the air". What this means is that, as many have argued before, the everyday can be absorbed into the circuits of capital to potentially create value. This, however, does not necessarily happen through deliberate acts of commodification. It may also occur through the unintended, non-deliberate, and random affective atmospheres people happen to enter into and participate in creating.

Notes

1 The normalization of "hygienic", consumer-oriented gay culture is historically new. As Berlant and Warner (1998: 560) argue, "In gay male culture, the principal scenes of criminal intimacy have been tearooms, streets, sex clubs, and parks" and other semi-public spaces.
2 I understand recreational sexuality as "commercial" because it produces value for capital even in the private sphere through classed aspirational fantasy work. I will expand this idea later.
3 Prostitution is legal but procuring is not (Laws of the State of Israel, Penal Law 5737-1977, article ten section 199a).
4 In 2012 and then in 2017 there were feminist campaigns that stressed, inter alia, the polluting of the city's streets. www.youtube.com/watch?v=6opo9d-R0lY&utm_source=atzuma. co.il&utm_medium=social&utm_campaign=petition (accessed January 1, 2017).
5 Laws of the State of Israel, Penal Law 5737-1977, article ten, sec 205C(a), and sec 214(A).
6 Laws of the State of Israel, Penal Law 5737-1977, C.10, Sec 204, 205.
7 www.nrg.co.il/online/54/ART2/344/523.html.
8 Laws of the State of Israel, Penal Law 5737-1977, C.10, Sec 214.
9 See footnote 4.
10 בס"ד (Aramaic). This caption is a Jewish religious custom. According to religious laws, it is forbidden to even look upon women, let alone visit prostitutes.

Bibliography

Agathangelou, Anna M. 2004. *The Global Political Economy of Sex: Desire, Violence, and Insecurity in Mediterranean Nation States*. New York: Palgrave Macmillan.

Allon, Fiona. 2004. "An ontology of everyday control: Space, media flows and 'smart' living in the absolute present." In *Media Space: Place, Scale and Culture in a Media Age*, edited by Nick Couldry and Anna McCarthy, 253–274. London: Routledge.

Amin, Ash. 2015. "Animated space." *Public Culture* 27(2):239–258.

Anderson, Ben. 2009. "Affective atmospheres." *Emotion, Space and Society* 2(2):77–81.

Anderson, Ben. 2012. "Affect and biopower: Towards a politics of life." *Transactions of the Institute of British Geographers* 37(1):28–43.

Anderson, Ben. 2014. *Encountering Affect: Capacities, Apparatuses, Conditions*. Burlington, VT: Ashgate.

Arvidsson, Adam. 2007. "Netporn: The work of fantasy in the information society." In *C'lick Me: A Netporn Studies Reader*, edited by Katrien Jacobs *et al.*, 69–76. Amsterdam: Institute of Network Cultures.

Arvidsson, Adam. 2013. "The potential of consumer publics." *ephemera* 13(2):367–391.

Attwood, Feona and Clarissa Smith. 2013. "Leisure sex: More sex! Better sex! Sex is fucking brilliant! Sex, sex, sex, SEX." In *Routledge Handbook of Leisure Studies,* edited by Tony Blackshaw, 325–336. London and New York: Routledge.

Azaryahu, Maoz. 2007. *Tel Aviv: Mythography of a City*. Syracuse, NY: Syracuse University Press.

Bannister, Jon, Nick Fyfe and Ade Kearns. 2006. "Respectable or respectful? (In)civility and the city." *Urban Studies* 43(5/6):919–937.

Bensinger, Gad J. 2007. "Trafficking in women for prostitution in Israel: A follow-up." *International Journal of Comparative and Applied Criminal Justice* 31(2):281–291.

Berlant, Lauren. 2004. "Introduction: Compassion (and withholding)." In *Compassion: The Culture and Politics of an Emotion*, edited by Lauren Berlant, 1–13. London and New York: Routledge.

Berlant, Lauren and Michael Warner. 1998. "Sex in public." *Critical Inquiry* 24(2): 547–566.

Bernstein, Elizabeth. 2007. *Temporarily Yours: Intimacy, Authenticity, and the Commerce of Sex*. London: University of Chicago Press.

Bernstein, Elizabeth and Elena Shih. 2014. "The erotics of authenticity: Sex trafficking and 'reality tourism' in Thailand." *Social Politics: International Studies in Gender, State & Society* 21(3):430–460.

Binnie, Jon. 2004. *The Globalization of Sexuality*. London: SAGE Publications.

Blum, Alan. 2003. *Imaginative Structure of the City*. London: McGill-Queen's University Press.

Böhme, Gernot. 2003. "Contribution to the critique of the aesthetic economy." *Thesis Eleven* 73(1):71–82.

Brook, Paul. 2013. "Emotional labour and the living personality at work: Labour power, materialist subjectivity and the dialogical self." *Culture and Organization* 19(4):332–352.

Büscher, Monika, John Urry and Katian Witchger (eds). 2010. *Mobile Methods*. London: Routledge.

Carlson, Jennifer D. and Kathleen C. Stewart. 2014. "The legibilities of mood work." *New Formations* 82(82):114–133.

Cnaan, Ram A. 1982. "Notes on prostitution in Israel." *Sociological Inquiry* 52(2):114–121.

Couldry, Nick and Anna McCarthy. 2004. *Media Space: Place, Scale and Culture in a Media Age*. London: Routledge.

Dean, Carolyn J. 2012. "Afterword: The agency of sex – Volition after Foucault." *South Atlantic Quarterly* 111(3):549–562.

Fox, Nick J. 2015. "Emotions, affects and the production of social life." *The British Journal of Sociology* 66(2):301–318.

Gal, Susan. 2002. "A semiotics of the public/private distinction." *Differences: A Journal of Feminist Cultural Studies* 13(1):77–95.

Gamson, Joshua and Moon, Dawne. 2004. "The sociology of sexualities: Queer and beyond." *Annual Review of Sociology* 30:47–64.

Gill, Rosalind and Christina Scharff (eds) 2011. *New Femininities: Postfeminism, Neoliberalism, and Subjectivity*. London: Palgrave Macmillan.

Green, Adam I., Follert, Mike, Osterlund, Kathy and Paquin Jamie. 2010. "Space, place and sexual sociality: Towards an 'atmospheric analysis'." *Gender, Work & Organization* 17(1):7–27.

Hardt, Michael and Antonio Negri. 2000. *Empire*. Cambridge, MA: Harvard University Press.

Hayward, Keith. 2004. *City Limits: Crime, Consumer Culture and the Urban Experience*. London: Routledge.

Hearn, Alison. 2008. "Meat, mask, burden: Probing the contours of the branded self." *Journal of Consumer Culture* 8(2):197–217.

Hubbard, Phil. 2002. "Maintaining family values? Cleansing the streets of sex advertising." *Area* 34(4):353–360.

Hubbard, Phil. 2016. "Sex work, urban governance and the gendering of cities." In *The Routledge Research Companion to Geographies of Sex and Sexualities*, edited by Gavin Brown and Kath Browne, 313–320. London and New York: Routledge.

Illouz, Eva 1997. *Consuming the Romantic Utopia: Love and the Cultural Contradictions of Capitalism*. Berkeley, CA: University of California Press.

Illouz, Eva. 2009. "Emotions, imagination and consumption: A new research agenda." *Journal of Consumer Culture* 9(3):377–413.

Jancovich, Mark. 2006. "The politics of playboy: Lifestyle, sexuality and non-conformity in American Cold War." In *Historicizing Lifestyle: Mediating Taste, Consumption and Identity from the 1900s to 1970s*, edited by David Bell and Joanne Hollows, 70–87. Aldershot, UK: Ashgate.

Jansson, André. 2002. "The mediatization of consumption: Towards an analytical framework of image culture." *Journal of Consumer Culture* 2(1):5–31.

Kaplan, Dana. 2011. "Sexual liberation and the creative class in Israel." In *Introducing the New Sexuality Studies* (second edition), edited by Steven Seidman, Nancy Fisher and Chet Meeks, 357–363. London: Routledge.

Kaplan, Dana. 2017. "Recreational sex not-at-home: The atmospheres of sex work in Tel Aviv." In *Sexuality and Gender at Home*, edited by B. Pilkey *et al.* London: Bloomsbury Academic.

Kennedy, Peter. 2010. "The knowledge economy and labour power in late capitalism." *Critical Sociology* 36(6):821–837.

Kingsbury Paul. 2011. "Sociospatial sublimation: The human resources of love in Sandals Resorts International, Jamaica." *Annals of the Association of American Geographers*, 101(3):650–669.

Knesset Protocol no. 88, 16.3.2011, Committee on the Status of Women and Gender Equality. www.knesset.gov.il/protocols/data/html/maamad/2011–03–16.html.

Kolar, Kat and Chris Atchison. 2013. "Recruitment of sex buyers: A comparison of the efficacy of conventional and computer network-based approaches." *Social Science Computer Review* 31(2):178–190.

Kotiswaran, Prabha. 2010. "Labours in vice or virtue? Neo-liberalism, sexual commerce, and the case of Indian bar dancing." *Journal of Law and Society* 37(1):105–124.

Latham, Alan and Derek P. McCormack. 2009. "Thinking with images in non-representational cities: vignettes from Berlin." *Area* 41(3):252–262.

Lee, Vered, 2012. "Hell du jour: Meet Israel's daylight prostitutes." *Haaretz* (11 October). Retrieved June 11, 2016 (www.haaretz.com/israel-news/hell-du-jour-meet-israel-s-daylight-prostitutes-1.469461.

Levenkron, Nomi. 2006. "Tel Aviv." In *Encyclopedia of Prostitution and Sex Work*, Vol. 2, edited by Melissa Hope, Ditmore, 472–473. London: Greenwood Publishing Group.

Löfgren, Orvar. 2003. "The new economy: A cultural history." *Global Networks* 3(3):239–254.

Löfgren, Orvar. 2014. "Urban atmospheres as brandscapes and lived experiences." *Place Branding and Public Diplomacy* 10(4):255–266.

Maddison, Stephen 2013. "Beyond the entrepreneurial voyeur? Sex, porn and cultural politics." *New Formations* 80/81:102–117.

Masterson-Algar, Araceli and Stephen Luis Vilaseca. 2015. "Text to street: Urban cultural studies as theorization and practice." *Journal of Urban Cultural Studies* 2(1/2):3–14.

Mazzarella, William. 2001. "Citizens have sex, consumers make love: Marketing KamaSutra condoms in Bombay." In *Asian Media Productions*, edited by Brian Moeran, 168–196. Honolulu, HI: University of Hawai'i Press.

McGuigan, Jim. 2016. *Neoliberal Culture*. Basingstoke, UK: Palgrave Macmillan.

Mears, Ashley. 2015. "Girls as elite distinction: The appropriation of bodily capital." *Poetics* 53:22–37.

Mould, Oli. 2014. "Tactical urbanism: The new vernacular of the creative city." *Geography Compass* 8(8):529–539.

Olsen, Bjørnar. 2003. "Material culture after text: Re-membering things." *Norwegian Archeological Review* 36(2):87–104.

Parker, Richard and Easton, Delia. 1998. "Sexuality, culture and political economy: Recent development in anthropological and cross-cultural sex research." *Annual Review of Sex Research* 9:1–19.

Paterson, Mark. 2009. "Haptic geographies: Ethnography, haptic knowledge and sensuous dispositions." *Progress in Human Geography* 33(6):766–788.

Pile, Steve. 2000. Calling cards. In *City AZ: Urban Fragments*, edited by Steve Pile and Nigel Thrift, 29–31. London and New York: Routledge.

Piller, Ingrid. 2010. *Sex in the City: On Making Space and Identity in Travel Spaces*. In *Semiotic Landscapes: Language, Image, Space*, edited by Adama Jaworski and Crispin Thurlow, 123–136. New York: Continuum.

Preciado, Beatriz. 2013. *Testo Junkie: Sex, Drugs, and Biopolitics*. New York: Feminist Press.

Prior, Jason and Andrew Gorman-Murray. 2014. "Housing sex within the city: The placement of sex services beyond respectable domesticity?" In *(Sub) Urban Sexscapes: Geographies and Regulation of the Sex Industry*, edited by Paul Maginn J. and Christine Steinmetz, 101–116. London: Routledge.

Roadway, Paul. 1994. *Sensuous Geographies: Body, Sense and Place*. London and New York: Routledge.

Silver, Daniel and Terry Nichols Clark. 2015. "The power of scenes: Quantities of amenities and qualities of places." *Cultural Studies* 29(3):425–449.

Smith, Nicola J. 2011. "The international political economy of commercial sex." *Review of International Political Economy* 18(4):530–549.

Steinmetz, Christine and Paul J. Maginn. 2015. "The landscape of BDSM venues." In *(Sub) Urban Sexscapes: Geographies and Regulation of the Sex Industry*, edited by Paul J. Maginn and Christine Steinmetz, 117–137. London: Routledge.

Szerszynski, Bronislaw and John Urry. 2006. "Visuality, mobility and the cosmopolitan: Inhabiting the world from afar." *The British Journal of Sociology* 57(1):113–131.

Thompson, John B. 2011. "Shifting boundaries of public and private life." *Theory, Culture and Society* 28(4):49–70.

Thrift, Nigel. 2004a. "Summoning life." In *Envisioning Human Geographies,* edited by Paul Cloke, Phillip Crang and Mark Goodwin, 81–103. London: Arnold.

Thrift, Nigel. 2004b. "Driving in the city." *Theory, Culture and Society* 21(4–5):41–59.

Thrift, Nigel. 2008. "The material practices of glamour." *Journal of Cultural Economy* 1(1):9–23.

Tsogas, George. 2012. "The commodity form in cognitive capitalism." *Culture and Organization* 18(5):377–395.

Tyler, Melissa. 2011. "Tainted love: From dirty work to abject labour in Soho's sex shops." *Human Relations* 64(11):1477–1500.

Venger, Olesya. 2014. A Paradox of Illegal Legality: Analysis of Online Escort Services Advertising on Backpage. Unpublished Dissertation, University of Georgia, USA.

Verbeek, Peter-Paul. 2010. *What Things Do: Philosophical Reflections on Technology, Agency, and Design.* University Park, PA: Penn State Press.

Warhurst Chris and Nickson, Dennis. 2009. "'Who's got the look?' Emotional, aesthetic and sexualized labour in interactive services." *Gender, Work and Organization* 16(3):385–404.

Weiss, Robert and Charles P. Samenow. 2010. "Smart phones, social networking, sexting and problematic sexual behaviors: A call for research." *Sexual Addiction & Compulsivity* 17(4):241–246.

Woltersdorff, Volker. 2011. "Paradoxes of precarious sexualities." *Cultural Studies* 25(2): 164–182.

Part II

Ideal of intimacy

Relational emotions

Chapter 5

Understanding authenticity in commercial sentiment

The greeting card as emotional commodity

Emily West

> There's something very insincere about these greeting cards we send back and forth to each other all the time. They're like these little one-dollar folded paper emotional prostitutes, aren't they? "I don't know what my feelings are, so I'll just pay some total stranger a buck to make up this little Hallmark hooker to do the job for me. So I can go, 'Yeah, I didn't write this, but whatever they wrote, I think the same thing.'" Wouldn't it be better if we just had one card that covered every occasion for everybody in one shot? Just "Happy Birthday, Merry Christmas, Happy Anniversary, Congratulations, It's a Boy and Our Deepest Sympathies. Signed, the whole office."
>
> (Opening Monologue from Seinfeld episode, "The Pledge Drive," Gammill and Pross 1994)

Jerry Seinfeld's rant about greeting cards puts a little more baldly what many of us may have thought or said about greeting cards. Paying money for a mass-produced expression of sentiment that is supposed to represent our feelings makes many people uncomfortable, and attracts plenty of flak in the entertainment media and popular press. Whether on sitcoms, in standup routines, comic strips, TV commercials, or the obligatory lifestyle features and opinion pieces that appear in newspapers and magazines before every major card-sending holiday, there is a good deal of cultural uncertainty expressed about the authenticity of the greeting card as a form of communication. It's telling that Seinfeld compares buying a greeting card with paying for sex, as it is the intrusion of commerce into intimacy that bothers many of us about greeting cards. At least in American culture, the authenticity of greeting cards remains uncertain, as they so clearly lie on or near the "commodity frontier" that Arlie Russell Hochschild (2003: 30) described, one of the "activities [that] seem . . . too personal to pay for."

What could be a more quintessential emotional commodity, or "emodity" as coined by Illouz, than the greeting card? Perhaps no other brand, at least in the United States, is as associated with emotion than Hallmark, estimated to control 44 percent of the greeting card market, including both paper and e-cards (Turk 2014). The core promise of Hallmark's brand is to deliver reliable and effective emotional products to use in interpersonal communication, most often for people with whom we are already close. And yet, the propriety of relying on the market to communicate personal emotions is in question. When we use a greeting card to communicate emotion, are we taking a shortcut, an easy way out? Are we becoming deskilled in the practice of connecting with others, or expressing our feelings with words? Are we allowing the market to intrude ever more into a "sacred sphere" of personality and intimate life? In other words, are greeting cards – or commodified sentiment – a threat to the authenticity of emotion?

These questions prompted me to undertake a project about authenticity in greeting card communication, as understood by both consumers and producers of cards. As an "ethnography of authenticity" (Illouz, Introduction to this volume), this mostly interview-based research produced insights into the space where emotion and the market meet, producing emodities. To be sure, understanding and opinion about the authenticity of greeting cards vary, particularly, I and others have found, depending on the cultural capital of consumers (Illouz 1997; Spaulding 1981 [1958]; West 2010a, 2010b). The notion that greeting cards are inauthentic because they are a form of communication mediated by an item produced for the mass market, thereby encumbering the expression of an individual's interiority, is not a universally held view, and indeed, much more likely to be found among people with more formal education. In contrast, from my interviews, a logic emerged that makes some sense of why so many people look to the market to help them express emotions to loved ones. Communicating emotion involves personal risk: how to do it and whether it will be well received or reciprocated is always at least somewhat uncertain. While contemporary ideologies of personal authenticity would suggest that in such a situation we should "look down deep into ourselves" in order to decide how to connect emotionally, in practice people look outside of themselves, to the symbolic resources of the public sphere. How do other people express emotion? What has worked in the past? What will be socially recognized as an expression of caring and connection? In this view, authenticity is a "social virtue," focused on effective connection and understanding between self and other (Guignon 2004: 151). Today, and for some time now, when we look to the world around us for such guidance, that world is infused with brands, marketing, and consumer products. The market is now a major, if not the primary, source of advice, resources, and certainty-producing strategies for social connection, including goods covered in this volume, such as music (Schwarz, Chapter 2 this volume) and self-help and coaching services provided by the positive psychology industries (Shachak, Chapter 6 this volume and Cabanas, Chapter 7 this volume).

The virtue of greeting cards, in particular, for this risk and uncertainty-management scenario is their status as consumer objects (Illouz, Introduction to this volume). Their tangibility brings concreteness and ambiguity-reduction to communicative exchange that reinforces the declarative quality of greeting card sentiment. Greeting cards are a paradigmatic case for considering what happens when commodities promise to "fix" emotions, both in the sense of presenting a solution to a communication problem, and in the sense of capturing a feeling in a tangible object.

The way people use greeting cards to navigate uncertain emotional waters speaks to another theme of this volume: the relationship between emotion and rationality. The emotions expressed in and through cards are not generally of the hedonistic variety. They are part and parcel of relationship work – usually relationship maintenance, and more rarely, transformation. Most often, they invoke a declaration and therefore renewal of existing emotional connections. The leading card-sending occasions in the United States are Christmas, Valentine's Day, Mother's Day, and birthdays, with the dominant emotions expressed being love, friendship, and appreciation (Greeting Card Association 2014a). The most emotional of these occasions are Valentine's Day and Mother's Day, and both are big business according to industry sources. About 132 million valentines are purchased overall in the United States for Valentine's Day, not including boxed valentines designed for children (Greeting Card Association 2014b; Hallmark 2015a). Similarly, for Mother's Day, 122 million cards are typically purchased in the US (Hallmark 2015b). For Valentine's Day, this means sales of about a billion dollars just on cards, compared to total spending of about 19 billion dollars for the holiday (Greeting Card Association 2014b).

Broadly speaking, greeting card sentiments signal recognition of the specialness of the recipient, and the importance of the recipient to the sender in his or her life. The feelings may be genuine, but those feelings are hard to separate from a rational assessment of one's relationships, and whether or how effort should be expended to maintain those relationships. In that sense greeting cards are part of the "rationalization of emotion management" that Schwarz suggests characterize people's uses of music (Chapter 3 this volume), or the "emotional utilitarianism" that Shachak (Chapter 6 this volume) recognizes in the techniques that positive psychology offers. This reflects a broader rationalization of emotion that Illouz (2007) has argued is emblematic of "emotional capitalism," and that so often goes hand-in-hand with processes of commodification. Greeting card selections may require a sober assessment of how a recipient will receive a given message, an exercise requiring equal parts cognition and emotional intelligence. Emotions are part of relationships, but those relationships are not expressions of pure emotion, neither are the efforts that go into creating and maintaining those relationships. As scholars such as Hochschild (2003), Di Leonardo (1987), and Miller (1998) have convincingly demonstrated, relationships and the emotions that sustain them require (often gendered) work.

As much as the public, tangible, and even commercial nature of greeting card sentiment can contribute a sense of security to emotional communication, these same characteristics are at the heart of why greeting cards are often viewed as inauthentic. People who use and make cards construct their understanding of authentic emotional communication by negotiating between two seemingly contradictory beliefs: that each individual is unique, and yet emotions and the ways we communicate them are socially shared, even universal. In fact, an industry term that guides the production of sentiment is "universal specificity" (Suddath 2014; West 2008). The emotional products of consumer culture, and greeting cards in particular, count on the utility of emotional scripts. And yet, it is the very scriptedness of cards that inevitably raises questions about their authenticity that must be constantly worked on and resolved, moment to moment, by both producers and users.

Beyond the scriptedness of any given card, there are other questions to raise about how the greeting card industry contributes to a particular emotion regime (Reddy 2001). Defined as socially privileged guidelines for expressing emotion, William Reddy's concept of emotion regime draws attention to how historically and socially contingent emotional styles are linked with dominant power interests. The greeting card industry is highly concentrated – in the United States about 65 percent of the greeting card market is controlled by two companies, Hallmark and American Greetings (Turk 2014). This profit-driven industry has a tremendous platform for shaping and reinforcing prevailing ideologies of emotion. The ubiquity of card practices suggests that they have been somewhat successful in making card-sending a "socially compulsory gesture" even in the digital age, at least for some occasions (Unity Marketing 2005; see also Fottrell 2013). Despite notable shifts in gender politics, it is remarkable how gendered greeting card use remains, with at least 80 percent of card purchases still made by women (GCA 2014a; West 2009). The industry as a whole does little to contradict the notion that sending cards is part of the gendered work of home and family. Finally, the industry has a vested interest in convincing consumers that they can depend on the market to help them communicate emotion, sometimes not so subtly undermining consumers' own abilities to express themselves. The take-home message is that the purchase of carefully selected commodities is the most effective way to communicate caring. The intellectual challenge remains how to integrate these kinds of critiques about the meta-communication of greeting cards as a cultural form with the sense- and culture-making of card users.

This brings us to the normativity question raised by Illouz (Introduction to this volume). As analysts and interpreters of culture, on what basis do we challenge some people's stated preference, often accompanied by compelling stories and impassioned testimonials, for the affective magic wrought by pre-printed sentiments on lovingly selected greeting cards? Pursuing an ethnography of authenticity brings us up close to the lived experience we seek to understand. Although it may not be strictly possible to experience emotions second-hand, people's actions and accounts testify to the emotional effectivity of their encounters with these commodities, as well as the ways in which they sometimes fail. Somehow, we must describe and honor their experiences while simultaneously holding in view the broader emotion regime that shapes the possibilities for these experiences to begin with.

A brief word about the study

My reflections on greeting cards as emotional commodities draw on research with North American producers and consumers of greeting cards, conducted between

2002 and 2005. The primary forms of data were fifty interviews with greeting card consumers, including mostly women but some men, ranging in age from eighteen to their eighties, concentrated mostly in the Northeast United States. I also interviewed seventeen people who work in the greeting card industry, and spent time at Hallmark Cards in Kansas City, Missouri. I attended eight Hallmark Writers and Artists on Tour events in three states, a public relations initiative taking place at this time in which members of the public had a chance to meet Hallmark creatives, ask them questions, and "share their own card stories." In addition, I consulted archival sources about cards and the card industry, followed news and public commentary on the same, attended the National Stationery Show in New York City, and collected many different kinds of greeting cards. Throughout these various forms of data collection, my guiding research question was how people understand authenticity (or the lack thereof) in a commercialized form of emotional communication.

The high risk territory of emotional connection

Consumer culture, and advertising in particular, has often been accused of promising emotional rewards through products that can ultimately never be delivered, thereby engineering never-ending demand (e.g., Campbell 1987; Leiss *et al.* 2005). Illouz counters this perspective by arguing that the market does, indeed, commodify emotions (Introduction to this volume). Since emodities are always the result of completion or "co-production" by the consumer (Ibid.: 7), then it follows that the emotional outcome of the market exchange remains fundamentally uncertain. Consumer objects and experiences can promote or facilitate a certain emotion, but the desired emotional use value is not guaranteed.

In talking to consumers about why they use cards, I came to understand that most people reject the view that greeting cards are some kind of sure-fire shortcut to communicating emotions to others. They were very clear about what they as consumers had to do to select the right card, complete it, and use it correctly to achieve the desired effect. Certainly, some consumers experience the commercial nature of greeting card sentiment as a threat to the possibility of authentic expression of the self. Yet, most of these consumers nevertheless find ways to participate in this "socially compulsory" gesture – sometimes by appropriating greeting card sentiment ironically, or by choosing cards that emphasize visual design rather than sentiment. That being said, many informants expressed genuine appreciation for how the sentiments in greeting cards assist them with emotional communication. Finding what seem like private thoughts and feelings reflected in the sentiments available in the marketplace can be very affirming, authorizing many people's desire to communicate those feelings. In this chapter I focus primarily on those consumers who do appreciate the utility of greeting card sentiments; elsewhere I have elaborated on how consumers who worry that pre-printed sentiments are an inauthentic expression of emotion nevertheless find ways to buy and send lots of cards (West 2010a).

Several respondents commented on the positive feelings they experience in "discovering" a pre-printed sentiment that matches their own feelings for a particular person or sending situation. For example, Daisy, a clerical worker in her 40s said:

> You'll be like, oh my gosh! I mean, if you read the card, you'll be like, that is me! You know or, that sounds just like you ... it is amazing how they just put it down and you're like, wooh, I could have said that!

Betty, also a clerical worker in her fifties, said something similar:

> [t]he messages in cards that you buy from the store, it just seems, if I read the words and I feel it, feel something for that person that I'm sending the card [to], I like to pick cards out like that.

Their descriptions of the process of finding the "right" card demonstrate how the initial emotional experience that cards produce takes place in the store, as the buyer reads sentiments as they shop for cards.

People commented that a card sentiment can communicate how much thought the sender put into the relationship and the occasion when picking it out. Of course, this perspective is more likely to be expressed by people *who themselves* put a great deal of effort into picking the "right" card. For example, when Salma, a working mother of three in her twenties, explains why she appreciates receiving cards, she assumes that others put as much effort into picking out cards as she does. She explains:

> You know, they actually looked in a store and picked out a card, you know, cause you can't just go in a store and pick out one. You know, usually I have like five in my hand before I decide, okay, I'm going to get this one, so I think that's why [a card means more than a written note or other form of communication].

My respondents often talked about the effort that goes into finding the perfect card in quite moral terms, as something that you are supposed to do to be a good person and do right by others. Heather, a woman in her thirties who was one of the most dedicated greeting card senders I spoke with, said "I would, you know, go through, I might look at twenty cards until I find the right one. Some people just don't care. They'll run in and grab anything, and I don't, I don't buy my cards that way." Cindy, a retired real estate agent, seemed to feel quite strongly about the effort that should go into picking out cards. She said:

> You just have to have patience and you have to care about what you're doing. It isn't just running in and grabbing any card and sending it. The idea of send-ing a card doesn't mean anything if you don't convey a message, how you feel about the person you're sending it to.

Among my respondents, those who pride themselves on finding the *right* card to send, particularly those who try to find a pre-printed sentiment that captures what they would like to say, tend to assume that others do the same.

College student Lesley commented on the excitement she feels upon finding a pre-printed card sentiment that captures her feelings, but accompanied this thought with the caveat that, "It's not because I don't want to think for myself, I don't want to say it," thereby acknowledging the cultural critique of cards as somehow displacing an authentic communication of sentiment. Other respondents were more comfortable admitting that card sentiments sometimes helped them express feelings they are unable or nervous to put into writing themselves. Some interviewees reported either that they find it difficult to express themselves through the written word in general, or that in particular for emotional messages they looked to card sentiments to find the "right words." These might be difficult emotions, such as sympathy at a time of loss, or expressions of love and attachment to the most important people in their lives. Indeed, the greeting card industry reinforces the notion that it can be hard to express ourselves by regularly producing sentiments known as "More than Words Can Say" or "Seldom Say," which explicitly reference the difficulty the sender has putting his or her feelings into words.

While this trope is common across sending situations for cards, it is particularly pronounced in cards designed for men to send to women. A typical example of this from Hallmark reads:

> For my Wife – I never have been good about telling you "I love you" enough or complimenting you as much as I should … but I hope somehow you know how glad I am to be your husband and that I love you more than anything in the world. Happy Birthday.

Card sentiments like this one position themselves as the vehicles by which inexpressive men are able to communicate emotionally to their loved ones. Card texts can be conceptualized as a publicly sanctioned set of instructions on how to communicate emotion. When these scripts invoke a gendered communication gap, they ultimately re-inscribe it. Greeting card industry marketing tends to reinforce the idea that men and women communicate very differently, but that greeting cards are the perfect solution to this communication gap (West 2009). This is especially true for card-sending occasions that men are expected to participate in but without the assistance of their wives – Valentine's Day in particular. While overall only 15–20 percent of cards are purchased by men, the figure rises to 45 percent for Valentine's Day (Greeting Card Association 2014b). Hallmark and American Greetings create larger cards at higher price points for men to buy on Valentine's Day and similar occasions, reasoning that because they feel anxious about what kind of card is expected, they will gravitate towards more expensive-looking cards (American Greetings Corporation 2000).

Ideally a greeting card sender recognizes his or her emotion reflected in the card in the store, selects and completes the card, and then the card effectively conveys the emotion to the recipient. However, it's no surprise that this outcome is far from guaranteed. The asymmetry of emotional experience that can occur between sender and recipient was humorously portrayed in an American television commercial for Budweiser beer in the early 2000s. The ad cuts back and forth between a young woman carefully looking at cards in a store, reading the sentiments, and a young man picking up a six-pack of beer at a different store. At the register, he sees a greeting card display and quickly grabs a card, hardly looking at it. Then the ad cuts to the couple at dinner, drinking their beer, presumably celebrating a special occasion. They each open their cards, and the woman almost cries with emotion at the card sentiment that her boyfriend had so carelessly selected for her. Although an ad for beer, this TV commercial taps into the cultural narrative that cards are women's work and men cannot be expected to express emotion effectively, demonstrating what a dominant trope this is across consumer culture.

However, the ad inverts the likely emotional effects of cards. In fact, my respondents argued that how *they* feel when picking out a sentiment is the more reliable emotional experience that cards produce. People are aware that the desired emotional effect of the card they send remains uncertain, particularly in sending situations where difficulties in communication or emotional connection already exist. One respondent, Shannon, pointed to the cards she receives from her father which seem to reflect his tastes and not take hers into account. The failure of the card to achieve emotional connection in this case is emblematic of a larger problem in their relationship. This example recalls another respondent, Tanya, who knows that her mother-in-law prefers cards with extended effusive sentiments because that's the kind she gives. But because Tanya isn't comfortable with using pre-printed sentiments to express herself, she sticks with the blank art cards that she feels represent her best, knowing that her mother-in-law will likely not appreciate them the way she does. In contrast, Jane has several elderly relatives to whom she regularly sends cards that she describes as "flowery" – in terms of both design and sentiment – not the kinds of cards she would like to receive, or that even resonate with her emotionally, except to the extent that they signify her desire to maintain her connections with her aging aunts.

Greeting cards are no emotional quick fix. Even if they touch the sender's heartstrings, they may fall flat at their destination. Or the sender may need to compromise finding something that represents her taste and feelings in order to find a card that will have the desired emotional effect. Within a broader belief that greeting cards are useful for emotional communication, consumers recognize the contingencies involved in their emotional effectivity. They draw attention to the emotional work and effort that they as a sender must carry out in order for the correct card to be identified for a given relationship or occasion. Whether this is merely a rhetorical move to distance themselves from being mere cultural dupes of commercial sentiment, or whether it's an accurate representation of this cultural practice is hard to determine once and for all. But awareness of ways that greeting cards can fail as emodities bolsters the notion that greeting cards offer a strategy for emotional connection, but one that still relies on consumer effort and execution.

For many consumers, just the right greeting card sentiment has a special ability to capture their feelings and convey them to others that their own words might never have. The existence of that sentiment in the marketplace affirms their feelings and the propriety of communicating them. As Berlant (2008) has argued, an attachment to conventionality should not be read merely as an attachment to the constraints of social order, but as an expression of desire for social belonging, which in turn implies its lack. The public, commercial nature of the card produces a sense of security in the inherently risky activity of emotional communication. This sense of authorization can function for both senders and recipients of cards, as suggested by the testimony of a woman who "felt less alone" after receiving a Hallmark card specifically for someone who has had a miscarriage (Radio-Times 2013). Realizing that this event happens often enough for Hallmark to make a card for it made it easier for her to imagine the community of women who have shared her difficult experience.

Even for those consumers who feel confident in their own ability to express emotion through language, many find something useful about the more formal and declarative communicative style of cards. Consider how two of my respondents explained the value they find in greeting card sentiments (West 2010b). Victoria said:

> [s]omeone you see every day, you're not going to tell them, I really respect you, I admire you as a person, you never do that. And a card, it's like a special occasion, you can actually tell them, hey, I really, you know, I like you (laughing).

Here is a similar thought from Sue:

> It's an event, and it's an opportunity for acknowledgement. So I treat it as such, and I make sure that I acknowledge them … And it's different than off the cuff. Off the cuff can be good but, you know, rehearsed is sometimes a little better.

The sense of "rehearsed" that Sue describes applies to the appropriation of a pre-printed sentiment, but also to how greeting cards require and then communicate a sender's forethought to a recipient. These greeting card users raise an important characteristic of emodities in general, and greeting cards in particular: their performativity.

Greeting cards as consumer objects: communicating time

The commercial nature of greeting card sentiment lends it a publicness, and that publicness has value to many consumers even for private, emotional communication. As Sue and Victoria argued, commercial sentiments bring a sense of occasion and preparation, and therefore a sense of commitment, to emotional communication. The mass-produced nature of cards might be what makes them such a target for accusations of inauthenticity, but their status as consumer objects is key to why many people recognize greeting cards as genuine expressions of feeling (Illouz, Introduction to this volume). Consider the comment of Pat, a retired teacher. Pat is generally speaking not a fan of greeting card sentiment, preferring to select cards on the basis of their design. However, she said:

> Even if there's a written message, somebody else's written message, it shows that you've cared enough to buy it, to address it, and to mail it! And those are three different steps, so it's supportive of whatever you're trying to convey.

Pat's comment, echoed by many others in my study, highlights how the labor of consumption – the time and effort of selecting goods in the marketplace, and then transforming them into possessions – can function as a form of emotional labor (Hochschild 1983; Miller 1998).

People's understanding of how cards work on this most basic level recalls John Durham Peters' (1999: 270) observation of why performance often communicates more powerfully than language alone:

> Touch and time, the two nonreproducible things we can share, are our only guarantees of sincerity. To echo Robert Merton, the only refuge we have against communication fraud is the propaganda of the deed. No profession of love is as convincing as a lifetime of fidelity.

Greeting cards, especially the paper variety rather than electronic greetings, function largely through this "propaganda of the deed." They allow consumers to not just "inform" the recipient about their feelings, but "perform" them (Rothenbuhler 1998: 23). While critics of greeting cards deride them as cheap and easy, most users view the effort involved in finding just the right card, in the right store, writing the right message, and delivering (or even better, mailing) it to be an effective way of demonstrating that they were thinking of the recipient. Indeed, the very asynchronicity and cumbersomeness of cards – especially now with so many options for instantaneous, convenient communication – is what makes them emotionally effective in the eyes of many. Miss Manners has advised that a good rule of thumb is "The more emotional the content, the more cumbersome should be the means of conveying it" (Martin 1997: 22), and in an age of instantaneous digital communication, the greeting card has never looked so cumbersome. In a cultural context where lives are understood to be busy and time scarce, even taking the time to select a card carries a premium. While at one time, cards were more likely to be compared unfavorably to handwritten letters, which for some represent more time and effort than a store-bought card, today cards are more likely to be compared to a phone call, email, or Facebook post. Even in 1926, the Greeting Card Association (the American trade association for this industry) presented letter writing as a quaint custom of a past era:

In the days of famous letter-writers like Lady Mary Wortley Montagu, the keeping up of a correspondence was a serious matter, for each letter had to be, as it were, an essay in friendliness. But nowadays, with more opportunity for personal association and less time that can be devoted to the writing desk, we must depend more and more upon outside help in keeping up our correspondence.

(GCA 1926:7)

The trade association highlighted the greeting card's time saving function but also reassured consumers that they were an appropriate substitute for handwritten letters, saying "Convenience and beauty alike commend them to busy and yet friendly folk" (Ibid.: 8). The case of greeting cards highlights the importance of the category of "time" in a consumer capitalist society. Consumer objects that signify time spent can be powerful statements of caring and connection in a culture where time is always experienced as a scarce resource, even by the retired and unemployed as Daniel Miller (1998) found in his ethnographic study of shopping in London.

Although from an objective standpoint greeting cards do seem like time-savers relative to handwritten notes or letters, or even compared to phone calls that can be hard to coordinate and may become protracted, from a subjective standpoint *most* consumers see them as requiring a significant amount of time and effort. My respondents pointed to the multiple steps in sending a card – leaving the house, visiting shops, going through the cards to find the best one, writing in the card, addressing it, stamping it, and mailing it – as crucial to endowing the card with emotional significance.

Hallmark's advertising campaign from the early 2000s capitalized on this aspect of greeting card communication, using the tagline: "They'll never forget you remembered." The television commercials depicted recipients opening cards with surprise and delight, and the tagline emphasized how the card represents the sender thinking of and remembering the recipient at a previous time and place. Hallmark's advertising campaign resonates with what people say about why they appreciate receiving cards. My interview respondents as well as many fans who attended Hallmark Writers on Tour spoke about how cards make them feel "remembered" and "thought of," and how they appreciate receiving cards from friends and family even when they don't particularly like the card itself, because it shows the sender was thinking of them. As college student Jess puts it, when comparing cards with the phone or email, "I guess it's the time issue, that it requires. And if someone sent you a card, and it arrives on time, then presumably they were thinking about this and it just shows more thought, I guess." Similarly, Salma, quoted earlier, said: "Cause anybody could just write a note, or pick up the phone. It takes effort to go out and put a stamp on it and send it." According to these responses and many others from people of different ages and backgrounds, what is appreciated is taking valuable "time out" and devoting it solely to the recipient.

One of my respondents reported that she couldn't bring herself to buy cards in a drugstore (where they are typically sold in the United States) because, ironically, it was *too* convenient, and so she would feel she had not put enough time into the purchase and therefore it would no longer be a valid sign of caring. For her, the time and effort necessary to show caring through greeting cards involves making a special trip to a greeting card store or gift shop, rather than picking a card up while running other errands. In her mind, shopping for a card to be used in "sacred" interpersonal communication must be kept separate from the contamination of shopping for other, profane everyday items.

The importance of the effort that goes into selecting cards for particular occasions with the recipient in mind was further highlighted by the comments of card stockpilers – people who keep a collection of cards at home to send when they don't have time to go out and make a special trip. Jean, a single professional and graduate student in her late thirties, keeps a stockpile of attractive blank cards at home to use when she wants to drop friends a quick note or a thank you. However, she explains that she would never use one of these blank cards for a specific occasion such as a birthday because she would "feel bad" about sending a card she hadn't clearly shopped for and picked out with their special occasion in mind. Further, if a friend is turning forty she will make sure to get a card that is captioned for a 40th birthday. The industry obliges consumers who have this concern by producing cards with quite specific captions, such as "To My Aunt on Passover," "Wedding for Mother and New Stepfather," or "Congratulations on Getting Your Driver's License." However, despite the fairly extensive specificity of the available captions (at least in larger card stores), one of the most frequent complaints that I have heard from consumers about the greeting card industry is not being able to find the exact caption or sentiment for a particular sending situation. Certainly the lack of cards from Hallmark specifically suited for a gay or lesbian wedding was a point of contention until they started to explicitly serve this market in 2008 (Associated Press 2008). Although Hallmark had previously produced cards that were consciously designed to be "sendable" for a gay or lesbian wedding or union, mere sendability has never been satisfying for most consumers given greeting cards' emotional logic. Certainly the callers into WHYY's Radio-Times for a 2013 show about greeting cards were not interested in cards that would be merely sendable for the situations that they felt were invisible or underserved in the market: cards for the incarcerated, for people who live in nursing homes, and Mother's Day cards that acknowledge difficult mother-child relationships. Most consumers seek specificity in captions, designs, and sentiments that speak to their identities, cultural experiences, and the precise emotion that they are trying to capture. Indeed, Hallmark increasingly emphasizes that they create cards for a wide range of relationships. For Mother's Day 2015, they explained that the brand "creates cards for hard-to-find situations such as birthday, foreign language, caregiver, goddaughter and cousin," and that, "Cards also exist to meet the needs of today's complex family relationships – stepmother, two moms, partner, former in-laws, dad-as-mom, dad's wife, birth mother, mother of my child, and anyone who is 'like a mother'" (Hallmark 2015b).

Rather than finding a reflection of one's personal experience or feelings in the marketplace to be a threat or something that diminishes one's originality or specialness, many consumers seek to find their experience and emotions affirmed in the market. Sending a hard-to-find card whose caption or pre-printed text captures something that feels specific about the recipient or sending situation advertises a certain level of time and effort on the part of the sender in the marketplace, recalling Shachak's argument (Chapter 6 this volume) about the "emotional performativity of the market" in shaping practices of emotion work as well as how value is perceived and measured. Illouz's conceptualization of the emodity emphasizes commodities, like greeting cards, that are designed to be completed by consumers with their own time and emotional labor. Ultimately, the performativity of using the market to express interpersonal feeling may be the most important reason that cards are widely read as representations of caring.

Greeting cards as consumer objects: communicating touch

Paper greeting cards effectively communicate time spent on the recipient, in the marketplace, which has come to serve as a powerful sign of caring. However, if we return to Peters' point about touch also being an ingredient of performative communication (that does not rely on language for its effectivity *or* affectivity), we also need to consider how the tangible card signifies touch between sender and recipient. The traditional ink-on-paper commercial card represents the *actual* physical labor of the sender in procuring, completing, and sending the card, therefore the recipient may feel connected to the sender through their respective touching of the same object. However, cards also frequently suggest work that the sender did *not* do through their design and lettering. The handmade look is often interpreted by consumers as more personal and as communicating caring better than cards that bear less evidence of the hand's work.

One of the cards I used in my interviews prompted some of my respondents to say that it reminded them of the kind of card they would dash into CVS (a large drugstore chain) to buy at the last minute. The card in question was a 99-cent card from Hallmark's "value" Warm Wishes line, although their reaction had less to do with the price than with the rather generic, computer-generated design of cake and presents and fairly non-committal copy inside: "Wishing you the happiest kind of birthday!" Shannon, a creative professional in her thirties, commented about this card:

> I'd pass right over that, it doesn't seem celebratory enough to me. This is more like one of those cards like, oh I was late, I just stopped in the CVS to grab a card. And this is what I found, it was the last one in the shop.

So in this sense, the card does not effectively communicate time spent in the marketplace, and risks being read as a last-minute gesture. In the same sample of birthday cards, I included another Warm Wishes selection with a design that had a hand-painted, watercolor design and copy with a "handwritten" appearance, and this card was often identified as more "thoughtful." About this second card, college student Rebecca said it seemed to indicate "more effort," whereas the other Warm Wishes card screamed "CVS" to her.

Cards that are handmade, or look handmade, even though they are purchased in the marketplace, bring an aura of caring that makes them extra special, and extra-appreciated when they are received, according to my informants. There are a variety of conventions in greeting card text and imagery that suggest the card is handmade when, in fact, it is mass-produced. For example, many greeting card texts resemble handwriting, either by using actual handwriting or calligraphy, or by having imperfect fonts that suggest the individuality and idiosyncrasy of handwritten text. While mechanized print announces its disassociation from physicality, handwriting is a "medium of the self" because of its connection to the body (Thornton 1996: xiii). Jaffe (1999: 119) writes of this convention, "Handwriting is one of the physical aspects of texts that gives them an 'aura' linked to the 'history of the hands that have touched them.'"

While some respondents explained that they liked cards with a handcrafted or hand-painted look best because they were more like "art," others said that they liked how it created the impression that the sender might have actually made it themselves, even when the card was clearly a commercial card and no one would likely be fooled. Several respondents were quite self-reflexive about their responses to these cards, like Emma who said, laughing, "I like the ones that look like you made them, even if you didn't." Similarly, responding to the Warm Wishes card with the hand-painted look, homemaker and amateur watercolorist Tina said:

> It does look like I might have made it by hand. Again, if I wanted to have them think, oh, she spent all this time you know, creating this just for me! Although Hallmark has its claim to fame on the back.

Even though people realized that the cards were mass-produced, they often responded to the handmade "look" of a card, pointing out brushstrokes, attachments, and the look of collage as features that contributed to this aesthetic.

The way that cards communicate the physical touch of the sender can also help us make sense of the fact that the majority of cards sent have very little written in them. I found this in my examination of various archives of saved cards (at the Smithsonian Institution of American History and the Historical Society of Pennsylvania), and this finding has been confirmed by Shank's (2004) archival research on greeting cards as well as by Hallmark archivist Sharman Robertson. The minimum expectation is to include a salutation and a signature, e.g., "Dear Mom," followed by the pre-printed sentiment, "Love Shirley," and indeed most saved cards include just this much written content from the sender. While some of my study participants were very focused on their own written message as the source of the card's authenticity (generally speaking those with more formal education), the evidence in archives as well as the kinds of sentiment-driven cards that the industry largely produces testify to a smaller amount of handwritten text being the norm. However, if the card communicates emotion and caring by representing the touch and time of the sender rather than the originality of his or her thoughts, this explains the more succinct approach to card completion as much as, if not more than, the notion that people are unable or unwilling to express themselves through words. It seems that leaving home and making a selection in the marketplace reads as valuable time spent on a loved one that serves as convincing evidence of under-lying emotion, more so than other strategies such as taking the time to compose heartfelt messages by hand.

Immaterial sentiment: e-cards

During the time period of my study, digital greeting cards – more commonly known as e-cards or e-greetings – were rising in popularity, a trend that has intensi-fied since. According to industry reports and the trade press, sales of paper cards are on a steady decline due to the new digital alternatives. Although the Greeting Card Association still claims that industry revenues in the US are between $7 and $8 billion a year (GCA 2014a), an independent report from IBISWorld describes a 3.8 percent annual decline in industry sales from 2009 to 2014, leading to current sales of $6.1 billion annually (Turk 2014). The major players are scrambling to respond by playing catch-up in the e-card world, which includes not only cards that are sent via email and social media, but using the online space for the customization of cards that consumers can send in either digital or paper form (Franzen 2013). The rise of e-cards is also influencing trends in paper cards. People may be buying fewer paper cards, but they are choosing ones that are more embellished, with more expensive-looking materials (New 2013; Thompson 2014). In other words, paper cards have become more gift-like in the context of an explosion in digital commu-nication, especially for occasions when paper cards are still somewhat obligatory, like Valentine's Day and Mother's Day.

How does the immaterial version of the greeting card complicate a communi-cative logic organized by "touch and time?" With the introduction of electronic greetings, the mass-produced greeting card now has a foil against which it is the morally better way of communicating emotion or messages of connection. From being the suspect "fast and easy gesture," the paper card now reads as the time-consuming, and therefore more caring, option in comparison to an e-card. And certainly card makers and marketers are capitalizing on this sentiment by pro-moting products that are not just tangible but celebrate this fact, through special papers, pop-ups, attachments, a handmade look, or designs that connote nostal-gia for a pre-internet age. By announcing their tangibility, these cards remind the recipient that the card has passed through the sender's own hands. Janet, a professional and graduate student in her forties, explains why she ultimately prefers receiving regular cards to electronic greetings, saying:

> I love getting a card that someone has written to me. You know opening that little envelope is like getting a little gift with the surprise of the picture. You get the surprise of the artistry that one doesn't get with an email. Even the email cards, some of them are trying, but you can't touch it, or see it later. So I think the tangibility of them is important to me. The tangible, touchable, tactile, visual sense, and the sense of being able to keep it is important to me.

Similarly, Sandra, a graduate student in her twenties, explained: "That's why I really have no interest in email cards. There's no texture to them, they're inside the machine, they're not real."

While ink-on-paper cards communicate because of how they represent time spent in the marketplace and capture the "aura" of the "hands that touched them" (Jaffe 1999: 119), e-cards operate according to a different logic – of timeliness versus time spent, and immediacy versus forethought. Digital greetings contribute to a broader sense of synchronous experience in online space even among friends and family who are at a distance. This produces intimacy and emotional connection in a different way than the asynchronicity of paper cards, which speak to time and effort on the sender's part that is unknown to the recipient until the card arrives.

E-cards were generally perceived by my respondents as having tenuous moral standing compared to traditional paper cards, mainly because they take less time and effort to send. Even though it is *possible* to spend a great deal of time looking for the perfect e-card (in fact, digital greetings can be even more specific and personalized, because they aren't limited in the same way by economies of scale), generally it was seen as the quick and easy option, especially because you don't even have to leave your home or office to send one. You might be in the virtual marketplace, but it's not quite the same process as transforming a commodity from the physical marketplace into a token of social expression (Miller 1998). In the end, the tangibility of the offline card seems crucial to how it signifies caring to many users, perhaps more so now that e-cards are an option. Homemaker and mother Tina explains this perspective clearly:

> I think they're fun. But I guess I've been using regular greeting cards for so long, I kind of feel cheated, it's almost like an afterthought, that someone said, oh my god it's their birthday, let me send them an e-card. Whereas with the other ones they take the time to look for it. Which I know you look for them on these web sites. But, it's just the going out and purchasing, and taking the time to write it or write a personalized message, or put a stamp on it and send it, just seems a little more personalized.

She goes on to say that she feels guilty sending them herself, even though she's conscientious about the selection process, "Because I keep thinking, do they think, like I do, like oh, she didn't take the time to go out and get me a card, so I'm getting an e-card." Tina struggles with the fact that sending an e-card *can* be a lot of work, but in the end this effort does not count, or is not as obvious to the recipient as the effort of picking out a paper card from a store. While Tina was over forty at the time of our interview, her attitude was not specific to a certain age bracket among my respondents. Many of my younger, web-savvy respondents felt the same about electronic greeting cards. Amanda, a college student, said she enjoyed sending electronic greetings in high school, but recently hadn't been sending them, saying:

> [i]t's not as personal online cause you can do it so easily and it takes two seconds, so why send it when, it takes more effort to go to a store and buy it, so it's more thoughtful of you if you go out and buy it rather than just send an email card.

While a few respondents did argue that the content and intent of a card was more important to them than the medium in which it was delivered, most of my informants did see electronic greeting cards as a somewhat poor substitute for paper cards. The interpretation of the e-card as a last-minute gesture may in fact be accurate, as a number of my respondents mentioned that they would normally only send an e-card if they had realized too late that a special occasion was coming. In fact, some early electronic greeting cards were invented under just those circumstances. Susan Polis and Steve Schutz, whose bluemountain.com was one of the first electronic greeting card sites, initially came up with the idea to put together an electronic version of one of their paper Blue Mountain cards for their son who was at college when they realized on the day of his birthday that they had forgotten to mail one (Schutz 2004). The electronic greeting proves that "hey, I remembered!" even if it is sent on the day of an occasion. Those consumers who only use e-cards in this way may tend to assume, when they *receive* an e-card, that it is also a "just-in-time" gesture.

A great deal of evidence points to the performative qualities of the card as an object, animated by the time and effort of the sender, as crucial to how it works as a form of emotional, interpersonal communication. Although finding the right sentiment or image for a card is something that some consumers report putting a great deal of effort into, they almost all agree that just the fact of sending a card has considerable communicative power. The physical and emotional effort that goes into selecting and sending a card is what my respondents consistently pointed to when explaining why greeting cards "work" as a form of communication, and how they are different from other forms of communication like phone calls, email, or face-to-face conversation. Their responses point to how the card as a material object is used for phatic communication – declaring and renewing an existing relationship – almost independent of its actual content. Even card users who send cards ironically, thereby distancing themselves from their own usage of commercial sentiment, nevertheless are participating in the core of the greeting card's emotional logic of touch and time. The commercial nature of the card actually supports this function of cards, by connecting the private, interpersonal nature of a relationship to a socially recognized communicative form, in a format that is designed with viewing and semi-public display in mind.

Conclusion: when ethnography and critique meet

In this chapter I have tried to disrupt what can be a too-easy dismissal of the greeting card as commercialized sentiment that reduces our individualized feelings to the lowest common denominator, a move that resonates with how Illouz problematizes a normative critique of emotions and their expression through commodities (Conclusion to this volume). While greeting card sentiment is almost another word for inauthenticity, especially in circles that are already critical of consumer culture such as the academy and other elites, an ethnographic perspective on their use reveals a distinct communicative logic in which genuinely felt emotional connection through these commodities is understood to be possible. While the mass-producedness of greeting cards would seem to be a built-in threat to their emotional authenticity, the publicness that accompanies their commercial nature brings a sense of recognition, certainty, and authorization to what can often feel like a high risk activity – expressing emotions in relational communication. Although we often imagine emotion as belonging to the private sphere of the individual, it's clear that emotions and their expression are fundamentally social, not least when they are exchanged between two people (a point that Illouz elaborates in the Conclusion to this volume). Scholars have distinguished between the category of emotion – which is socially recognized and for which there are available discourses in the public sphere – and the category of affect, which may be experienced and even be observable, but for which there may not be language or recognizable cultural forms (Kavka 2008; Wetherell 2012). Illouz (2007) argues that one of the defining features of emotional capitalism is "the transformation of the public sphere into an arena for the exposition of private life, emotions, and intimacies" (2007: 108).

The commercial mass-producedness of cards contributes to their performativity as emotional commodities. Even if someone can't find just the right words to express an emotion or recognize an occasion (either within themselves or in the marketplace), the card signifies time and effort, which is offered as a kind of proof or evidence of caring. The status of cards as consumer objects is key to this communicative logic, and in the age of digital connection, cards are becoming even more object-like in order to draw attention to the sender's touch and time.

Having made the case for why greeting cards "work" as emotional communication for so many (but certainly, not all) consumers, based on the understandings and experiences they shared with me, I also want to make space for critiques of emodities that this analysis fails to address, and indeed, the new critiques that it raises. While the market functions as a resource for identifying and expressing emotion, it is clearly also then likely complicit in emotion regimes that regularize ideas about emotion and link them to broader dynamics of power and subjectification. Certainly, the greeting card industry contributes to particular ideologies about emotion, both in its marketing and its products. Although from a feminist perspective it would be desirable for the industry to promote more equity among men and women in terms of expectations for emotional expressivity, as well as the labor of sending cards to maintain social relationships, the industry has largely conceded defeat in converting men into regular card senders. Indeed, many cards and ads use the idea that men and women have trouble communicating about emotion as a selling proposition for their products that are presented as the solution to this problem, thereby only reinforcing it. Similarly, while no doubt communicating emotion to loved ones is high stakes, the greeting card industry only highlights this belief and undermines people's confidence in their own abilities to express or convey emotion when they present cards as the solution to this problem (West 2008). Although it seems unlikely that the industry has invented this communication problem out of whole cloth and somehow imposed this belief on consumers, it certainly has a vested interest in reinforcing and reproducing it. Even if public symbolic resources are inherently valuable in bringing a sense of formality and authorization to interpersonal communication, why must those resources be so insistently commercial? Reliance on greeting cards highlights the lack of widely known alternatives for emotional language, scripts, and gestures in the larger public sphere.

Perhaps most troubling is why "spending" time and effort in the marketplace is such a hegemonic standard for signifying caring. My informants never discussed the value of a card in terms of its price, which is interesting since almost all cards actually have the sale price printed on the back, where both sender and recipient can easily see it. The money paid for the card becomes almost invisible compared to its representation of the sender's time and effort, offered as evidence of feeling. If performativity is key to effectively conveying emotion, then what are the alternatives for performing caring when shopping is so privileged as its sign? Even the DIY approach to creating cards and tokens is effectively captured by the market with the increasing options for creating customized cards digitally, either using software on a home computer or through an online service. No doubt a committed DIY population exists that eschews commercial solutions in creating their homemade expressions of caring. But will the truly homemade gestures – the handwritten letter, the card crafted from scraps – actually be read reliably as a sign of time, effort, and caring, as intended? At least a few of my informants volunteered that they see greeting cards as more emotional and sentimental than handwritten notes or letters, suggesting that a DIY approach is not on equal footing with commercial cards among at least some segments of the public.

Although greeting card sales in the United States are on the decline, this emotional commodity, or "emodity," shows no signs of disappearing soon. As digital technologies transform our modes of interpersonal communication, the authenticity of gestures that effectively convey feeling in an interaction-rich environment are under continual negotiation. Whether the greeting card will continue to be privileged as an authentic expression of emotion ultimately remains to be seen.

Bibliography

American Greetings Corporation. 2000. "The Business of Valentine's Day." *PR Newswire*, January 20. Retrieved April 8, 2016 (www.prnewswire.com/news-releases/the-business-of-valentines-day-72140157.html).

Associated Press. 2008. "Hallmark says 'I Do' to gay marriage." *Today*, August 2. Retrieved June 30, 2014 (www.today.com/id/26328361/ns/today-today_style/t/hallmark-says-i-do-gay-marriage-cards/#.U7GR-6ivyCQ).

Berlant, Lauren. 2008. *The Female Complaint*. Durham, NC: Duke University Press.

Campbell, Colin. 1987. *The Romantic Ethic and the Spirit of Modern Consumerism*. New York: Blackwell Publishing.

Di Leonardo, Micaela. 1987. "The female world of cards and holidays: Women, families, and the work of kinship." *Signs* 12: 440–453.

Fottrell, Quentin. 2013. "Why Facebook can't kill the greeting card." *Market Watch* (*The Wall Street Journal*), April 16. Retrieved June 30, 2014 (www.marketwatch.com/story/why-facebook-wont-kill-the-greeting-card-2013–04–15?pagenumber=1).

Franzen, Carl. 2013. "Sorry for your loss: Hallmark struggles to update its card empire." *The Verge*, September 4. Retrieved June 30, 2014 (www.theverge.com/2013/9/4/4579832/sorry-for-your-loss-hallmark-struggles-to-update-its-card-empire).

Gammill, Tom and Max Pross. 1994. "The pledge drive." Episode no.89 of *Seinfeld*, Season 6, Episode 3, First Broadcast October 6, 1994. Script transcribed by Dave (ratboy). Retrieved July 1, 2014 (www.seinfeldscripts.com/ThePledgeDrive.html).

Greeting Card Association (GCA). 1926. *Greeting Cards: When and How to Use Them*. New York: Greeting Card Association.

Greeting Card Association (GCA). 2014a. "About greeting cards: General facts." *Greeting Card Association: About the Industry*. Retrieved July 1, 2014 (www.greetingcard.org/AbouttheIndustry/tabid/58/Default.aspx).

Greeting Card Association (GCA). 2014b. "Greeting card sales to help fuel Valentine's Day record spending; Projected $1B in card sales." *Greeting Card Association: About the Industry*, February 11. Retrieved July 1, 2014 (www.greetingcard.org/AbouttheIndustry/IndustryInformation/tabid/100/CBModuleId/446/ArticleID/234/Default.aspx).

Guignon, Charles. 2004. *On Being Authentic*. New York: Routledge.

Hallmark. 2015a. "Valentine's Day." *Hallmark Corporate Information*. Retrieved May 20, 2015 (http://corporate.hallmark.com/Holiday/Valentines-Day).

Hallmark. 2015b. "Mother's Day." *Hallmark Corporate Information*. Retrieved May 20, 2015 (http://corporate.hallmark.com/Holiday/Mothers-Day).

Hochschild, Arlie Russell. 1983. *The Managed Heart: Commercialization of Human Feeling*. Berkeley, CA: University of California Press.

Hochschild, Arlie Russell. 2003. *The Commercialization of Intimate Life: Notes from Home and Work*. Berkeley, CA: University of California Press.

Illouz, Eva. 1997. *Consuming the Romantic Utopia: Love and the Cultural Contradictions of Capitalism*. Berkeley, CA: University of California Press.

Illouz, Eva. 2007. *Cold Intimacies: The Making of Emotional Capitalism*. Malden, MA: Polity Press.

Jaffe, Alexandra. 1999. "Packaged sentiments: The social meaning of greeting cards." *Journal of Material Culture* 4: 115–141.

Kavka, Misha. 2008. *Reality Television: Affect and Intimacy*. New York: Palgrave Macmillan.

Leiss, William, Stephen Kline, Sut Jhally and Jacqueline Botterill. 2005. *Social Communication in Advertising: Consumption in the Mediated Marketplace*. 3rd ed. New York: Routledge.

Martin, Judith. 1997. *Miss Manners' Basic Training™: Communication*. New York: Crown Publishers.

Miller, Daniel. 1998. *A Theory of Shopping*. Ithaca, NY: Cornell University Press.

New, Catherine. 2013. "Even as American greetings struggles, small card companies find a new way to thrive." *Huffington Post*, April 4. Retrieved June 30, 2014 (www.huffing tonpost.com/2013/04/04/american-greetings-small-card-companies_n_3000946.html).

Peters, John Durham. 1999. *Speaking into the Air: A History of the Idea of Communication*. Chicago, IL: University of Chicago Press.

Radio-Times with Marty Moss-Coane. 2013. "Greeting cards and their meaning." *WHYY*, July 11. Program available for streaming online. Retrieved April 8, 2016 (http://whyy.org/cms/radiotimes/2013/07/11/24036/).

Reddy, William M. 2001. *The Navigation of Feeling: A Framework for the History of Emotions*. New York: Cambridge University Press.

Rothenbuhler, Eric. 1998. *Ritual Communication: From Everyday Conversation to Mediated Ceremony*. Thousand Oaks, CA: SAGE Publications.

Schutz, Susan P. 2004. *Blue Mountain: Turning Dreams into Reality*. Boulder, CO: Blue Mountain Press.

Shank, Barry. 2004. *A Token of My Affection: Greeting Cards and American Business Culture*. New York: Columbia University Press.

Spaulding, Sheila. 1981/1958. *Social Psychology of Interpersonal Relations as Expressed in Greeting Cards*. New York: Clearwater Publishers.

Suddath, Claire. 2014. "Writing Mother's Day cards at Hallmark: An inside look." *Bloomberg*, May 1. Retrieved May 19, 2017 (www.bloomberg.com/news/articles/2014-05-01/writing-mothers-day-cards-at-hallmark-an-inside-look).

Thompson, Derek. 2014. "Why are greeting cards so expensive?" *The Atlantic*, February 14. Retrieved June 30, 2014 (www.theatlantic.com/business/archive/2013/02/why-are-greeting-cards-so-expensive/273086/).

Thornton, Tamara P. 1996. *Handwriting in America: A Cultural History*. New Haven, CT: Yale University Press.

Turk, Steven. 2014. *IBISWorld Industry Report 51119: Greeting Cards & Other Publishing in the US*, March. Retrieved June 30, 2014 (http://clients1.ibisworld.com/reports/us/industry/default.aspx?indid=1235).

Unity Marketing. 2005. *Greeting Card Market is Experiencing a Generational Shift, Unity Marketing Reports*. Retrieved February 10, 2010 (www.unitymarketingonline.com/reports2/cards/pr2.html).

West, Emily. 2008. "Mass producing the personal: The greeting card industry's approach to commercial sentiment." *Popular Communication* 6(4):231–247.

West, Emily. 2009. "Doing gender difference through greeting cards: The construction of a communication gap in marketing and everyday practice." *Feminist Media Studies* 9(3):285–299.

West, Emily. 2010a. "A taste for greeting cards: Distinction in a denigrated cultural form." *Journal of Consumer Culture* 10(3):362–382.

West, Emily. 2010b. "Expressing the self through sentiment: Working theories of authentic communication in a commercial form." *International Journal of Cultural Studies* 13(5):451–469.

Wetherell, Margaret. 2012. *Affect and Emotion: A New Social Science Understanding.* Thousand Oaks, CA: SAGE Publications.

Part III

The ideal of mental health and self-improvement

Emotional self-monitoring as commodity

Chapter 6

(Ex)changing feelings

On the commodification of emotions in psychotherapy

Mattan Shachak

Emotional change, regulation and expression have long played a crucial role in ethical programs, collective rituals, religious practices and moral narratives. Modern psychology, however, brought a radical transformation to the ways in which emotions are understood; the role assigned to them in shaping modern self-hood and sociability; the practices used to address, change and control them; and their moral horizon, i.e. mental health and personal well-being (Danziger 1997; Dixon 2003; Gergen 1995; Mestrovic 1997; Williams 2001; Wouters 2004). The psychological model of the person offers new forms of secular and amoral framework for self-knowledge and self-improvement in which reflection on one's emotions and their management are paramount (Lears 1983; Rieff 1966). This outlook has several features: it reshapes the way in which individuals assign meaning and value to their social relations, commitments, conduct, duties, pleasures and feelings through the construction of emotions as private psychological entities available for reflection and valuable for moral orientation; it relies on the formulation of scientific knowledge about emotions through technologies of objectification, classification, empirical observation and measurement (Furedi 2004; Rose 1996; Taylor 1989); it devises individualized practices of reflexivity to identify, monitor, change and regulate emotions (Crossley 2006; Illouz 2008); and it offers a generic yet easily personalized narrative to make sense of the relations between emotions, events, objects, relationships and the self (Bellah *et al.* 1986; Cushman 1996; Lasch 1979).

The transformation modern psychology brought to the cultural models and practices by which we understand emotions and act upon them, is intertwined with yet another distinctive feature of twentieth-century society and economy: the fact that the person and her emotions have become the target of an industry selling mental health, self-realization and emotional well-being. Throughout the twentieth century, and particularly since the 1960s, the psy-industries have been integrated into the welfare state (Porter 1987) and considerably enlarged the scope of their actions, audiences and markets, as they progressively expanded their aims from healing the pathological suffering of patients, to increasing the well-being and emotional health of clients (Illouz 2008). Simultaneously, along the move from industrial society to consumer society considerable changes have taken place in the dominant psychologies and their ideas and practices for the management of human beings (Brinkmann 2008).

Today, psychological counselling of various persuasions, new age therapies, coaching sessions, emotion management workshops, self-help books and psycho-pharmacological drugs all try to construct standard and simple verbal, imaginative and bodily techniques to quickly induce specific emotional changes, whether by expert knowledge and professional techniques (psychological, pharmaceutical, genetic) or by professionalizing popular ideas and techniques to the same end. They offer to reshape one's psychological-emotional make-up through a variety of emotional commodities: to reduce depression, relieve stress, anger or anxiety, promote self-esteem, satisfaction, resilience or well-being, or increase a couple's intimacy. These phenomena highlight the changes in the institutional settings and economic mechanisms by which the psychological models of emotions and the self are (re)produced, disseminated and practised/consumed.

It seems then that the growing focus on emotions in the psy-industries and their rising economic value in corporations and consumer culture (Dittmar 2007; Hardt 1999; Hochschild 1983; Illouz 2008; Van Maanen and Kunda 1989) are intertwined with the rising cultural value of emotions in the constitution of self-identity, social relations and well-being (Beck and Beck-Gernsheim 2002; Giddens 1991; Illouz 2008, 2013). Thus, the interaction of the cultural and the economic in producing the value of emotions underlies the rise of psy-practices in western societies. But how are the economic and the cultural interwoven in the constitution of modern ideas and practices of emotions and selfhood?

The critical literature on the commodification of emotions examines areas where the economic and the emotions collide or come together, namely the corporate world, the service economy and consumer culture. In the realm of work, it is argued that emotions – previously private – are now commodified as yet another stage in the commodification of labor in the service and information economy, in which the worker's emotions are incorporated into economic practices and the worker's emotion-work becomes central in producing economic value for corporations (Fineman 1993, 2000; Hardt 1999; Hochschild 1983, 1979; Illouz 2008; Swan 2010). In the realm of consumption, it is claimed that the romantic spirit of modern consumerism provides consumers with emotional experiences through new experiential commodities (Friedberg 1993) and promotes an individualistic "imaginative hedonism" (Campbell 1987). These approaches contribute to our understanding of the increasing value of emotions for labor and consumption, but they usually do so on the theoretical premises of the opposition between emotions and the economy, and thus see the intertwinement of the emotions and the economy as a new form of labor exploitation, a consumerist delusion or the colonization of life-worlds by economic rationality.

In this chapter, however, I take a different path. I examine how changes in the therapeutic repertoires and practices of emotions are interrelated with macro institutional changes – academic, professional, bureaucratic, economic – in which they develop, as well as with micro changes in the structure and goal of the therapeutic interaction; the role and meaning of money in the constitution of therapeutic relationship and exchange (i.e. Zelizer 1996, 2005); and the promises of therapy regarding emotional self-transformation. I outline the simultaneous development of two processes: the commodification of psychotherapy, i.e. the gradual infusion of market and consumer logic into the production, dissemination and consumption of therapeutic knowledge and techniques; and the growing focus on emotions and their rising value for mental health and personal well-being in mainstream psychological theory, research and practice, from psychoanalysis to cognitive behavioural treatment, and later to the quasi-professional practice of life coaching.

I draw on the idea that culture and the economy co-produce ideals and technologies of selfhood and emotions, that cultural ideals such as emotional authenticity, emotional self-transformation and emotional health are co-produced with and objectified through the market in the form of emotional commodities, or emodities (Illouz, Introduction to this volume). I seek to understand repertoires and practices of emotion-work and emotional self-fashioning as moral technologies which underlie a form of sociation or morality, that is to say, a set of techniques the person performs on themselves with or without the help of others in order to achieve a moral goal (Foucault 1988), which in this case is deeply embedded in the logic and performativity of the market. The chapter aims to illustrate the co-production of emotions through the emergence and development of therapeutic technologies for effective and efficient modification of specific emotions by focusing on the role of psychologists in providing repertoires and practices for understanding emotions and acting upon them.

I suggest that in order to understand the transformations in the psychological repertoires of emotions, their role and meaning in therapy and the therapeutic practices constructed for emotion-work, we have to account for two interrelated aspects of this process: the *emotional performativity of the market*, i.e. how economic (market) practices and rituals reorganize not only social relations of exchange and measures of value, but also repertoires of emotions, practices of emotion-work and the social conditions for actual emotional experiences; and the *economic performativity of emotions*, i.e. how new repertoires of emotions and technologies for their management and transformation give rise to new forms of value, economic practices, commodities and markets. The interrelation of these processes gives rise to the objectification of emotions as central components of mental health, well-being and self-fashioning, and constructs emotions as objects of choice for individual consumption. The mutual constitution of culture and the economy are analysed by addressing the common grounds on which different institutions and actors interact in constituting emotions as social, economic and moral objects. I argue that this common ground consists in the construction of certain emotions as valuable, measurable, calculable and manageable objects, and that it emerges through the interaction of knowledge systems, professional practice, the State and the market. The interrelations of the four realms are intricate, and include frictions, tensions and discrepancies, but they result in the co-production of emotions as commodities.

In the first section I discuss the rise of the emotional as a distinct realm of professional intervention since the turn of the century in Freudian psychoanalysis. I analyse the relationship between its ideas about emotions in the theory of drives, the central therapeutic technique of transference, the symbolization of money in the therapeutic relationship, its function in balancing the mental economy of the client, and its relation to the goal of therapy. In the second section I turn to examine the reformulation of psychological theories of emotions and practices for their modification in the emerging cognitive behavioural and humanistic approaches in the second half of the twentieth century, and their interaction with academic, professional, political and economic processes, such as the paradigm shift towards positivism and empiricism; the rising administrative, legal and commercial efforts to establish psychotherapy as a standard, evidence-based and effective health care service. I analyse the ways in which emotions are objectified, rationalized and pathologized through new technologies of classification, differentiation, measurement and evaluation, which enable the commensuration of emotions with other objects such as health, productivity or economic value (i.e. Carruthers and Espeland 1998; Espeland and Stevens 1998). In the third section I present the hybrid semi-professional and market-oriented practice of life coaching and its elaboration of previous frameworks and techniques for emotion-work and self-transformation for the enhancement of personal well-being while constructing emotions as objects of personal choice. This chapter draws on a fieldwork I conducted in the life-coaching industry in Israel, including interviews with coachers and coaches (Shachak 2013). In the concluding discussion, I focus on the ethical meaning and consequences of contemporary notions and practices of emotions, their importance for understanding contemporary cultural and commercial processes, and their effects on normative modes of subjectivity and sociability. I claim that this co-production, in its contemporary form, enacts a morality based on *emotional utilitarianism*, which interweaves emotional authenticity and self-interest by bestowing great value on emotions and desires, their reflexive observation and management as subjective experiences and life goals. But at the same time this emotional utilitarianism relies on the logics, practices and rituals of the market to provide such experiences, which radically rationalizes and objectifies emotions as instruments or resources of productivity in both institutional and individual levels, albeit with different aims and meanings.

This chapter presents the cultural process by which emotions are constructed as objects of choice and consumption through therapeutic interpretive framework and technologies of emotion-work and self-transformation. Similar technologies and repertoires of emotions are performed in other sites examined in this volume, such as music (Schwarz, Chapter 2 this volume), tourism (Benger Alaluf, Chapter 1 this volume) and cinema (Gilon, Chapter 3 this volume).

Modern psychology and the rise of the emotional

From its birth in the late nineteenth century, modern psychology worked to delineate the emotional as a distinct realm of intellectual and scientific observation, and a new site for professional practice in which money payment is an integral part. In 1894 Sigmund Freud published (in French) a classical paper entitled "The justification for detaching from neurasthenia a particular syndrome: the anxiety neurosis". In this article, Freud deploys clinical and theoretical reasons for the creation of the new disease. Although he still conceived anxiety neurosis as a disease of the nervous system, Freud constituted it as a separate and independent disorder and offered a psychological rather than a physiological treatment for it. Freud, alongside other psychologists, worked to establish new categories of disorders, such as "neurosis", "panic" and "phobia", by detaching previously known symptoms from their earlier meaning, and gathering them into what was then claimed to be *independent* clinical conditions. The notion that these symptoms could all be the *manifestation* of a unitary construct called "anxiety" was alien to pre-Freudian psychiatry (Berrios 1996).

As Kenneth Gergen (1995) argues, the construction of the modern psychological conception of emotions emerged in relation to the romantic tradition on the one hand, and the physiological discourse on the other, in order to be "scientific" yet allow the establishment of a new field of academic inquiry and a new professional practice. Such psychological discourse about emotions serves as symbolic capital of high order and was used as a cultural distinction mechanism for psychologists in the professional and academic fields. Moreover, as Kurt Danziger (1997) notes, the very category of "emotions" has been constructed, elaborated and disseminated by psychologists from the second half of the nineteenth century onwards in order to establish a new cultural repertoire to speak of those human phenomena which had previously been represented through moral and religious categories such as passions, desires and sentiments.

The emerging psychological language brought with it new repertoires and practices of emotions. However, in order to better grasp the changing meaning and role of the "emotional" in psychotherapy, we need a better understanding of psychoanalytic repertoires and practices of emotions, and the transformations they have undergone during the second half of the twentieth century.

Psychoanalytic theory focuses on the pathogenic nature of *repressed or disavowed affect* and stresses the importance of uncovering and acknowledging their origins during the analytic process. As a *psychology of drives*, psychoanalysis views emotions and affects as symptoms of deeper mental processes, that is to say, signs which exist on the visible surface of the psyche and originate from unconscious mechanisms which repress, channel, tame or discharge inner "blind" drives. According to Freud, the repression of the original affects enables the mental energy underlying them to be subverted to other objects in a way that is not intelligible to the individual. Thus, affects are key in understanding mental processes and pathologies, but they are not independent mental entities.

Analytic approaches saw no therapeutic value in modifying specific emotions. Even if it could be done, it would have little meaning for the patient's mental health. The therapeutic goal is not to directly induce positive emotional experiences, but to transform neurotic suffering into common unhappiness (Breuer and Freud 1955 [1893–1895]), by uncovering the unconscious processes by which affects are formed through transference. In the process of transference, the patient's emotional and sexual drives and attachments, originally directed towards others – mainly the father and mother – are transferred onto the analyst in the course of therapy. The analyst uses this process to make transparent the representational relations between emotional symptoms, their objects and the self, by uncovering their unconscious origins and thus loosening their grip on their current (contingent) object. In this practice, understanding emotions and their objects as symptoms, representations and metaphors and working to acknowledge their underlying mental mechanisms encapsulates a therapeutic potential.

Perhaps counter intuitively, the highly intimate and emotionally ridden relationship required for a successful transference, is based upon the economic and professional features which underpin this relationship. Here, money plays a crucial role in the construction of the analytic relationship and the achievement of a successful transference, however, it is not a payment for a predefined outcome, since its outcome and duration are not predetermined. Freud argues that:

> Free treatment ... enormously increases some of a neurotic's resistances – in young women, for instance, the temptation which is inherent in their transference relation, and in young men, their opposition to an obligation to feel grateful, an opposition which arises from their father-complex and which presents one of the most troublesome hindrances to the acceptance of medical help. The absence of the regulating effect offered by the payment of a fee to the doctor makes itself very painfully felt; the whole relationship is removed from the real world, and the patient is deprived of a strong motive for endeavoring to bring the treatment to an end.
>
> (Freud 1958 [1913]: 128)

How can the de-personalizing or alienating quality of money payment produce intimacy, and how is it woven into the psychoanalytic process? On the very basic level, money buys the analyst's time, expertise and attention for a long-term relationship and bridges the initial strangeness between analyst and patient. Moreover, as Freud notes, money payment enables the exclusion of the therapeutic relationship from other forms of social relations, attachments and commitments of both parties, and brings about a form of confidentiality and intimacy and thus enables the loosening of the grip of normative forms of emotional expression and encourages free association. Finally, money is used to balance and structure both the therapeutic relationship and the economic exchange by excluding further commitments and settling any interpersonal debt or obligation by the patient to the analyst.

On the analytical level, the initial strangeness between analyst and patient and the exclusive relationship built upon it, as Freud stresses, are crucial for the achievement of a successful transference. The symbolization of money and ritualization of payment are used for balancing the patient's mental economy of drives and affects. In this case, the emotional and the economic features are woven together in the constitution of the therapeutic process and relationship, in which strangeness and intimacy should be dialectically sustained and overcome in order to successfully create a transference relation. These features underlie and enable transference and the revelation of the subconscious origins of emotional attachment. The social structure of payment in this case, we must add, is an interpersonal exchange of money between the patient and the analyst, with no institutionalized mechanisms for the financing of therapy by a third party (insurance, for example) or for the measurement and evaluation of its effectivity in delivering a predefined outcome.

The centrality of the concepts of the subconscious, resistance and denial in understanding the self and creating the relationship, creates a role hierarchy which does not permit a simple contractual relationship. This is because the receiver of the service is not an equal partner in the transaction, he is a "patient", his accounts and judgments of the process or its outcomes are irrelevant for the professional evaluation of the outcome/goods exchanged; his willingness and trust are irrelevant to the success of the treatment; and his desires are to be analysed rather than met (Freud 1958 [1913]).

The constitution of the goods psychoanalysts offer is based on expertise and the authority of science, but not on statistical evidence for efficacy in providing specific predefined outcomes. Freud claimed his therapeutic technique is superior to other therapies and based the efficacy of his new professional practice on the theoretical underpinnings of his method, his personal clinical experience and the presentation of case histories of his patients. The mental goods Freud offers might not be well defined by time or specific effect, but they definitely promise to be a good bargain for any middle-class patient:

> As far as the middle classes are concerned, the expense involved in psychoanalysis is excessive only in appearance. Quite apart from the fact that no comparison is possible between restored health and efficiency on the one hand and a moderate financial outlay on the other, when we add up the unceasing costs of nursing-homes and medical treatment and contrast them with the increase of efficiency and earning capacity which results from a successfully completed analysis, we are entitled to say that the patients have made a good bargain. Nothing in life is so expensive as illness – and stupidity.
>
> (Freud 1958 [1913]: 129)

Psychoanalysis is cost-effective despite its high economic costs, Freud argues, since it offers the middle class a *priceless* and *incommensurable* good: mental health. However, as effective as psychoanalysis is claimed to be for one's mental health, its outcomes cannot be predetermined, specified or subjected to standard measurement. Although affects and emotions have gained new meaning and prominence in psychoanalytic theory and "emotion-talk" became the core of its practice, Freud refrained from promising the transformation of specific emotions, or from devising standardized techniques and measurement methods for successful therapy. The basis for this stand is epistemological, but as a consequence the cost of the treatment does not aim to commensurate a specific mental good or a predefined outcome.

Freud was sceptical towards "statistics", which he equated with the rudimentary procedures of behavioural research as it was in the early 1900s, and rejected, for theoretical reasons, the ability to use standardized measurement techniques to evaluate the efficacy of therapy and to compare therapeutic techniques. He claimed the clinical material available to the investigator is that diverse and heterogeneous as to make meaningful comparisons all but impossible. In addition, he fiercely attacked critics who disparaged his treatment results (Freud 1963 [1916]). During the first half of the twentieth century, psychoanalysis gained dominance in both psychological theory and the practice of professional psychotherapy in America, mainly by psychiatrists, and established the basis for the first two editions of the *Diagnostic and Statistical Manual of Mental Disorders of the American Psychiatric Association* (hereafter, DSM) (Hale 2000). Moreover, it was a fertile cultural ground for the development of various psychodynamic approaches and reshaped popular conceptions of emotions and the self (Illouz 2008).

However, the academic shift towards positivism in the constitution of psychological knowledge and the search for an empirical, comparative and statistical evidence of psychotherapy, generated a radical change in the regimes of truth and justification governing psychological knowledge; the ways in which emotions are constituted as scientific objects; the methods through which they are observed; the practices of knowing and interpretive repertoires which constitute this knowledge; and finally, the therapeutic practice itself, which, as we will see in what follows, was increasingly required to become quantitatively measurable, to focus on modifying specific pathologized emotions and moods and to demonstrate cost-effectiveness.

Figuring out emotions: changing moods, measuring feelings

Freud's approach was soon contested by critics who demanded to be shown hard empirical statistical evidence. From the 1950s, a growing number of psychiatrists, psychologists and other behavioural scientists demanded studies based on "hard" data – that is, on records that progressed beyond uncontrolled clinical observations – in order to evaluate therapy "objectively", by numbers (Mitchell 2004). The growing demand for positivist knowledge and effective practice was a means for overcoming an epistemological problem regarding the validity of psychological knowledge. However, it was also a result of wider institutional and technological changes involving scientific, administrative, legal and commercial institutions and actors, which had a structuring effect on the production of psychological knowledge and therapeutic practice.

First, the formalization of psychotherapy as a standard health care service became a welfare policy goal in post-war America, and a new object of private and public insurance programs so that mental health costs could be reimbursed. Moreover, effectiveness became a dominant principle for the reproduction of academic psychological knowledge as it became an administrative requirement for federal funding from NIMH to university-based clinical training programs that provided the core training for the mental health professions (Deleon *et al.* 2011; Pickren and Schneider 2005; Vandenbos *et al.* 1992). At the same time, "emotional damage" was increasingly recognized by the tort law as an independent cause for compensation, which psychologists were assigned to assess (Nolan 1998). Moreover, the emergence and exponential growth of the psychological drugs' market from the 1950s – especially antidepressants and tranquilizers – was enabled by the regulatory framework of the state and the positivistic epistemology of science, which demanded measurable, effective and specific transformation of pathologized emotions (Deleon *et al.* 2011; Shorter 2009; Tone 2009). And finally, the quest for quantification was enabled by several socio-technical developments such as new classification systems and measurement technologies of pathologized moods and emotions, and the use of statistical models and computer technology for building and handling large data sets.

Thus, providing evidence-based and cost-effective solutions for changing specific moods and emotions has gradually become a yardstick for experts, policy makers, industry and consumers for the evaluation and consumptions of therapeutic technologies, and set new standards for the reproduction of psychological knowledge and practices. Moreover, it reshaped the professional categorization and classification of moods and emotions and expanded their pathologization, which reached its peak with the publication of DSM-III in 1980 (Conrad 2007; Horwitz and Wakefield 2007, 2012; Kutchins and Kirk 2003; Rose 2009). And finally, it became a central feature of consumers' normative expectations for instant mood modifying commodities (Shorter 2009; Tone 2009).

While psychoanalysis had difficulties in co-opting with this demand for comparative, controlled treatment studies, new brief methods of psychotherapy, such as cognitive, behavioural and humanistic therapies, worked to meet these demands and have been able to demonstrate some positive results in clinical trials in some disorders, notably depression, anxiety and stress (Hale 2000). Each of the emerging psychologies worked to gain professional prestige, scientific legitimacy and governmental funding, in order to fortify their ideas and practices and gain advantage over other approaches, by providing empirical evidence for the efficacy of their therapeutic technique for specific disorders through the emerging methodologies and technologies of psychotherapy research. This in turn, pushed further the efforts to construct technologies of specification, classification, measurement and evaluation of emotions, and the consolidation of emotion-specific technologies. However, the production of positivist knowledge was not easily settled with common notions of emotions.

The opposition to mentalistic notions of emotions and the fortification of empiricism and positivism in post-war American psychology was most prominently carried out by behaviourism (Mills 1998). In this approach, mental states that cannot be empirically observed and objectively formulated are scientifically non-existent, and the notion of the unconscious denounced as myth. Thus, it narrowed the psychological interest in the emotions to observable conditioned responses to stimuli, and denounced the intra-psychic and experiential aspects of emotions as spiritualistic and mentalist relics that would soon be overcome by science. As Elizabeth Duffy (1941) claimed:

> I am aware of no evidence for the existence of a special condition called "emotion" which follows different principles of action from other conditions of the organism. I can therefore see no reason for a psychological study of "emotion" as such.

In a similar tone, Skinner (1953:160) suggested that "The 'emotions' are excellent examples of the fictional causes to which we commonly attribute behavior". On the practical level, behaviourism aimed at developing standardized and empirically proven techniques for behaviour engineering, which in relation to emotions focused on *modifying undesirable affective states* such as anxiety and depression.

However, the reduction of emotions to the behaviourist stimulus-response model was soon contested. From the late 1950s onwards, along with the rise of the computer metaphor of the mind, the growing interest in personal experience and the spreading normative model of the emotional self, behaviourism was challenged by new psychological approaches: humanistic and cognitive psychologies. These approaches granted emotions with theoretical and practical primacy in accounting for and shaping subjective experience and individual behaviour, and reconceptualized them in a manner more amiable to the rising institutional demand for measurement and quantification. The positivist approach was not renounced by this shift in the psychological paradigm of emotions; rather, it was reintegrated into the new paradigm and practices in making emotions visible and measurable, in focusing on their desirability or functionality, and aiming at effectively changing specific emotions.

Following Carl Rogers (1942), humanistic approaches promoted a view of emotions as a system of orientation that provides the organism with adaptive information or an intuitive judgment mechanism; a set of authentic personal needs of higher level; and an important motivator for personal change. Thus, the central action the therapist carries out in therapy is the acceptance and clarification of the client's feelings and emotions, or states of emotional ambivalence, which encourage the emergence of positive emotions and personal change (Greenberg and Safran 1989).

In a slightly different vein, Albert Ellis and Aaron Beck, among others, worked to develop a cognitive approach to emotions mainly by theorization, research and treatment of the spreading "epidemic" of mood and affective disorders, especially depression (Beck 1970), anxiety (Clark 1986) and stress (Lazarus 1993, 1999). According to this view, emotions result from the individual's intuitive appraisals and beliefs, and the meaning given to an event determines the emotional response to it (Beck 1976; Ellis 1962). Constructs such as automatic thoughts, irrational beliefs, negative or maladaptive cognitions about the world, the future and the self, are posited as mediating between events and "maladaptive" emotional responses to them. Thus, cognitive therapists focus on the elimination of these emotional responses through self-instructional training (Arknoff 1992). Although rational in orientation (Pilgrim 2011), this approach was radically focused on explaining and transforming affects and behaviours through emotion-specific techniques, as the central goal of a short and issue-specific therapeutic treatment (Kendall and Bemis 1983).

Despites their differences, in both humanist and cognitive approaches emotions are no longer seen as symptoms of determinist unconscious psychological mechanisms or signs of pathology – since the concepts of unconscious and the theory of drives were altogether abandoned – but as the product of a dynamic interplay between personal, social and environmental factors. As scientific and therapeutic objects in themselves, emotions are conceived to be manageable by simple, specific and effective techniques. According to this rising view, "treating the symptoms" is good enough if it provides desirable experiences and promotes adaptive behavioural changes.

By the 1960s, even the successors of psychoanalysis, the ego psychologists, gradually changed their perception of emotions and the idea of selfhood underpinning it. As Ely Zaretsky notes, along the thinning of their lines, while trying to reconcile psychoanalysis with academic psychology and philosophy, ego psychologists abandoned the notion of drives in favour of notions of affects and feelings, which, as opposed to drives and their intra-psychic nature, are intrinsically inter-subjective and thus oriented towards representations of the self and others. Depression, for example, was no longer viewed as a matter of "oral frustration", but rather of lower self-esteem and negative beliefs about the world, the future or the self. As American psychoanalysis turned from the Ego to the Self, the distinction between analytic and non-analytic approaches became blurred, and analytic language has shifted from "conflict", "defense" and "sexual and aggressive drives" to "dilemma", "adaptation", "learning" and "motivation in general" (Zaretsky 2004).

Put more simply, as Jacoby notes (1975: ix), "In a crowded market no American psychologist could advertise Freud's therapeutic goal, transforming hysterical unhappiness into everyday unhappiness". Thus, the goal and logic of therapy became to provide clients with simple techniques and repertoires to identify, clarify, monitor and document their emotions, to become aware of their meaning and consequences, and to be able to change specific maladaptive, dysfunctional or undesirable emotions through self-instructional training. Thus, overcoming sadness or fear, aspiring to experience more intimacy in a relationship, feeling better about oneself or desiring to reduce anger, became legitimate therapeutic goals, and desirable commodities.

How can emotions – conceived of as subjective mental states – be constructed as measurable and manageable scientific, professional and economic objects, and what enabled the construction of specific techniques for their modification a source of value and a site of exchange? The co-production of emotions as scientific and professional objects and at the same time as commodities is the result of the interaction of four arenas – expert knowledge systems, professional practice, the State and the market. I argue that this co-production is enabled by the establishment of a common institutional ground in which mental entities are constructed and managed, at both micro and macro levels, through the construction of what Callon and Muniesa (2005) call *calculative agencies*. Emotions can be inserted into calculative spaces and processed by calculative agencies thanks to psychological knowledge and practices for their specification, classification, measurement and commensuration for a variety of uses in different institutional settings. But how can emotions, conceived of as subjective experiences, be measured, and how are those measurement technologies used in different institutional settings? Let's take depression as an example.

The diagnosis, assessment and treatment of pathologized moods and emotions rely on standardized technologies of measurement and evaluation of emotions through formalized questionnaires for self-report. One of those emotions measurement technologies is the Beck Depression Inventory, which was introduced by Aaron Beck in 1961, one of the forerunners to cognitive psychology research and treatment of depression. It is a mood-measuring device that detects the presence of depression and rates its severity, through 21 multiple-choice, self-report questionnaire about how the subject was feeling during the week prior to the test. This mood measurement technology, which has become one of the most widely used instruments for measuring depression for both clinical practice and academic research, is put to different uses in different institutional contexts. The consequences of such commensuration technology and practice are complex and varied, according to their uses in specific institutional contexts (Espeland and Stevens 1998), for example, to expand what is considered relevant in bureaucratic decisions, to evaluate objects and convert forms of value, or to enable calculation and facilitate decision making.

In academic and professional contexts, the measurement scale constitutes depression in particular and pathologized emotions in general as research objects which can be observed, evaluated, compared and managed, in order to formulate their causes and effects for diagnostic purposes and scientific explanations. In administrative and policy contexts, however, this commensuration technology enables the inclusion of mood and emotion issues in the construction of health policy goals, to calculate their social and economic costs and benefits, and to bring emotions into a calculative space (Callon and Muniesa 2005) in which they are posed and evaluated in relation to other objects, such as health, longevity or work productivity, and taken into account in more complex calculations alongside other policy objects. In some cases, it changes the terms of what can be talked about, how we value and how we treat what we value (Espeland and Stevens 1998), by infusing moods and emotions into such valuations and consideration. And finally, it enables the reformulation of social, economic and political problems in terms of moods and emotions, and vice-versa: to pose emotions as political, economic and social problems. So depression can be evaluated for its costs to public health institutions, corporate productivity or citizens' well-being.

In a slightly different use, more common in the commercial and corporate context, making emotions commensurate with other "variables" – such as academic and educational success, work productivity, effective advertising, well-being or successful social relationships – makes it possible to economically evaluate certain emotions for their costs or utility in specific domains, such as the stock exchange, corporate labor, marketing, professional health services or social policy. This process of commensuration not only enables the comparison and equivalence of qualitatively different mental and physical objects, but also constitutes their interrelations and promotes a view in which their conversion into one another is possible. Although commensuration is not a necessary condition for commodification, when it comes to abstract commodities, such as emotions, it not only *measures* an object, but *constitutes* it. Moreover, in late capitalist societies, measurement and commensuration become necessary processes since they enable not only the objectification and comparison, but also the evaluation of objects and courses of action, to convert different forms of value to economic value and vice-versa. Most basically, they enable the conversion of emotions as calculable objects into information, bringing them into the different calculative spaces of the information economy for a variety of uses – academic, professional, economic, social and political.

In the therapeutic field, however, emotion measurement techniques are used as a *technology of reflexivity*, which focus on emotional self-monitoring, the assessment and documentation of mood changes, evaluation of the progress of therapy and production of emotional self-transformation. This practice constitutes a form of emotions work by which individuals are led to identify, chart, name, classify and document their emotions and experiences, and to perform certain techniques on themselves in order to produce desirable emotions and relieve undesirable or pathologized ones. The client uses this technique in "homework" assignments between sessions: each time he experiences a strong emotion, such as anger, fear or sadness, he is instructed to write in a journal a detailed account of the time, place and trigger for the incidence that brought about the emotional experience, its intensity, duration and bodily effects, and to describe the emotional and behavioural strategies he implemented in order to "cope" with the emotional reaction, to better manage the specific emotion and better control the behaviour derived from it.[1]

Such strategies consist in a variety of linguistic, imaginative and bodily practices, such as "exposure in reality" or "imaginary exposure" for the treatment of stress and phobias and other "maladaptive" emotions; "cognitive restructuring" (Beck 1976) of negative or maladaptive beliefs; and various "relaxation" and "coping" techniques for the management of stress and anger. These therapeutic techniques promote an *emotional mode of reflexivity*, i.e. a way of attending to one's psyche and interpreting the self and others by focusing on moods and feelings, attitudes towards emotions and emotional dispositions, their causes and effects. It stresses the importance of diminishing "negative emotions" for one's well-being. Simultaneously, it constitutes emotions as objects which can be transformed and managed through strategic action, in order to achieve a desirable emotional make-up.

Quantification and commensuration, which are central in the administrative, academic, professional and commercial institutional contexts for different reasons, are used here as a vehicle for the objectification of subjective experiences, granting them value, defining the goal of emotion-work and pursuing their re-engineering. Moreover, these practices of emotional self-monitoring and self-transformation enable the objectification, singularization and differentiation of emotions (Appaduari 1986), and make the existence of "anger", "fear" or "sadness" a distinct natural aspect of subjective experience. This in turn facilitates the commodification of specific emotions, by devising emotion-specific technologies.

The construction of scientific knowledge on emotions and the search for effective and specific intervention techniques for mood and emotion modification are reflexive in a double sense: on the individual level, these emotion/mood measurement techniques are used as diagnostic tools and a framework and practice of self-inspection, emotional self-monitoring and transformation; and on the macro, institutional level, these techniques are used to standardize disorders and provide information about the efficacy of intervention "upwards" for the purpose of knowledge production and macro efficacy monitoring. At both levels they function as a routine feedback loop which shapes the reproduction of (self) knowledge and therapeutic practice.

We have seen so far how the co-production of emotions as commodities by economic and cultural institutions has reshaped the ways in which psychological knowledge and therapeutic techniques are produced, justified and evaluated. Simultaneously, the therapeutic relationship – the site where emotions are transformed, produced and consumed – went through a significant change as well. It became a *contractual relationship*, which offers effective delivery of predefined emotional commodities; the subjects of therapy shifted from patients to clients, or "educated consumers", who have the right to choose the course of care on their own, according to their judgment and preferences; the aim of professional psychotherapy became to increase the client's well-being and be attentive to the client's needs, wants and desires; and finally, as the possibilities to finance therapy grew and included third-party insurance reimbursement, the role of money became to commensurate the outcome – a specific emotional and behavioural transformation.

The techniques of emotions and mood therapy were rapidly popularized and incorporated into self-help books and counselling practices. In 1980, the year DSM-III was published, David Burns, a Stanford psychiatrist and one of Beck's students, published his bestselling book *Feeling Good: The New Mood Therapy*. The book offers cognitive behavioural techniques of mood modification and emotional self-transformation for self-help. The author offers his readers ways to "Recognise what causes your mood swings, Nip negative feelings in the bud,

Deal with guilt, Handle hostility and criticism, Overcome addiction to love and approval, Build self-esteem, Feel good everyday". The popularization of CBT techniques for mood modification restructures their aim to enhance positive emotions and personal well-being, while addressing the wide "normal" public and the whole spectrum of emotions. Another of Beck's students, Martin Seligman, who worked on the research and treatment of depression in Pennsylvania University, would during the next two decades, develop an academic version of the "feeling good" idea, by establishing a new branch in American psychology devoted to the production, enhancement and maintenance of positive emotions: positive psychology (Cabanas, Chapter 7 this volume).

Emotional utilitarianism and self-realization: the case of life coaching

Before the rise of positive psychology, however, similar practices of emotion-work emerged on the market of self-improvement services in light of new demands from the changing corporate world. During the 1980s, executive coaching emerged in American corporations as a semi-professional consultancy practice for new leadership and management development programs, aiming at enhancing managerial performance and motivation, work satisfaction and organizational productivity (Kampa and Anderson 2001; Kilburg 1996). Executive coaching and its emotion management techniques aim to perform in corporations what Michael Hardt (1999) calls "affective labor": to produce motivation, interpersonal relations, communication skills and a variety of positive feelings such as ease, well-being, satisfaction and excitement to facilitate the construction and maintenance of social networks and peer relations, which came to be central resources in the new flexible corporate environment. Moreover, it enables the practice of authority without overt demonstration of power (Illouz 2008).

Quite parallel to their growing demand in corporations, coaching services begun flourishing in the market of self-improvement for everyday personal life as well, as a joint venture of corporations, psychotherapists and cultural entrepreneurs. Coaching addresses a variety of audiences, offering clients help to improve their performance by setting goals, and working strategically to achieve them in all aspects of personal daily life such as career, family and social relations, romantic life, leisure activities and lifestyle fashioning. Unlike other therapeutic practices, coaching did not emerge as an academic discipline, a system of knowledge or a school of thought. Rather, it emerged more organically from within the market of self-improvement by eclectically utilizing a variety of well-established therapeutic and entrepreneurial techniques and repertoires to forge a new practice of self-realization. It offers a "tool kit" of standardized techniques which can be easily customized to the personal needs of the client, aiming at efficiently increasing economic, social and emotional rewards in all aspects of life. It constructs a pure contractual relationship between coach and client, which is often formalized through a standard written contract with defined goals and timetable, focusing on the needs and desires of the client, and offering a short, goal-oriented, relationship for their achievement in 8–12 sessions.

Coaching adopts some common cognitive and humanistic repertoires and techniques of emotional self-transformation, but weaves them into a highly entrepreneurial discourse. As we are about to see, here, emotions have a dual meaning: they are interpreted as objects of desire and an intuitive and authentic yardstick for the evaluation of situations, courses of action, objects and relationships, which qualify the authentic goals of one's life project and the best way to achieve them. At the same time, emotions are treated as objects of utility which should be evaluated for their costs and benefits in a given situation, alongside other utility objects, when practising personal choice.

Coaching denounces the medicalizing discourse of psychology and the practice of diagnosis according to standardized classification categories. Instead, it problematizes the self through economic categories. It aims at locating the client's authentic self, the areas of life where it should be expressed and experienced, and the most effective ways for its realization. Instead of diagnosis, coaching turns to self-assessment through mapping one's current life situations, personal resources, strengths and barriers in relation to a desirable goal. Mapping one's current life, locating the areas in which action is needed and the construction of a prospective plan of self-realization are done through conversation and leading questions, but also through self-assessment tools and exercises.

One of the common tools is the "Wheel of Life": a round diagram, on which the client is asked to assess her current level of satisfaction in different areas of life, on a scale of 1–10, which includes categories such as career, family and friends, money, romance, personal growth, fun and recreation, health, physical environment (see Whitworth *et al.* 2007). The idea is to map one's current life according to the yardstick of satisfaction in order to locate the sites where change should be induced, and to come up with a plan to improve one's overall satisfaction by setting goals and working to achieve them. Satisfaction (or dissatisfaction) in this case is an emotional scale which is used to evaluate the discrepancies between one's expectation and one's actual situation. Dissatisfaction can be identified in virtually all situations: feeling not rewarded enough in a job or a relationship; frustration from the gap between the individual's social image and one's desired self-image; feelings of detachment in unsupportive environment; frustration over not making the most out of situations, relationships and activities, etc. As a category of evaluation, it is inclusive, flexible and subjective enough to evaluate everything in relation to the self and its aspirations. It can lead the individual to enhance satisfaction by changing attitudes and beliefs: by reshaping expectations, preferences, comparison model or whatever one values; or it can lead to a new understanding of the situation and encourage action in new directions which are prospectively more desirable and rewarding. In both cases, it encourages the individual to define her self-interest *and* sources of emotional authenticity, by addressing the self and her emotions as both the ultimate criteria of evaluation and as objects for manipulation by certain techniques.

As a technology of commensuration, however, it is used quite differently from the commensuration techniques devised for the diagnosis and research of pathologized emotions mentioned earlier, and has little, if any, use for administrative or research purposes. In this case, *commensuration is used primarily as a technology of the self*, to enable choice and facilitate decision making without appealing to objective criteria, by establishing a subjective, common measure to compare qualitatively different life situations, to evaluate them, delineate a zone where action is required, outline different courses of action, calculate the best alternative, and carry it out. This instrumental and quantitative approach to emotions is used to insert certain emotions – actual as well as desirable – into a common calculative space alongside other objects such as social relationships, leisure, career and economic considerations, and thus enables the individual to distinguish forms of value in the situation and formulate social situations as sites of personal choice. Moreover, it enables the individual to make actual choices in concrete situations in which emotions are taken into account, and facilitate processes of attachment to and detachment from relationships, objects and social activities.

Satisfaction helps the client to define the actual present self and to focus on sites where action is required. Coaching's mode of reflexivity acts simultaneously to define the virtual prospective self, to be actualized and experienced in the near future by constructing a desired future – desired self-image, wanted lifestyle, aspirations concerning career, and social, familial and romantic relationships. The construction of the authentic virtual self is accomplished through techniques of self-imagination: questions directing and encouraging the individual to develop, imagine and verbally articulate personal dreams, fantasies and visions of their aspired life. One of the self-help coaching books presents it as a string of questions:

> What is it that you desire and keeps slipping away? Imagine that you have it, whatever it is, now what? … Now that you have it, what does it give you that you didn't have before? What does it look like? What do you feel when you have it? Do you see yourself differently now that you have it? Do others see you differently now? And what about your daily life – is it significantly changed and better in any way?

> (Blanchard and Human 2004: 24)

This passage illustrates how imagination is used not only for the construction of fantasies (Campbell 1987) but also as means of self-experimentation to probe personal aspirations and their prospective contribution to one's self-image, social recognition and life improvement in order to evaluate their authenticity, i.e. their prospective emotional effect and the degree of their desirability. The imaginative construction of the desired life and self-image serves as a personal compass to facilitate individual orientation in current social relationships, to produce positive and future oriented emotions such as hope and excitement, to induce motivation and action, and to facilitate choice from different courses of action.

The gap between the actual self and the virtual one is bridged by the construction of a prospective narrative, which is designed to produce a strong future orientation, hope, excitement, enthusiasm, a sense of self-worth and a sense of control, while its ultimate telos is individual happiness.

The "traditional" social practice which confronts the fragility and uncertainty of the future consists in promise keeping, interpersonal commitment, trust and coercive social norms which are enforced through feelings of shame, guilt, loyalty and debt. In contrast, the prospective narrative offered by coaching is an attempt to devise an individualized way of confronting this problem and its existential consequences, by projecting the self into the future through the construction of a desired self-image and a personal life project which is carried out rationally. This narrative is translated into a concrete project including a work plan, timetable, stages and performance measures. As part of this project, the actual self is reassessed: the client's personality traits, tendencies, competencies, habits, beliefs, ways of thinking, acting and feeling are reformulated in terms of strengths/ resources or barriers, in relation to the specific goal the client sets for herself, and the social context in which it is to be realized.

In this utilitarian framework, however, there is no intention to classify emotions into simple categories of positive and negative; rather to evaluate the emotional – alongside the economic and social – costs and benefits in relation to specific ends or a specific situation of decision making. Fear, for example, can be a "barrier" if it inhibits action or narrows down choice, but so is "too much" comfort. A widely used technique requires the client to delineate his "comfort zone" – where one feels familiar, at ease, in control and experiences low distress – in order to see the possibilities it denies of him, and then to practise leaving the "zone", to generate change and gain new rewards and experiences (see Whitmore 2009; Whitworth *et al.* 2007). Thus, enhancing personal performance sometimes demands experiencing yet overcoming the fear, stress and uncertainty this risk induces, for the future gains it may entail. As Ruth, a 42-year-old coach, put it:

> [s]ometimes clients come up against barriers they have placed there themselves: limiting beliefs, fears, fears of success, fears of failure, etc. It's easy, because if you put these obstacles in front of you, and you understand it, you can change and transform it.

The same goes for various emotions and feelings. Anger management is required when confronting one's boss, for the sake of one's career, not because anger is bad but because it damages one's interests in this particular situation. Coaches offer clients techniques for empowering useful and productive emotions as resources for action in a situation, and techniques for controlling or eliminating damaging ones. These techniques, as those described earlier, draw on some CBT techniques of changing or "restructuring" cognitions and beliefs in order to produce adaptive behaviours and positive feelings. However, they differ in some significant respects: they address a wide variety of emotions and do not focus on "disordered" emotions. Moreover, they do not assess emotions on the basis of their being adaptive to a given function or ideals of normalcy and health, but on their utility to a given end in a specific situation, or their personal desirability. While the experience of emotions is subjective, the criteria for "adaptive" emotions and behaviours in CBT is not. It represents the reasonable or "rational" reaction to a situation, or a manner of functional behaviour. In coaching, however, the criteria are completely subjective and appeal to one's authentic desires, preferences and interests. Thus, while at times the emotions are to be adapted to a situation, at other times, the situation is to be changed to fit one's emotional life project. This requires practices of attachment and detachment in relation to specific others, cultural objects, activities and situations. For example, Meital, a 26-year-old columnist in a local newspaper decided to leave her job despite her success, because she was not receiving recognition from her co-workers:

> I don't want to be in a place where I am not appreciated after giving so much of myself. So I decided it was time to move on. That's it. I made the most of this place. Now it's time to move on. I need this new adrenalin, it is vital for me.

In addition to the techniques of mood management and emotional self-transformation described earlier, coaching offers to regulate emotions through framing social relationships according to the anthropological assumption of self-interest: in cases one is getting angry or hurt by someone's behaviour or attitude, the language of self-interest is evoked to dismantle any harmful intersubjective intention on behalf of the offender. Relating the action to the other's self-interested intention of gaining some personal benefits – which is, needless to say, legitimate and natural – enables to reduce "negative" emotions, avoid the behaviours related to them, construct a depersonalized relationship and promote cooperation on the basis of pursuing one's own ends.

In summary, the case of coaching demonstrates a distinct form of the co-production of emotions in the following respects: first, it is not constrained within a theoretical framework or a specific knowledge system; rather, it draws on a variety of approaches and techniques according to "what works" for the client. In addition, it aims to meet the demands of different actors in the market effectively, be it organizations or individuals, granting clients what they desire, enhancing their performance, satisfaction, self-esteem and a sense of self-worth, not through the constitution of classification systems, knowledge and diagnostic procedures, but rather by offering effective, efficient, quick and relatively cheap techniques. That is to say, coaching does not represent a progress or refinement of knowledge of emotions or the self, but a sophistication of the commodification processes of existing ideas and practices with the aim of increasing economic, social and emotional performance, be it for CEOs and workers in organizations, or for the individual's personal well-being. And finally, it offers a utilitarian, entrepreneurial and extremely individualized interpretive framework for understanding and reshaping the self, one's emotions and social relationships. Thus, the meaning of commodified emotions in this case goes beyond the emotional experiences produced by this practice, such as hope, excitement, optimism, enthusiasm and desire. It constitutes a general cultural and moral framework which promotes a form of entrepreneurial mode of attending, monitoring and consulting emotions, as part one's self-concept and social relationships, and a set of practices of emotions work one performs on oneself in order to regulate and control one's emotions and experiences.

This form of emotion management is an interesting mixture of what Campbell (1987) calls *regulation of emotions*, i.e. the cultural conventions on *when* and *how* we should *express* wanted emotions, and *suppress* unwanted emotions, with what he calls *emotional control*, i.e. the ability to decide on the type and intensity of the emotions they want to feel. These techniques can produce emotional capital (Illouz 2008), but their primary meaning as commodities is fusion with economic repertoires and practices of cost-benefit calculation, personal choice and maximization of emotional reward. Experiencing too much or not enough excitement, intimacy, love or empathy in the realms of friendship, romance or family will bring about the same techniques of emotions regulation in order to reach the optimal emotional experience, hand in hand with the optimal general gains out of the situation.

Conclusion

Modern selfhood and morality are shaped by the ideal of emotional authenticity *and* the rational calculation of self-interest, and both repertoires are institutionalized in the language and practice of psychotherapy. Critic of the commodification of therapeutic knowledge and practices of emotion-work, however, draw on the ontological distinction between emotions and the economy. They point out the commodification of emotions in psychotherapy in two central ways: first, the utilization of therapeutic knowledge, categories and classification schemes – which were produced by academic and professional actors for certain scientific and therapeutic uses – for economic uses, nourishing new cultural industries and creating new commodities, markets, forms of labor and value (Hochschild 1983, 2003; Illouz 2008). Second, the infusion of economic rationality into the production and consumption of therapeutic repertoires and techniques, demanding standardization of practices and prices, commensurability of outcomes (being able to produce specific, predefined and measurable outcomes), time efficiency, effectiveness, problem specificity and ability to meet the demands of various social actors (corporations, welfare state, insurance companies or individual consumers).

What we have seen in this chapter, however, presents a third meaning of commodification of self and emotions, which has two central features: the infusion of economic and consumerist repertoires (cost-benefit calculation, self-interest, utility, efficiency, limited contracts, personal choice, planning, self-management, profit seeking, maximization of satisfaction and happiness) into the construction of subjectivity and social relationships; and the construction of self-identity, emotions and sociality according to criteria of productivity (emotional, social and economic) in achieving a project of self-realization. The utilitarian model thus became a cultural repertoire which provides moral orientation in various social spheres. But as it expands the model of "homo economicus" far beyond the realm of "pure" economic action into all life spheres, it constitutes emotions as central measures of value in the formation and management of "pure relationships" (Giddens 1991) in which emotional authenticity and emotional reward are paramount. "Purity" in both cases is of course misleading. The framework of co-production and the concept of emodities enable us to rethink the ontological distinction between the economic and the cultural in shaping emotions and selfhood, by examining the ways in which they are intertwined. From this perspective, the economy and consumer culture provide the social and cultural infrastructure of repertoires, practices and rituals which enable a certain mode of emotional self-transformation and emotional experience.

To conclude, I would like to ask: If "Authenticity is the experience generated by the co-production of emotions and consumer practices" (Illouz, Introduction to this volume), what is the ethical form forged by it and what is the role and meaning of emotions in it? The idea of co-production indicates that the market not only objectifies emotions and produces emotional experiences through objects and rituals, but it reshapes the ethics and practice of sociation – the ways in which humans associate and dissociate – by framing emotions as objects of personal choice. We can identify two features of this moral form: the subjectification of moral imperatives and commitments; and the infusion of "personal choice" into the realm of emotions and sociation as a source of value and legitimation in itself.

This model of selfhood holds a dual role for emotions in the construction of social relationships: first, it makes "emotional rewards" a standard of worth and the yardstick by which social relationships and activities are to be measured and evaluated, which encourages personal choice of temporal commitments according to the actual or prospective experiences they provide and their contribution to one's sense of authenticity; and second, it takes emotions to be essential resources for the construction of relationships in various social spheres in which their expression is managed strategically according to one's self-interest. This ethical framework promotes a suspension of objective moral categories of right and wrong, good and bad, as standards of evaluation in favour of a *subjective hedonic (emotional) calculus* which becomes a central moral technology, and gives rise to an ironic model of selfhood: the autonomous emotional self.

At the end of the 1950s, Martin Buber criticized the intellectual discourses on guilt: on the one hand, the theologians took it as a metaphysical concept, and on the other, psychologists (mainly analysts) took it as an individual psychological state. Both approaches, Buber noted, ignore its very basic ethical meaning, as a personal experience which exists in the face and in relation to the other.

In this ethical framework, the meaning and value of emotions as inter-subjective, collective and ritualized entities is on the retreat (Wilce 2009). Instead, emotions come to play a central role in the construction of the intra-subjective relationship between the person and oneself. It enables guilt to be detached from blame and fault, from debt and remorse, so as to become "a sense of guilt" which one can manage through individual mental exercises rather than through an inter-subjective ritual of forgiveness. Similarly, anger is dismantled from its moral claim upon others; love is separated from commitment, from the banalities of daily life and the sorrows cast by fortune and chance, to embrace exclusively a choice for excitement and intimacy; suffering and sadness entirely lose their moral meaning to become a pathology one should overcome by individual rituals of optimism; and happiness becomes a positive and optimistic ideal emotional make-up, rather than the telos of the virtuous life, the life (morally) well lived.

Counterintuitively, it seems that the repertoires and practices of consumer culture help to reproduce the cultural view of emotions as individualized and psychological phenomena which are central to one's well-being and authenticity, by objectifying emotions and enabling the experience of some emotions as individual objects of choice through rituals of consumption. Contemporary co-production of emotions draws heavily on the psychologized and individualized repertoires of emotions, and through their performativity, they reproduce a social reality which enables them to validate and sustain this view of emotions and their ethical separation from concrete others. This, in turn, promotes a new ethical framework which assigns new functions and meanings to emotions.

Note

1 Today, a variety of mobile Apps for mood and emotions monitoring and management offer this technology to the wider public.

Bibliography

Appadurai, Arjun. 1986 (ed.). *The Social Life of Things*. New York: Cambridge University Press.

Arknoff, Diane and Carol Glass. 1992. "Cognitive therapy and psychotherapy integration." In *History of Psychotherapy: A Century of Change*, edited by Donald Freedheim, *et al.*, 657–694. Washington, DC: American Psychological Association.

Bandura, Albert. 2004. "Swimming against the mainstream: The early years from chilly tributary to transformative mainstream." *Behaviour Research and Therapy* 42:613–630.

Beck, Aaron. T. 1970. "Cognitive therapy: Nature and relation to behavior therapy." *Behavior Therapy* 1:184–200.

Beck, Aaron. T. 1976. *Cognitive Therapy and the Emotional Disorders*, New York: New American Library.

Beck, Aaron. T, John A. Rush, Brian F. Shaw and Gary Emery. 1979. *Cognitive Therapy of Depression*. New York: Guilford.

Beck, Ulrich and Elisabeth Beck-Gernsheim. 2002. *Individualization. Institutionalized Individualism and Its Social and Political Consequences*. London: SAGE Publications.

Bellah, Robert N., Richard Madsen, William M. Sullivan, Ann Swindler and Steven M. Tipton. 1986. *Habits of the Heart. Individualism and Commitment in American Life*. London: University of California Press.

Bergin, Allen E. and Lambert, Michael J. 1978. "The evaluation of therapeutic outcomes." In *Handbook of Psychotherapy and Behavior Change* (2nd ed.), edited by Sol L. Garfield and Allen E. Bergin. London: Wiley.

Berrios, German E. 1985. "The psychopathology of affectivity: Conceptual and historical aspects." *Psychological Medicine* 15:745–758.

Berrios, German E. 1996. *The History of Mental Symptoms: Descriptive Psychopathology since the Nineteenth Century*. Cambridge, UK: Cambridge University Press.

Blanchard, S. and Human, M. 2004. *Leverage Your Best Ditch the Rest: The Coaching Secret Top Executives Depend On*. London: HarperCollins.

Breuer, Joseph and Freud, Sigmund. 1955 [1893–1895]. "Studies on hysteria." In *The Standard Edition of the Complete Psychological Works of Sigmund Freud* (Vol. 2), edited and translated by James Strachey, 1–305. London: Hogarth Press, 1955.

Brinkmann, Svend. 2008. "Changing psychologies in the transition from industrial society to consumer society." *History of the Human Sciences* 21(2):85–110.

Busfield, Joan. 1986. *Managing Madness: Changing Ideas and Practice*. Cambridge, UK: Polity Press.

Callon, Michel and Fabian Muniesa. 2005. "Peripheral vision economic markets as calculative collective devices." *Organization Studies* 26(8):1229–1250.

Campbell, Colin. 1987. *The Romantic Ethic and the Spirit of Modern Consumerism*. New York: Blackwell.

Carruthers, Steve and Wendy Espeland. 1998. "Money, meaning, and morality." *American Behavioral Scientist* 41(10):1384–1408.

Clark, David. M. 1986. "A cognitive approach to panic." *Behaviour Research and Therapy* 24:461–470.

Conrad, Peter. 2007. *The Medicalization of Society: On the Transformation of Human Conditions into Treatable Disorders*. Baltimore, MD: The Johns Hopkins University Press.

Crits-Christoph, Paul, Jacques P. Barber and Mary Beth Connolly Gibbons. 2011. "University of Pennsylvania Center for Psychotherapy Research." In *History of Psychotherapy: Continuity and Change*, edited by John C. Norcross, Gary R. VandenBos, Donald K. Freedheim, 370–374. Washington DC: American Psychological Association.

Crossley, Nick. 2006. *Contesting Psychiatry. Social Movements in Mental Health*. Abingdon, UK: Routledge.

Cushman, Phillip. 1996. *Constructing the Self, Constructing America: A Cultural History of Psychotherapy*. Burlington, VT: Da Capo Publishing Inc.

Danziger, Kurt. 1997. *Naming the Mind: How Psychology Found Its Language*. London: SAGE Publications.

DeLeon, Patrick, Mary Beth Kenkel, Linda Garcia-Shelton and Gary R. VandenBos. 2011. "Psychotherapy: 1960 to the present." In *History of Psychotherapy: Continuity and Change*, edited by John C. Norcross, Gary R. VandenBos and Donald K. Freedheim, 39–62. Washington, DC: American Psychological Association.

Dittmar, Helga. 2007. *Consumer Culture, Identity and Well-Being: The Search for the 'Good Life' and the 'Body Perfect'*. London: Psychology Press.

Dixon, Thomas. 2003. *From Passions to Emotions: The Creation of a Secular Psychological Category*. Cambridge, UK: Cambridge University Press.

Duffy, Elizabeth. 1941. "The conceptual categories of psychology: A suggestion for revision." *Psychological Review* 48:177–203.

Ellis, Albert. 1962. *Reason and Emotion in Psychotherapy*. New York: Lyle Stuart.

Espeland, Wendy and Stevens, Mitchell. 1998. "Commensuration as a social process." *Annual Review of Sociology* 24:313–343.

Fineman, Stephen. 1993. "Organizations as emotional arenas." In *Emotion in Organizations*, edited by Stephen Fineman, 9–35. London: SAGE Publications.

Fineman, Stephen. 2000. "Commodifying the emotionally intelligent." In *Emotion in Organizations*, edited by Stephen Fineman, 101–114. London: SAGE Publications,

Foucault, Michel. 1988. *Technologies of the Self: A Seminar with Michel Foucault*. Boston, MA: University of Massachusetts Press.

Freud, Sigmund. 1958 [1913]. "On beginning the treatment." In *The Standard Edition of the Complete Psychological Works of Sigmund Freud* (Vol. 12), edited and trans. by James Strachey *et al.*, 121–144. London: Hogarth Press.

Freud, Sigmund. 1963 [1916]. "Analytic therapy." In *The Standard Edition of the Complete Psychological Works of Sigmund Freud* (Vol. 16), edited and trans. by James Strachey *et al.*, 448–463. London: Hogarth Press.

Friedberg, Anne. 1993. *Window Shopping: Cinema and the Postmodern*. Berkeley, CA: University of California Press.

Furedi, Frank. 2004. *Therapy Culture: Cultivating Vulnerability in an Uncertain Age*. London: Routledge.

Gergen, Kenneth. 1995. "Metaphor and monophony in the 20th-century psychology of emotions." *History of the Human Sciences* 8(2):1–23.

Giddens, Anthony. 1991. *Modernity and Self Identity: Self and Society in Late-Modern Age*. Oxford, UK: Polity Press.

Greenberg, Leslie S. and Safran, Jeremy D. 1989. "Emotion in psychotherapy." *American Psychologist* 44:19–29.

Hale G. Nathan. 2000. "American psychoanalysis since World War II." In *American Psychiatry After World War II, 1944–1994*, edited by Roy W. Menninger and John C. Nemiah, 77–102. Washington, DC: American Psychiatric Press.

Hardt, Michael. 1999. "Affective labor." *Boundary 2*, 26(2):89–100.

Hochschild, Arlie. R. 1979. "Emotion work, feeling rules and social structure." *American Journal of Sociology* 85(3):551–575.

Hochschild, Arlie. 1983. *The Managed Heart: Commercialization of Human Feeling*. Berkeley, CA: University of California Press.

Hochschild, Arlie R. 2003. *The Commercialization of Intimate Life: Notes from Home and Work*, Berkeley, CA: University of California Press.

Horwitz, Allan V. and Jerome C. Wakefield. 2007. *The Loss of Sadness: How Psychiatry Transformed Normal Sorrow into Depressive Disorder*. Oxford, UK: Oxford University Press.

Horwitz, Allan V. and Jerome C. Wakefield. 2012. *All We Have to Fear: Psychiatry's Transformation of Natural Anxieties into Mental Disorders*. Oxford, UK: Oxford University Press.

Illouz, Eva. 2008. *Saving the Modern Soul: Therapy, Emotions and the Culture of Self-Help*. Berkeley, CA: University of California Press.

Illouz, Eva. 2013. *Why Love Hurts*. Oxford, UK: Polity.

Jacoby, Russell. 1975. *Social Amnesia: A Critique of Contemporary Psychology*. Boston, MA: Beacon Press.

Kampa-Kokesch, Sheila and Mary Z. Anderson. 2001. "Executive coaching: A comprehensive review of the literature." *Consulting Psychology Journal: Practice and Research* 53(4):205–228.

Kendall, P. C. and Bemis, K. M. 1983. "Thought and action in psychotherapy: The cognitive-behavioral approaches." In *The Clinical Psychology Handbook*, edited by M. Hersen, A. E. Kazdin and A.S. Bellack, 565–592. New York: Pergamon.

Kilburg, R. 1996. "Toward a conceptual understanding and definition of executive coaching." *Consulting Psychology Journal: Practice and Research*, 48(2):134–144.

Kutchins, Herb and Stuart A. Kirk. 2003. *Making Us Crazy*. London and New York: Simon and Schuster.

Lasch, Christopher. 1979. *The Culture of Narcissism. American Life in an Age of Diminishing Expectations*. New York: Norton.

Lazarus, Richard. 1993. "From psychological stress to the emotions: A history of changing outlooks." *Annual Review of Psychology* 44:1–21.

Lazarus, Richard. 1999. *Stress and Emotion: A New Synthesis*. Dordrecht, The Netherlands: Springer.

Lears, TJ. Jackson. 1983. "From salvation to self-realization: Advertising and the therapeutic roots of the consumer culture, 1880–1930." In *The Culture of Consumption*, edited by Richard Wightman and Jackson Lears, 1–38. New York: Pantheon.

Mayes, R. and Horwitz, A. V. 2005. "DSM-III and the revolution in the classification of mental illness." *Journal of the History of the Behavioral Sciences* 41(3):249–267.

Mestrovic, Stjepan. 1997. *Postemotional Society*. London: SAGE Publications.

Mills, John A. 1998. *Control: A History of Behavioral Psychology*. New York: New York University Press.

Mitchell, Joel. 2004. "The place of qualitative research in psychology." *Qualitative Research in Psychology* 1:307–319.

Nolan, James. 1998. *The Therapeutic State: Justifying Government at Century's End*, New York: New York University Press.

Pickren, Wade E. and Stanley F. Schneider. (eds) 2005. *Psychology and the National Institute of Mental Health: A Historical Analysis of Science, Practice, and Policy*. Amsterdam: American Psychological Association.

Pilgrim, David. 2011. "The hegemony of cognitive-behaviour therapy in modern mental health care." *Health Sociology Review* 20(2):120–132.

Polsky, Andrew. 1991. *The Rise of the Therapeutic State*. Princeton, NJ: Princeton University Press.

Porter, Roy. 1987. *Mind Forg'd Manacles: A History of Madness in England from the Restoration to the Regency*. Harmondsworth, UK: Penguin.

Rieff, Philip. 1966. *The Triumph of the Therapeutic: Uses of Faith After Freud*. Chicago, IL: University of Chicago Press.

Rogers, Carl. 1942. *Counseling and Psychotherapy: Newer Concepts in Practice*. Oxford, UK: Oxford.

Rose, Nikolas. 1996. *Inventing Our Selves: Psychology, Power, and Personhood*. Cambridge, UK: Cambridge University Press.

Rose, Nikolas. 2009. "Normality and pathology in a biomedical age." *Sociological Review* 57:66–83.

Shachak, Mattan. 2013. "The commodification of the self: The case of life coaching." In *Ökonomisierung der Wertesysteme: Der Geist der Effizienz im mediatisierten Alltag*. Stuttgart, Germany: Steiner.

Shorter, Edward. 2009. *Before Prozac: The Troubled History of Mood Disorders in Psychiatry*, Oxford, UK: Oxford University Press.

Skinner, B. F. 1953. *Science and Human Behavior*. New York: Macmillan.

Strupp, H. Hand and Hoeard, Kenneth I. 1992. "A brief history of psychotherapy research." In *History of Psychotherapy: A Century of Change*, edited by Freedheim, Donald *et al.*, 309–344. Washington, DC: American Psychological Association.

Swan, Elaine. 2010. *Worked Up Selves: Personal Development Workers, Self-Work and Therapeutic Cultures*. Basingstoke, UK: Palgrave Macmillan.

Taylor, Charles. 1989. *Sources of the Self: The Making of the Modern Identity*. Cambridge, MA: Harvard University Press.

Tone, Andrea. 2009. *The Age of Anxiety: A History of America's Turbulent Affair with Tranquilizers*. New York: Basic Books.

Vandenbos, Gary, Nicholas A. Cummings and Patrick H. DeLeon. 1992. "A century of psychotherapy: Economic and environmental influences." In *History of Psychotherapy: A Century of Change*, edited by Freedheim, Donald *et al.*, 65–102. Washington, DC: American Psychological Association.

Van Maanen, John and Gideon Kunda. 1989. "Real feelings: Emotional expressions and organization culture." In *Research in Organizational Behavior*, edited by B. Staw and L.L. Cummings. Vol. 11. London: Elsevier.

Whitmore, John. 2009. *Coaching for Performance: Growing Human Potential and Purpose*. 4th edition. London: Nicholas Brealey Publishing.

Whitworth, Laura, Karen Kimsey-House, Henry Kimsey-House and Phillip Sandahl. 2007. *Co-Active Coaching: New Skills for Coaching People towards Success in Work and Life*. Mountain View, CA: Davies-Black Publishing.

Wilce, James M. 2009. *Language and Emotions*. Cambridge, UK: Cambridge University Press

Williams, Simon 2001. *Emotion and Social Theory: Corporeal Reflections on the (Ir) Rational*. London: SAGE Publications.

Wouters, Cas. 2004. "Changing regimes of manners and emotions: From disciplining to informalizing." In *The Sociology of Norbert Elias*, edited by Steven Loyal and Stephen Quilley, 193–211. Cambridge, UK: Cambridge University Press.

Zaretsky, Eli. 2004. *Secrets of the Soul: A Social and Cultural History of Psychoanalysis*. New York: Alfred A. Knopf.

Zelizer, Viviana. 1996. *The Social Meaning of Money*. Princeton, NJ: Princeton University Press.

Zelizer, Viviana. 2005. *The Purchase of Intimacy*. Princeton, NJ and Oxford, UK: Princeton University Press.

Chapter 7

"Psytizens", or the construction of happy individuals in neoliberal societies

Edgar Cabanas

> "We have invented happiness", say the last men, and they blink.
> (Friedrich Nietzsche, *Thus Spoke Zarathustra*)

The Hollywood movie *The Pursuit of Happyness* was a worldwide hit in 2006, with a total revenue of $307,077,300 at the box office. The movie is based on the true story of Christopher Gardner, an African-American undergraduate and lower-middle-class family guy who tries very hard to prevent his 5-year-old son, Christopher, and his wife, Linda, from sinking into poverty. It is the early 1980s; Ronald Reagan has delivered bad economic news on television; and Gardner's family situation is dramatic: they can barely pay their rent, bills, or for Christopher's day care (on whose nursery wall the word happiness is misspelled as "happiness", giving the title of the film). But in spite of all this, Gardner is optimistic. He is persistent, talented, and has a deep longing for a better career path. One day, standing in front of a prestigious stock brokerage firm, Gardner stares at the faces of the brokers leaving work: "They all look very happy", he claims; "Why cannot I be like them?" Gardner has now a goal he is determined to pursue: to become a stock broker at that company. He wants a share of the American Dream, and thanks to his charms and social skills, Gardner manages to get into a highly competitive and unpaid internship program at the company. Gardner tells his wife Linda about his intention of becoming a broker, to which she sarcastically replies, "Why not an astronaut?" Linda is depicted as Gardner's counterpart: she represents the whiner, the pessimist; the kind of person who brings others down and does not support their dreams. She is a miserable and unhappy character. She is also depicted as a quitter, abandoning the family just when things seem that they could not get any worse. Without the economic support of his wife, Gardner finds himself completely broke. He and his son are kicked out first from their apartment, and then from a motel, so they are forced to move to a homeless shelter. Gardner, nevertheless, does not allow himself to be overcome by the circumstances. He works day and studies night, struggles to maintain the appearance of success amongst the program's CEOs and his Ivy League competitors, and manages to take good care of his son. Gardner is highly determined and motivated: "Do not ever let somebody tell you that you cannot do something. You got a dream, you have to protect it. If you want something, go get it. Period", (sic.) Gardner tells his son while they play basketball. Gardner finishes at the top of the program and finally gets his dream job. "This is happiness", he claims at the end of the movie.

The most interesting aspect of the film is not what it says about the notion of happiness per se, but what it says about its pursuit and about the kind of citizen that rightfully achieves it. Gardner is not depicted as an exception to the norm, but as an exemplification of what the norm should be. In this way, the movie intensifies, through the character of Gardner, those key moral values and psychological features which underlie the individual pursuit of happiness and, at the same time, depicts one of the dominant kinds of subjectivity in contemporary societies, i.e., individualistic (the individual rises by himself despite his social circumstances, eschewing any kind of dependence on others), autonomous, and personally responsible (failures and successes are the outcome of personal choices), authentic and true to oneself (everyone is naturally equipped with a set of skills which one has to discover and implement in order to make the best of them), self-motivated, determined, and highly emotionally competent (an intrinsic inclination to persevere with optimism and hopefulness in the pursuit of one's own goals, and skillful in deploying interpersonal abilities).

Interestingly, the depiction of Gardner in the film almost perfectly matches the description that happiness researchers have supplied about the psychological features of happy individuals. For instance, in the influential article "Happiness is everything, or is it? Explorations on the meaning of psychological well-being", positive psychologist Carol Ryff defines well-being as an "optimal psychological functioning" achieved by people who possess the following six individual dimensions: self-acceptance (which describes someone who "possesses a positive attitude toward the self"), positive relations with others ("has warm, satisfying, trusting relationships with others"), autonomy ("is self-determining and independent; able to resist social pressures to think and act in certain ways; regulates behavior from within; evaluates self by personal standards"), environmental mastery ("has a sense of mastery and competence in managing the environment; makes effective use of surrounding opportunities"), purpose in life ("has goals in life and a sense of directedness"), and personal growth ("has a feeling of continued development; sees self as growing and expanding") (Ryff 1989: 1072; see also Peterson *et al.* 2005). From this point of view, happiness is rendered as an utterly individualistic endeavor, with any problematization of the political, economic, or social circumstances completely obliterated from the analysis. Indeed, positive psychologists claim that the role played by political, economic, and social aspects in the happiness of individuals is, at most, secondary, either because they contribute very little, or because trying to influence or change those circumstances seems not to be worthwhile in terms of the individual's cost-benefit analysis of their personal well-being (e.g., Seligman 2002).

From a sociological standpoint, the similarities between the depiction of the character of Gardner and the psychological characteristics of happy individuals provided by positive psychologists are not surprising. Both the cinematographic and the academic accounts should be understood as cultural expressions of a highly individualistic and psychological model of citizenship that is characteristic of and dominant in neoliberal societies, i.e., as self-governed beings whose behaviors and aspirations are mainly constrained by, linked to, and based on their own personalities, tastes, choices, motivations, emotions, beliefs, goals, dreams, and life-projects, all of them conceived as inherent aspects of the "psyche", which have the capacity to be satisfied, developed, and mastered through acts of choice and consumption. Indeed, this model renders individuals as what we might call *psytizens*, defined as "an individualistic and consumerist kind of subjectivity that renders citizens as clients whose full functionality as individuals is tied to the pursuing and development of their own happiness" (Cabanas 2016).

This kind of subjectivity is the result of a process of individualization and psychologization which has progressively transformed the political and social orders of accountability within neoliberal societies, rendering its structural deficits, contradictions, and paradoxes in terms of psychological features and individual responsibilities (Lipovetsky 1983); therefore, aspects such as work become more and more a matter of personal strengths, creativity, and entrepreneurship; education a matter of individual competences and talents; health a matter of habits and life-styles; love a matter of interpersonal likeness and compatibility; identity a matter of choice and personality; social progress a matter of individual growth and thriving, and so on. The corollary is a widespread collapse of the social in favor of the psychological (Crespo and Freire 2014), with Politics (with a capital P) being gradually replaced by therapeutic politics (with a small p) (McLaughlin 2010), and with the discourse of personal happiness progressively taking over the discourse of individualism in the definition of the neoliberal model of citizenship (Cabanas 2013).

On the grounds of this sociological diagnosis, this chapter aims to account for the emergence, expansion, and consolidation of a "happiness industry" which is based on the commodification of happiness at multiple levels – ranging from positive psychological techniques offering individuals efficient self-management of their emotions, cognitions, and motivations, and including a wide variety of self-help literature, coaching and professional advice, pharmaceutical goods, body-shaping products, tourism and experiential marketing, and even cinema. It is argued that these happiness "emodities", namely psy goods and services aimed at increasing the happiness of individuals, simultaneously presuppose and target the construction *psytizens*. It is also argued that happiness emodities are effective because they are not limited to offering fleeting moments or states of pleasure, tranquility, evasion, hope, or reassurance, but mainly because they presuppose and target a determinate "structure of feelings" (Williams 1977), a specific way of being, acting, and understanding the world, which is particular to and consistent with the neoliberal notion of citizenship. In this respect, I do not understand happiness as an emotion so much as a specific and normative kind of subjectivity which is intensely and predominantly defined in emotional and psychological terms and practices. Therefore, this chapter defends the idea that ideological and economic analyses should go hand in hand, since the former informs about the kind of subjectivity which is simultaneously targeted and presupposed by the happiness industry, and the latter informs about the consumerist logic under which that kind of subjectivity is constructed.

The first part of this chapter addresses the ideological analysis. It tackles happiness as a notion which has proved useful in neutralizing and legitimizing the individualist ideology of neoliberalism into seemingly non-ideological terms, showing how it conceals its ideological implications by being presented as a natural and self-evidently universal goal (naturalization), as well as a scientific, objective, and quantitative variable (commensuration) which can be established as a neutral criterion to guide a wide array of educational, organizational, economic, and political decisions and interventions. The academic fields of positive psychology and happiness economy are presented as two of the authoritative sources which have most influenced and contributed to the institutionalization of both phenomena. The institutionalization of happiness is crucial to understanding its commodification, since it is on the basis on this institutionalization that happiness has become a legitimate commodity which promises to turn individuals into fully functioning *psytizens*.

The second part of the chapter addresses the economic analysis, focusing on how the "happiness industry" commodifies happiness as a set of psychological techniques aimed at shaping the three main features of the *psytizen*, i.e., "emotional rationality", that is, individuals' ability to master their own feelings, thoughts, and motivations in order to take full responsibility for coping with their problems, to hierarchize their priorities, and to pursue their goals efficiently; "authenticity", that is, individuals' ability to make self-fulfilling, reflexive, and strategic choices amongst a highly plural and heterogeneous corpus of market options on the basis of conforming to their inner self-image; and "flourishing", that is, individuals' capacity to continuously exercise and work on their positive emotions and thoughts in order to grow personally and constantly engage in looking for new ways to increase their levels of well-being.

Rekindling, legitimizing and institutionalizing the neoliberal discourse of individualism

Happiness has become part of a commonsensical discourse through which the neoliberal ideology of individualism is rekindled, legitimized, and institutionalized in seemingly non-ideological terms through the discourse of science. One of the main differences between the notions of individualism and happiness in neoliberal societies is that while the former seems culturally and ideologically laden, the latter does not, so it can convey similar values without appearing to be doing so. Happiness conceals its ideological undertones by presenting itself as a universal human goal, and as a natural psychometrical property which can be objectively measured and scientifically studied. As a universal human goal, happiness is no longer considered "WEIRD" (western, educated, industrialized, rich, and democratic) (Henrich *et al.* 2010), but something that applies to all human beings equally. The commensuration of happiness, or its depiction as a quantitative and objective variable, has been also fundamental to its neutralization and institutionalization as a first-order criterion for making and justifying a wide array of social, political, and educational decisions and interventions (Espeland and Stevens 2008).

The academic fields of positive psychology and happiness economics are two of the authoritative sources which have most contributed to the diffusion and institutionalization of happiness in the fields of psychology, education, and politics since the 2000s. Founded in 2000 as a "new" and "alternative" field to "traditional psychotherapy" (Seligman and Csikszentmihalyi 2000), the originators of positive psychology claimed that the "scientific study of happiness and human flourishing" is not a historically and culturally bounded endeavor, but a universal enterprise yielding results which can be expanded "to other times and places, and perhaps even to all times and places" (Seligman and Csikszentmihalyi 2001: 90). According to positive psychologists, human happiness underlies the successful achievement of many desirable outcomes in life, such as a superior mental and physical health; greater longevity and less medication use and substance abuse; high-quality social relationships and greater prosocial behavior; fulfilling marriages and more stable romantic relationships; better coping with the ever-changing circumstances of daily life; work performance and career success; and higher income in the future, to name just a few (e.g., Boehm and Lyubomirsky 2008; Fredrickson 2013; Lyubomirsky *et al.* 2005; Seligman 2008).

These studies also claim that happiness essentially depends upon individual cognitive, motivational, and emotional variables, rather than upon political, social, or economic ones. This idea has been expressed in what positive psychologists have called "the happiness formula", according to which genetics accounts for about the 50 percent of individuals' happiness; psychological factors account for about 40 percent; and individuals' life circumstances such as income, education, social status, race, gender, etc., account for the remaining 10 percent (e.g., Seligman 2002). Accordingly, Ed Diener *et al.* concluded in one of their studies that individualism is the feature most consistently related to subjective well-being, even ahead of other aspects such as income, or human rights, thus explaining why individualistic cultures (e.g., the United States and Australia), in contrast with non-individualist or collectivist ones (e.g., Bangladesh and Cameroon), tend to produce happier individuals. The explanation was that in individualistic cultures individuals have "more freedom to choose his or her own life course", they are "more likely to attribute success to themselves", and they have more chances "to pursue their individual goals" (Diener *et al.* 2009: 67).

Regardless of the many criticisms directed at the foundational assumptions of positive psychology since the late 2000s, as well as criticisms addressed to other aspects such as its presumed novelty (Fernández-Ríos and Novo 2012; Kristjánsson 2012), its ethnocentrism and universalist aspirations (Christopher and Hickinbottom 2008), its religious roots (Cabanas and González 2012; Ehrenreich 2009; García *et al.* 2015), its resemblance to self-help literature (Cabanas and Huertas 2014), its theoretical contradictions and flaws (Miller 2008; Pérez-Álvarez 2012), its methodological problems (Brown *et al.* 2013; Lazarus 2003; Simmons *et al.* 2011), or even its therapeutic efficacy (Mongrain and Anselmo-Matthews 2012; Pérez-Álvarez 2013), the expansion and influence of positive psychology in academic, institutional, and organizational spheres has continued apace. In fact, since the foundation of positive psychology at the turn of the century, the amount of academic research on happiness and related topics such as subjective well-being, positive emotions, flourishing, optimism, or resilience has quadrupled (Schui and Krampen 2010).

Within a decade, positive psychologists have swiftly created a broad institutional network, widely disseminated through PhD and Master's degrees programs in Applied Positive Psychology; courses and speeches marketed to human resources personnel, coaches, and popular audiences; symposia and workshops all over the world; numerous websites from which they collect data and provide questionnaires; and numerous academic journals, such as the *Journal of Happiness Studies*, founded in 2000, the *Journal of Positive Psychology*, founded in 2006, and the *Journal of Applied Psychology: Health and Well-Being*, founded in 2008, to name a few. The dramatic expansion of this network, founded in 2003 and mainly coordinated by Martin Seligman from the Positive Psychology Center at the University of Pennsylvania, has been economically backed by a wide array of institutions, corporations, foundations, agencies, and governments, such as the United States government (which has invested $145 million in the "Comprehensive Soldier Fitness" program mainly developed by positive psychologists with the intention of improving military motivation and soldiers' resilience to post-traumatic episodes); Coca-Cola (which, in collaboration with positive psychologists and other happiness professionals, has created 'The Happiness Institute' in countries such as the United States, Australia, Germany, New Zealand, Russia, and Spain which invests in research into efficient methods of increasing corporate productivity, or promote "organizational citizenship behavior" in workers); the National Institute of Mental Health (to provide universities, colleges, and high schools with happiness-based prevention programs against depression and anxiety); the Robert Wood Johnson Foundation (seeking methods to reduce health costs and to extend people's longevity); or even institutions such as the John Templeton Foundation (which has invested more than $8 million in a coordinated project on positive psychology to develop the field of "Positive Neuroscience" and to study the role of spirituality in successful living, amongst others) (e.g., Seligman 2005).

Interdependently, the field of happiness economics has exponentially grown since the mid 2000s. Consistently with many core positive psychology's assumptions, and following the lead of Richard Layard, one of the most prominent representatives in the field, happiness economists claim that happiness must be considered "the ultimate goal that enables us to judge other goals by how they contribute to it", a "self-evident" good for all human beings, so a better society would be any society where the majority of individuals are either happy or pursue the achievement of happiness (Layard 2005: 111). Happiness economists advocate for the adoption of happiness as a scientific and individualist criterion for measuring economic utility and guiding public policies.

To this regard, the main focus of the field is to design quantitative indicators and measurement techniques which can overcome the problems associated with the quantification and comparison of subjective emotions, and hence improve the reliability and validity of individual happiness as a scientific and objective index of common good (e.g., Frey and Stutzer 2006). Several global surveys on well-being and life satisfaction, as well as data collection methodologies such as the "Experience Sampling Method" (to collect real-time objective and emotional information on individuals' everyday life experiences), the "Day Reconstruction Method" (asking people to reflect on how satisfied they feel at different times during the day), the "U-Index" (monitoring the proportion of each day that individuals spend in an unpleasant state), or "Brain Imaging" (using fMRI to look for brain correlates of positive and negative emotions) (e.g., Kahneman and Krueger 2006), have been developed in the last decades with the aim of improving the measurement of emotions, cognitions, and attitudes, on the one hand, and of proving the strength of happiness as a scientific construct, on the other.

According to these scholars, thanks to these methodologies "researchers have [already] succeeded in doing what Bentham could not accomplish: to devise a way of measuring how happy people are and how much pleasure or pain they derive from the ordinary events and conditions of their lives" (Bok 2010: 204). From their point of view, evidence seems solid enough: cultures can be compared by their levels of happiness, and nations and institutions can adopt this as a criterion to guide their public and private policies.

Indeed, in 2012 the United Nations declared 20 March the "International Day of Happiness", proclaiming "happiness and well-being as universal goals and aspirations in the lives of human beings around the world", and defending "the importance of their recognition in public policy objectives" of nations. Echoing this statement, and advised by some prominent happiness economists and positive psychologists, the Organization of Economic Cooperation and Development recommends adopting well-being measures in national accounting systems, something to which countries such as the United States, United Kingdom, Chile, Japan, Israel, Spain, and Australia, to name just a few, have already signed up. The purpose is to develop a "Gross National Happiness" (GNH) index which goes beyond Gross National Product (GNP) and extensions of it such as the "Measure of Economic Welfare", "Economic Aspects of Welfare", "Index of Sustainable Economic Welfare", or "Human Development Index" for guiding policies and measuring social and economic progress.

Alongside large organizations, health institutions, and governmental policies, schools and higher education are major fields for the application of positive psychological interventions on emotional intelligence, positive emotions, positive thinking, resilience, optimism, and self-motivation – they are also fields in which the positivist and individualist bias of happiness-based interventions are especially manifest. For instance, the "Social and Emotional Aspects of Learning" program, inspired by the work of Daniel Goleman and introduced to British primary schools in 2007, aims to teach students how to "manage their emotions", "feel optimistic about themselves", and "learn to feel good about themselves", arguing that these and other techniques should be incorporated into the curriculum (Miller 2008). For its part, the "Penn Resiliency Program" addresses North American late elementary and middle school students with the aim of teaching them tools such as how "to detect inaccurate thoughts", "to challenge negative beliefs by considering alternative interpretations", and to "cope with difficult situations and emotions", arguing that its application should not be circumscribed to schools but also applied to the domestic sphere (Reivich et al. 2005). Similarly, the PERMA (Positive emotion, Engagement, Relationships, Meaning, Achievement) program, applied both in the US Army and schools, distinguishes itself from programs seeking to enhance well-being through the removal or reduction of negative factors by aiming at the cultivation of positive emotions (Seligman 2011; Waters 2011). Further, the "Pinnacle Program" and "GRIT" studies address college students with the aim of assessing individual differences in talent, emotional mastery, and self-motivational abilities in order to foster genius, teach perseverance toward ambitious goals, and prevent discouragement (e.g., Duckworth et al. 2007).

The implementation of these kinds of intervention at the turn of the twentieth century inherits:

> [t]he legacy of the humanistic psychology of the 1950s to 1970s, with its emphasis on positive self-fulfillment and self-education, and of what one could call the *adaptability psychologies* of the 1980s and 1990s, referring to literatures addressing coping, self-esteem, self-efficacy, self-determination theory, multiple intelligences, and emotional intelligence.
>
> (Kristjánsson 2012: 86, italics in the original)

The hope that such interventions would have positive effects is not new, and it has sustained numerous educational programs over the course of the second half of the last century, despite several disappointments.

One of the most prominent (and failed) attempts stems from the *Self-Esteem Movement* in the 1980s and 1990s, at which time an apparent epidemic of low self-esteem had caused the term to take root in popular jargon. This movement claimed that virtually every social and individual problem could be traced back to a lack of self-esteem: "many, if not most, of the major problems plaguing society have roots in the low self-esteem of many of the people who make up society" (Smelser 1989: 1). Nathaniel Branden, a leading figure of this movement, stated that there was not "a single psychological problem – from anxiety and depression, to fear of intimacy or of success, to spouse battery or child molestation – that is not traceable to the problem of low self-esteem" (Branden 1984: 12). For instance, in 1986 a Task Force on Self-Esteem and Personal and Social Responsibility was funded by the governor of California for several years, with an annual budget of $245,000, to help solve problems such as crime, teen pregnancy, drug abuse, and school underachievement. Although this and similar attempts were subsequently proved unsuccessful, in the 1990s the National Association for Self-Esteem took over these previous attempts and launched a new program of intervention, this time deploying scholars as well as popular North American self-help writers, such as Jack Canfield or Anthony Robbins. The results proved no better, encountering several theoretical and methodological problems on the way.

Indeed, Roy Baumeister and colleagues (Baumeister *et al.* 2003) concluded their extensive analysis of the Self-Esteem Movement stating that they "have not found evidence that boosting self-esteem (by therapeutic interventions or school programs) causes benefits" (2003: 1), and that "perhaps psychologists should reduce their own self-esteem a bit and humbly resolve that next time they will wait for a more thorough and solid empirical basis before making policy recommendations to the American public" (2003: 3). The Self-Esteem Movement, which is highly reminiscent of many of the assumptions and aims of the current interventions of positive psychologists in the educational sphere, is a good example of how cultural and ideological artifacts often play a leading role not only in sustaining certain psychological premises and social interventions despite strong evidence against them, but also in motivating certain kinds of psychological researches and interventions in the first place.

Happiness is currently a highly political concept, and it has been in Anglo-Saxon cultures since at least the advent of modernity. This is acknowledged by happiness economists and positive psychologists alike. They recognize that happiness has political as well as economic, educational, and social implications in contemporary societies. What they do not acknowledge, though, is that the study of happiness might be also politically and culturally motivated: that is, that there might be an ideological agenda as well as a cultural bias behind its scientific study and its political, economic, and social applications. Happiness researchers try to escape any cultural, historical, or ideological questioning by upholding to the science-value dichotomy, insisting that their scientific approach prevents their definition of the happy individual from being laden with moral principles, ethical prescriptions, and ideological values. However, this argument has been widely and compellingly contested, and this is one of the reasons why sociological approaches might better explain the remarkable rise and consolidation of the contemporary neoliberal notion of happiness.

Happiness and *psytizenship*: constructing subjectivity through the consumption of happiness

Since the mid 2000s, neoliberal societies have witnessed a "happiness turn" (Ahmed 2010), in which the imperative of happiness has become ubiquitous, permeating every layer of the social realm: from media to academia, and including the entertainment industry, schools systems, health institutions, corporations, public and private organizations, and popular literature. Undoubtedly, positive psychologists and happiness economists have vastly contributed to this "happiness turn", gaining significant authority, power, and widespread influence. If, as Roger Smith (1997) and Kurt Danziger (1997) claimed, humanist psychology shares a great deal of responsibility for the transformation of postwar western societies into psychological societies, it would be no great leap to infer that positive psychology, together with happiness economics share a great deal of responsibility for the fact that these psychological societies have become flooded with the necessity, if not the imperative, to achieve happiness. Happiness has become the norm of what is good, desirable, and healthy in neoliberal societies, both for individuals and societies alike, such that failure to conform to it becomes a sort of stigma (e.g., Ehrenreich, 2009; Lipovetsky, 2007). As Alenka Zupančič (2008: 5) notes:

> [t]here is a spectacular rise of what we might call bio-morality (as well as morality of feelings and emotions), which promotes the following fundamental axiom: a person who feels good (and is happy) is a good person; a person who feels bad is a bad person.

To this regard, the neoliberal discourse of happiness should not be viewed as a general and abstract idea of wellness and satisfaction. Instead, it should be regarded as a particular set of "ought to's" that define and prescribe a particular "structure of feelings" (Williams 1977), that is, a specific way of being, acting, and understanding the world, which is highly individualistic and emotionally saturated. Happiness does not only stand out as an emerging and pervasive ideology that stresses the insource of responsibility, delineates a new moral regime that defines what is right and wrong, promises rewards for those who engage in psychic self-development, and punishes those who fail to conform to it (Cederström and Spicer 2015). Happiness also stands out as a new and pervasive model of selfhood which defines individuals of neoliberal societies as *psytizens*.

By coining the term *psytizen*, the chapter aims at stressing the psychologicist bias and individualistic kind of subjectivity that underlie the neoliberal discourse of happiness. It also aims at emphasizing the core neoliberal assumptions and the consumerist rationale that lies beneath this discourse, which turns the achievement and development of happiness into something essential for the political definition of a fully functioning citizen and, simultaneously, into something essentially dependent upon the consumption of positive "psy" commodities offered by the growing "happiness industry".

In what follows, I will analyze the three main features that define the *psytizen*, namely, "emotional rationality", "authenticity", and "flourishing", showing how psychological, political, and economic discourses converge in the definition of happy individuals. I will also comment upon the "happiness industry" which emerges around the offer-demand of happiness commodities in the form of "know-how" scientific knowledge, positive psychotherapeutic services, positive psychological techniques, and happiness applications, all of them sold and purchased under the promise of helping individuals to turn the symbolic value of their happiness into an emotional and economic asset.

Responsible psytizens, or emotionally rational individuals

The neoliberal notion of happiness combines the modern Romantic ideal of the emotional as the set of inner dynamics that drives human action with the rational and utilitarian demand for self-control as the ability to manage, contain, and channel these emotions with the goal of maximizing individual self-interest. On the one hand, under this notion, passions and desires have ceased to be indeterminate and inapprehensible states, and have become emotions which can be rationalized, localized, classified, and managed; on the other, rationality has ceased to be a matter of virtue, discipline, and commitment to certain axiological and ethical principles, instead becoming a psychological ability, rooted in natural mental mechanisms, which presumably allows the "self" to be completely governed by the "self". This latter aspect accounts for one of the main differences between the classic liberal and the neoliberal ethics of self-government: while classic liberalism sharply distinguished between how individuals behave (naturally) from how individuals ought to behave (ethically), neoliberalism claims instead to derive its ethics from human nature, justifying self-government under the assumption that individuals are inherently equipped with psychological mechanisms of self-control. Thus, the demand of self-government, characteristic of the liberal ideal of the "self-made man", can now be understood as a psychological problem, not an ethical, ideological, or political one.[1]

In this regard, notions such as "emotional intelligence" are no longer considered oxymoronic, but rather a feature of a wider social demand for emotional rationality, with emotions falling into the sphere of individual responsibility. Indeed, emotions are at the center of the self-care therapeutic *ethos* of contemporary societies: they are considered one of the principal sources of happiness, health, and social adaptation, but also the source of suffering, maladjustment, and disorders, so individuals must strive for their correct regulation and management. Accordingly, the claim for emotional self-regulation stands out as one of the key elements motivating consumption. Eva Illouz (2007, 2008, 2012), for instance, has coined the term "emotional capitalism" to show the intimate relationship between the demand for emotional self-control and the logic of consumption in advanced capitalist societies. Thus, a whole market emerges around the demand for psychological techniques which allow consumers to increase their self-regulation skills, assertiveness, creativity, communicative abilities, coping competencies, interpersonal aptitudes; in a word, what positive psychologists call their "psychological capital" (e.g., Luthans *et al.* 2007).

The "happiness industry" is one of the most salient symptoms of the wider socio-economic trend of "emotional capitalism". Taking the notion of self-control as one of the primary variables explaining individual happiness and well-being, "children, adolescents, and adults who consistently exercise the muscle of self-control are happier, more productive, and more successful individuals" (Peterson and Seligman 2004: 38), positive psychologists, as well as a multitude of self-help writers, counselors, motivational speakers, and coaches – where the latest trend is the so-called "self-coaching", a training aimed at turning workers into their own coaches – provide a multitude of happiness-based techniques for emotional and cognitive self-regulation. These techniques promise individuals that they will succeed in expanding their self-governing abilities in order to increase performance, build positive and profitable relationships, manage anger, develop healthy habits, cope with risk and uncertainty, rationalize everyday failures in a positive and productive manner, and so on. There are multiple examples of these techniques, ranging from those consisting in changing emotional styles, to those focused on making frequent positive self-affirmations; training hope; practicing gratitude and forgiveness; developing resilience; or cultivating optimism (e.g., Carver *et al.* 2010; Lopez *et al.* 2003; Reivich *et al.* 2005). One of the most popular happiness-based techniques is "mindfulness", which, like the previously mentioned techniques, has had a significant impact on the theoretical teachings of business studies and on managerial practices within organizations. Mindfulness training programs instruct individuals to focus intensely on their emotions and bodily signals, in order to reach full self-control and optimize their effects on personal well-being. Mixing spiritual counseling with positive science, mindfulness professionals promise to help workers reduce stress and anxiety, and offer organizations an effective service for increasing workforce performance, reducing absenteeism, and creating a more solid and emotionally healthy corporate culture. Although there is no clear evidence that mindfulness is as effective as it is claimed to be, many corporations such as Google, Inc., and institutions such as the US Marine Corps, have widely incorporated mindfulness services into their managerial policies (Cederström and Spicer 2015).

Happiness-based techniques do not aim to deeply or structurally change the psyche; on the contrary, they are offered as a service focused on those practical aspects which can be easily understood, controlled, managed, and changed by individuals themselves, as well as to produce short-term and calculable benefits. Thus, instead of entailing thorough psychological analyses, these techniques focus on providing quick diagnoses and easy guidelines to help individuals reinforce their sense of autonomy and their ability to turn everyday drawbacks into productive stimuli to action. In this sense, happiness-based techniques detach from more time-consuming therapeutic approaches and embrace a more eclectic, gentle, and self-reassuring approach to problem-solving, thus making them both more accessible to every individual and more easily marketable by being commodified as scientific techniques that produce practical, quick, and measurable results.

In the first place, happiness-based techniques obliterate the unconscious, in contrast to other therapeutic approaches based on the notion of self-knowledge, e.g., psychoanalysis and, to a lesser extent, humanist psychology. The "psyche" in its totality is now available, knowable, and open to manipulation by the individual. Nothing is ineffable and beyond his "inner glance". The unconscious mind by definition implies a lack of agency: that is, certain aspects of the psyche are located in an inner and inaccessible space where individuals are unable to examine themselves; this completely disappears here.

Second, happiness-based techniques provide individuals with a non-technical and more colloquial language about the "psyche" (optimism, hope, self-affirmations, gratitude, satisfaction, etc.), facilitating their use and understanding. This is especially relevant when individuals are depicted as "self-therapists", since they are not only required to frequently apply these techniques for themselves (with little or no mediation of a therapist), but depicted as the ones that have the most complete knowledge and understanding about their own needs, goals, problems, fears, etc.

Third, happiness-based techniques do not turn self-control into a struggle or into something self-critical or judgmental; on the contrary, emotional and cognitive self-regulation is presented as a gentle process in which individuals must focus on their achievements, strengths, positive feelings, and memories, and avoid any negative emotion, memory, or self-valuation.

Authentic psytizens, or displaying and consuming "authentic selves"

Positive psychologists define authenticity as "presenting oneself in a genuine way and acting in a sincere way", "being without pretense", and "taking responsibility for one's feelings and actions" (Peterson and Seligman 2004: 29). They also claim that individuals who act authentically achieve great and positive outcomes "as a result of their focus on what they do best" (Hodges and Clifton 2004: 258). Although the notion of authenticity is not a new idea –it was already present in the cultural and political movement of Romanticism in the second half of the nineteenth century, in some positive liberal approaches to liberty and individualism at the end of it, in many religious and new age movements during the twentieth century, especially in the United States, and it was one of the hallmarks of humanist psychology in the second half of the twentieth century – positive psychologists have played an essential role in its naturalization by framing it within an evolutionist perspective.

The most influential approach in this regard is Peterson and Seligman's "hierarchical classification of positive traits", a counter positive version of the DSM-IV-R (Peterson and Seligman 2004). This classification puts forward the existence of six universal "virtues" (wisdom, courage, humanity, temperance, justice, and transcendence), which are claimed to be "grounded in biology through an evolutionary process that [was] selected for these aspects of excellence as [a] means of solving the important tasks necessary for [the] survival of the species" (2004: 13). These virtues are depicted as psychological categories whose practice and everyday display receive the name of "strengths". According to Peterson and Seligman, there are three features which all strengths share. First, they have to fulfill the individual, that is, to give her a sense of authenticity, invigoration, and excitement. Second, they tend to produce desirable outcomes for those individuals that put them into practice. Third, since they are natural traits, they possess a high degree of generality across situations and stability across time (Ibid.). In short, positive psychologists claim that individuals are naturally equipped with a certain set of inner psychological potentialities which entail "a particular way of behaving, thinking, or feeling that is authentic and energizing to the user" (Linley and Burns 2010: 4).

Along with the notion of self-control, authenticity underlines the individualist component of contemporary subjectivities. It also stands out as a first-order social demand, since personal authenticity strongly relates to high levels of well-being, social adaptation, and labor performance in multiple realms of life. In the personal realm, an authentic life is synonymous with a healthy one. Authenticity not only provides individuals with high levels of self-acceptance, since authentic individuals do not act against their true nature, but also provides them with a sort of buffer against vulnerabilities which help them to cope with eventual psychological problems. Authenticity is also synonymous with adaptation and competence, with fully functioning citizens who measure up to their tasks and circumstances because they willingly display "the best version of themselves". In the social realm, authenticity is synonymous with autonomy and independence, with individuals who are not afraid to express their true identities and life-styles. Authentic individuals are those who shape their selves according to their tastes, their preferences, and their values, and who act on their own choices. They are also depicted as more reliable, since authentic individuals are presumably more congruent and spontaneous as they do not hide themselves behind a "façade". In the organizational realm, authenticity is synonymous with high performance and work success, since authentic individuals presumably tend to choose the tasks to which they are naturally suited and prepared – a sort of psychologized version of the notion of "vocation". In the economic realm, authenticity is synonymous with utility: that is, authenticity becomes a fundamental criterion for making self-fulfilling, reflexive, and strategic choices between a highly plural and heterogeneous corpus of market options on the basis of conforming to self-image, since every choice made by individuals at any moment is not only liable to shape them, but it is also liable to appreciate or depreciate their value as a person.

As authenticity stands out as a first-order social demand, it is also an essential commodity for the emerging "happiness industry". Positive psychologists offer a wide range of methodologies enabling individuals to spot their inner and authentic skills and capabilities, and put them into practice. Clients have at their disposal a whole variety of tools, such as the ISA (Individual Strengths Assessment) and the VIA (Values in Action) questionnaire. These are all good examples of therapeutic services in which therapists and clients engage in a mutual exchange relationship through which authenticity, instead of being "discovered", is negotiated and co-produced. For instance, Linley and Burns (2010) describe the ISA as a set of questions which help people "to look for strengths within themselves", giving enough liberty to therapists to "tailor" the sessions in a way that "the client understands, values, and engages with the strengths" and the final outcome "fits the needs and expectations of the client" (2010: 10). As was the case with self-control, happiness-based techniques and methodologies aiming to spot the authentic selves of individuals do not address deep psychological problems, traumas, or negative aspects; rather, they offer clients a kind, painless, and quick process of self-discovery which only focuses on positive experiences, memories, and perspectives. On the one hand, Linley and Burns emphasize that "the questions that make up the ISA are all designed to encourage people to talk about their great experiences, their enjoyment, their best successes, who they are at their core, and when they are at their best" (2010: 10), since clients who focus on negative aspects tend to narrow their attentional focus, disengage, and withdraw. On the other hand, methodologies such as the ISA promise that within a few therapeutic sessions and follow-ups clients are able to interiorize the self-discovery process and work on themselves on their own. Through the use and application of these psychotherapeutic services, individuals purchase a scientific method to discover their "authentic selves" at the same time as they learn how to turn the symbolic value of their authenticity into a powerful emotional and economic asset.

Drawing from professional and popular fields such as coaching and self-help literature, authenticity is commodified under the notion of "personal branding", a notion that has yielded a multitude of books, magazines, websites, and training programs. "Personal branding" is a primary instance of the commodification of authenticity and an example par excellence of self-commodification, merging the concepts of product development and promotion with the idea of authenticity to aim at the explicit self-packaging of individuals. Defined as "the art of investing in oneself in order to improve one's chances of success, satisfaction and employability", "personal branding" depicts individuals as brands who must define what makes them different, authentic, and indispensable to others; what strengths and virtues they can offer that are distinguishable and profitable to others; what personal values they inspire in others; and what strategies individuals can undertake in order to trade themselves most productively as a brand and hence improve their chances of work and business success. Once one's idiosyncrasy has been defined, the individual also has to learn the arts of self-expression and persuasion, acquiring social skills which allow him to influence people and manage relationships efficiently. "Personal branding" is also a symptom of the process of individuals becoming responsible for their successes and failures, depicting and legitimizing a highly individualized economic and professional world, and strongly resonating with the by-your-own-bootstraps *mythos* characteristic of neoliberal ideology (Lair *et al.* 2005).

Besides a fundamental aspect of several therapeutic services and techniques offered by the "happiness industry", authenticity plays an essential role in defining the symbolic value of several other material and immaterial goods at a wider economic level. For instance, in the book *Authenticity: What Consumers Really Want*, James Gilmore and Joseph Pine situate the notion of authenticity at the core of the emerging field of the "experience economy" (Gilmore and Pine 2007). They analyze how the notion of authenticity, applied to individuals, spaces, events, and objects alike, takes the shape of a new business imperative, since it determines the economic value of the products and services provided by the industry of leisure and entertainment. This is evident in the industries of tourism, music, and customization (see correspondingly Benger Alaluf, Schwarz and West, this volume).

Flourishing psytizens, or "self-made men" whose "selves" are never completely or fully "made"

At the turn of the twentieth century, positive psychologists had already produced a vast literature relating happiness with life success, presupposing the broadly accepted idea that successful outcomes in different realms of life lead to happiness and satisfaction. In recent years, however, positive psychologists have contested their own original assumption, asserting now that the relationship between happiness and life success should be better understood in the reverse direction: that is, that happiness is what causes successful outcomes, not the other way around. Thus, while they acknowledge that past research demonstrated a strong relationship between happiness and life success, they now claim that this research failed to grasp the "correct" causality between the variables, since individuals' success "is in large part a consequence of their happiness" (Lyubomirsky *et al.* 2005: 804).

The causal relationship between happiness and life success is explained through notions such as the "upward spiral" of happiness (e.g., Fredrickson 2009). According to this idea, since happy persons are more motivated, perform better, build more positive relationships, cope better with uncertainty, etc., than non-happy and unhappy people, the former presumably achieve a wider number of early successes in life than the latter, thus resulting in a cumulative advantage which increases the probability of achieving subsequent successes. Happiness presumably triggers a sort of "Matthew Effect" – defined as a process of cumulative advantage in which early achievement rewards the successful with greater resources, a more rapid growth rate, and higher motivation – so higher happiness levels would lead individuals to a series of short-term achievements which set the tone for long-run ones, thus explaining why happy people end up better off than non-happy individuals (Judge and Hurst 2008).

A popular model accounting for this effect is Barbara Fredrickson's "Broaden-and-Build Theory" (Fredrickson 2009, 2013) according to which positive emotions, unlike negative ones, increase awareness and cognitive processes in a way that widens individuals' outlook on the world and allows them to attain more information about their surroundings: that is, creating a broadening effect. Positive emotions also enable individuals to "produce" durable and effective "personal resources such as competence (e.g., environmental mastery), meaning (e.g., purpose in life), optimism (e.g., pathways thinking), resilience, self-acceptance, positive relationships, as well as physical health", resources "upon which people draw to navigate life's journey with greater success" (Fredrickson 2013: 3): that is, a build effect. From this perspective, people who exploit these "broaden-and-build effects" of positive emotions are considered people who "flourish", that is, individuals who "live within an optimal range of human functioning, one that connotes goodness, generativity, growth, and resilience" (Fredrickson and Losada 2005: 678). In other words, happy individuals are those who flourish because they "do good by feeling good" (Fredrickson 2013).

Once a causal relationship between happiness and life success is established, positive psychologists claim that this relationship holds mainly when happiness is not a temporary, fleeting or a passing state. Presumably, happiness is much more a matter of frequency than of intensity, so low-grade but frequent positive emotions and feelings define happiness better than intense but low-frequency ones (Boehm and Lyubomirsky 2008). As positive psychologists state, "frequent positive affect is the hallmark of happiness" (Lyubomirsky *et al.* 2005). To this regard, Lahnna Catalino and Barbara Fredrickson (2011) reported in the article "A Tuesday in the life of a flourisher: The role of positive emotional reactivity in optimal mental health" that people who experience more frequent positive states thrive because they make more out of routine activities, better capitalize on pleasant events in their lives, and build more personal resources over time than people who do not. Thus, higher and frequent positive emotional ratios seem characteristic of "chronically happy people", that is, of individuals in a permanent process of flourishing and self-improvement.

As noted elsewhere (Cabanas and Illouz 2016; Cabanas and Sánchez-González 2012, 2016), underlying the neoliberal notion of happiness is the idea that individuals are "self-made men", albeit "self-made men" whose "selves" are never completely or fully "made", as it is presupposed that they can always become fuller and better. As Beck and Beck-Gernsheim (2002) note, the "fundamental incompleteness of the 'self'" lies at the core of the second phase of modernity in which neoliberal capitalism arose, as it is undoubtedly useful for a market that links the ideal of limitless self-improvement to the principles of insatiable consumption and productivity. The "happy self" is always incomplete by definition, demanding the continuous and frequent exercise of positive emotions, affects, and cognitions in order to attain success in any objective which the individual may pursue. Achieving the highest possible levels of happiness through the constant investment of time and effort in oneself becomes a necessity, especially when argued that it is scientifically proven that happiness underlies every successful outcome which individuals achieve in life.

To this end, the "happiness industry" provides consumers with a wide array of commodities supporting the continuous self-improvement of individuals (see also Shachak, Chapter 6 this volume). Based on the scientific findings of positive psychologists, happiness commodities are sold as products, techniques, and services which increase individuals' chances of achieving short-term and cumulative successes in different spheres of their lives. There are products and advice on beauty, fashion, fitness, nutrition, sex, marriage, relationships, and business, for all genders, including psychological techniques and self-assessment methods for mastering and improving assertiveness, public speaking, stress and anger management, relaxation and meditation, flow, resilience, cognitive flexibility, etc., academic literature, therapeutic advice, professional consultation, specialized seminars, innumerable self-help books, magazines, and blogs, and even "wearable technology".

Let us examine one of the latest examples of the intimate relationship between the repertoires and methodologies on flourishing, and the self-improvement commodities of the happiness market: the application *Happify*.[2] *Happify* is one of several applications for smartphones and computers available for users daily to monitor and work on their happiness (see also *Track Your Happiness*, *Happy Life*, *Happy Habits: Choose Happiness*, *Happier*, *The H(app)athon app*). These applications all claim to be based on scientific research into happiness – indeed, most of them not only resemble the Day Reconstruction Method, but also include the advice of positive psychologists, consultants, motivational speakers, etc. Commonly sold under the label "Health and Fitness", these applications share the aim of monitoring in real time the emotional state of individuals to provide them with examples of how to cultivate their positive emotions and thoughts, and to instruct them in how to achieve higher goals in different spheres of their lives. It is also possible for users to share this real-time data with other users and friends, sharing tips and entering online challenges for "who is happier". To use the application *Happify*, users first have to sign in specifying their personal goals. Then, the application provides them daily with customized activities and advices to help them "get there". For instance, the exercise "Today's Grateful Moment" inspires and instructs users in how to break free of negative thinking patterns and cope with tough situations. The application rewards users with happiness scores when tasks are performed well, tracking their improvement as they go, and feeding back with an array of personal statistics.

Happify was released in 2012, and during its beta period alone it was tested by 100,000 users. The application costs $12.95 per month, or $239.96 for the life-time version. *Happify* is one of the most remarkable applications of a virtual market of happiness and self-development which has already produced millions of dollars in revenue and which is growing exponentially (Howells *et al.* 2014; Miller 2012). To give but one example, in 2014 in Chicago *The Happiness App Challenge*[3] was launched as an international competition offering $50,000 in prizes to developers, designers, and entrepreneurs from 152 countries to create applications which "make people happy" and help to "increase the world's happiness quotient". Besides a lucrative market, applications might also be the future of happiness research and interventions for their high accessibility, versatility, and cost-effectiveness.

Conclusion

The cultural advent and expansion of neoliberal ideology and advanced capitalism during the second half of the last century not only brought about drastic structural economic, political, and institutional transformations, but also changes on the infrastructural level, to use Herbert Marcuse's expression. Neoliberalism brought a new "structure of feelings" which simultaneously presupposes and demands from individuals certain ways of being, thinking, and acting while precluding, banning, and even stigmatizing others. These ways of being, thinking, and acting correspond to a highly individualistic and psychologized notion of citizenship that takes individual happiness as a normative lifestyle which is specifically targeted, shaped, and achieved through the consumption of happiness commodities within a wider happiness industry. We have called this neoliberal notion of citizenship *psytizenship* to highlight its psychological and emotional core.

The happiness industry emerges parallel to the increasing depiction of happiness as a natural, commensurable, and scientific criterion which, on the one hand, determines the standard of what is a fully functioning individual, and, on the other, legitimizes a technocratic and neo-utilitarian style of decision-making at the institutional and national level. The rapid commodification of happiness in multiple forms leans on these neoliberal ideological assumptions and demands, which explain not only the emergence of the happiness industry, but also its effectiveness. At the same time, the success and expansion of the happiness industry becomes itself an explanation for why the market for and power of happiness to shape the lives of individuals have intensified and consolidated in the last decades.

The rise of the happiness industry also explains the great extent to which individuals have internalized happiness as a *modus vivendi*. Individuals in neoliberal societies tend to take for granted that happiness is a natural and scientific psychological feature which shapes (and should shape) the way they relate to themselves and to others. These are no longer strange notions to anybody; rather, what is now strange is that they might be strange to somebody. It is no longer strange that happiness can be purchased either, be it as a concrete experience (e.g., spending a day at Disneyland, or having a drink with some friends), as a set of psychological services and techniques which help to cope with stress, anxiety, and frustration, or as a symbolic value which can be turned into an economic and social asset (e.g., to increase employability, work performance, social mobility, and future income). Indeed, happiness has come to play a central role in the economic practices of neoliberal societies, since the economic worth of commodities is no longer distinguishable from their emotional value; that is, from their power to simultaneously reflect and construct certain subjectivities (Illouz, Introduction to this volume). As previously mentioned, I do not see happiness in this context as an emotion, but rather as a specific and normative subjectivity which is mainly defined in emotional and psychological terms and practices, and characterized by the demand for emotional rationality, authenticity, and flourishing, or permanent self-improvement. This is what makes happiness commodities so effective and successful: that they do not limit themselves to selling fleeting and pleasurable states, but rather an ideologically aligned, socially desirable, and morally unproblematic lifestyle.

Happiness advocates claim that those who criticize happiness do so in the absence of an alternative to human suffering. This is simply not so, because happiness is not the alternative to suffering; on the contrary, happiness generates its own forms of suffering, discontent, and social segregation. Neoliberal societies blame those who suffer for their failure to be happy, just as it blames smokers and the physically unfit for their failure to live a healthy life, the unemployed for their failure to develop their working projects, or the hopeless for not being hopeful and sufficiently optimistic. Within this conjuncture, and despite some displays of skepticism and resistance, it is not surprising that happiness therapies, services, and products – all of which convey the message that turning our priorities inwards in order to unlock, control, and improve our inner selves is the only way to navigate, cope, and thrive in a frantic, unstable, and competitive society – have become extremely popular. Happiness turns citizens into *psytizens* by making them bear the responsibility for the inherent structural economic and political contradictions and paradoxes of society, so criticisms addressed to this dominant notion of happiness, as well as to its increasing commodification, are in fact criticisms directed against these contradictions and paradoxes, which are, instead of the "psyche", the principal loci of human suffering in neoliberal societies.

Notes

1 For an example of how the psychological discourse of self-regulation is useful to depict Attention Deficit Hyperactivity Disorder (ADHD) as a natural disorder, see Shachak *et al.* 2013.
2 http://my.happify.com/
3 www.happinessapps.com (Retrieved January 21, 2016).

Bibliography

Ahmed, Sara. 2010. *The Promise of Happiness*. Durham, NC: Duke University Press.
Baumeister, Roy. F., Jennifer. D. Campbell, Joachim. I. Krueger and Kathleen. D. Vohs. 2003. "Does high self-esteem cause better performance, interpersonal success, happiness, or healthier lifestyles?" *Psychological Science in the Public Interest* 4(1):1–44.
Beck, Ulrich and Elisabeth Beck-Gernsheim. 2002. *Individualization. Institutionalized Individualism and Its Social and Political Consequences*. London: SAGE Publications.
Boehm, Julia. K. and Sonja, Lyubomirsky. 2008. "Does happiness promote career success?" *Journal of Career Assessment* 16(1):101–116.
Bok, Derek. 2010. *The Politics of Happiness. What Government Can Learn from the New Research on Well-Being*. Princeton, NJ: Princeton University Press.

Branden, Nathaniel. 1984. "In defense of self." *Association for Humanistic Psychology* (August-September):12–13.

Brown, Nicholas J. L., Alan D. Sokal and Harris L. Friedman. 2013. "The complex dynamics of wishful thinking: The critical positivity ratio." *The American Psychologist* 68(9):801–113.

Cabanas, Edgar. 2013. "La felicidad como imperativo moral: Origen y difusión del individualismo 'positivo' y sus efectos en la construcción de la subjetividad". (Doctoral dissertation). Universidad Autónoma de Madrid, Madrid. (www.educacion.gob.es/teseo/mostrarRef.do?ref=1064877).

Cabanas, Edgar. 2016. "Rekindling individualism, consuming emotions: Constructing 'psytizens' in the age of happiness." *Culture & Psychology* 22(3):467–480.

Cabanas, Edgar and José Carlos Sánchez González. 2012. "Las raíces de la psicología positiva." *Papeles del Psicologo* 33(3):172–182.

Cabanas, Edgar and Juan Antonio Huertas. 2014. "Psicología positiva y psicología popular de la autoayuda: Un romance histórico, psicológico y popular". *Anales de Psicología* 30(3):852–864.

Cabanas, Edgar and Eva Illouz. 2016. "The making of a 'happy worker': Positive psychology in neoliberal organizations". In *Beyond the Cubicle: Insecurity Culture and the Flexible Self*, edited by Allison Pugh. New York: Oxford University Press.

Cabanas, Edgar and José Carlos Sánchez-González. 2012. "The roots of positive psychology." *Papeles del Psicólogo* 33(3):172–182.

Cabanas, Edgar and José Carlos Sánchez-González. 2016. "Inverting the pyramid of needs: Positive psychology's new order for labor success." *Psicothema* 28(2):107–113.

Carver, Charles S., Michael F. Scheier and Suzanne C. Segerstrom. 2010. "Optimism." *Clinical Psychology Review* 30(7):879–889.

Catalino, Lahnna I. and Barbara L. Fredrickson. 2011. "A Tuesday in the life of a flourisher: The role of positive emotional reactivity in optimal mental health." *Emotion* 11(4):938–950.

Cederström, Carl and André Spicer. 2015. *The Wellness Syndrome*. Cambridge, UK: Polity Press.

Christopher, J. C. and S. Hickinbottom. 2008. "Positive psychology, ethnocentrism, and the disguised ideology of individualism." *Theory & Psychology* 18(5):563–589.

Crespo, Eduardo and José Celio Freire. 2014. "La atribución de responsabilidad: De la cognición al sujeto". *Psicologia & Sociedade* 26(2):271–279.

Danziger, Kurt. 1997. *Naming the Mind*. London: SAGE Publications.

Diener, Ed, Marissa Diener and Carol Diener. 2009. "Factor predicting the subjective well-being of nations". In *Culture and Well-Being. The Collected Works of Ed Diener*, edited by Ed Diener, 43–70. Dordrecht, The Netherlands; Heidelberg, Germany; London and New York: Springer.

Duckworth, Angela L., Christopher Peterson, Michael D. Matthews and Dennis R. Kelly. 2007. "Grit: Perseverance and passion for long-term goals." *Journal of Personality and Social Psychology* 92(6):1087–1101.

Ehrenreich, Barbara. 2009. *Smile or Die: How Positive Thinking Fooled America and the World*. London: Granta Books.

Espeland, Wendy Nelson and Mitchell L. Stevens. 2008. "A sociology of quantification." *European Journal of Sociology* 49(3):401–436.

Fernández-Ríos, Luis and Mercedes Novo. 2012. "Positive pychology : Zeigeist (or spirit of the times) or ignorance (or disinformation) of history?" *International Journal of Clinical and Health Psychology* 12(2):333–344.

Fredrickson, Barbara L. 2009. *Positivity*. New York: Crown.

Fredrickson, Barbara L. 2013. "Updated thinking on positivity ratios." *American Psychologist* 68:814–822.

Fredrickson, Barbara L. and M. F. Losada. 2005. "Positive affect and the complex dynamics of human flourishing." *American Psychologist* 60(7):678–686.

Frey, Bruno S. and Alois Stutzer. 2006. *Happiness and Economics: How the Economy and Institutions Affect Human Well-Being*. Princeton, NJ: Princeton University Press.

García, Roberto, Edgar Cabanas and José Carlos Loredo. 2015. "La cura mental de phineas p. quimby y el origen de la psicoterapia moderna". *Revista de Historia de la Psicología* 36(1):135–154.

Gilmore, James H. and Joseph B. Pine. 2007. *Authenticity. What Consumers Really Want*. Boston, MA: Harvard Business School Press.

Henrich, Joseph, Steven J. Heine and Ara Norenzayan. 2010. "The weirdest people in the world?" *The Behavioral and Brain Sciences* 33:61–83; discussion 83–135.

Hodges, Timothy D. and Donald. O. Clifton. 2004. "Strengths-based development in practice". In *Positive Psychology in Practice*, edited by Alex, P. Linley and Stephen Joseph, 256–258. Hoboken, NJ: John Wiley & Sons, Inc.

Howells, Annika, Itai Ivtzan and Francisco Jose Eiroa-Orosa. 2014. "Putting the 'app' in happiness: A randomised controlled trial of a smartphone-based mindfulness intervention to enhance wellbeing." *Journal of Happiness Studies* 17(1):163–185.

Illouz, Eva. 2007. *Cold Intimacies: The Making of Emotional Capitalism*. Cambridge, UK: Polity Press.

Illouz, Eva. 2008. *Saving the Modern Soul. Therapy, Emotions, and the Culture of Self-Help*. London: University of California Press.

Illouz, Eva. 2012. *Why Love Hurts: A Sociological Explanation*. Cambridge, UK: Polity Press.

Judge, Timothy A. and Charlice Hurst. 2008. "How the rich (and happy) get richer (and happier): Relationship of core self-evaluations to trajectories in attaining work success." *Journal of Applied Psychology* 93(4):849–863.

Kahneman, Daniel and Alan Krueger. 2006. "Developments in the measurement of subjective well-being." *Journal of Economic Perspectives* 20(1):3–24.

Kristjánsson, Kristján. 2012. "Positive psychology and positive education: Old wine in new bottles?" *Educational Psychologist* 47(2):86–105.

Lair, Daniel J., Katie Sullivan and George Cheney. 2005. "Marketization and the recasting of the professional self: The rhetoric and ethics of personal branding." *Management Communication Quarterly* 18(3):307–343.

Layard, Richard. 2005. *Happiness: Lessons from a New Science*. London: Allen.

Lazarus, Richard S. 2003. "Does the positive psychology movement have legs?" *Psychological Inquiry* 14(2):93–109.

Linley, Alex and George. W. Burns. 2010. "Strengthspotting: Finding and developing client resources in the management of intense anger." In *Happiness, Healing, Enhancement: Your Casebook Collection for Applying Positive Psychology in Therapy*, edited by G.W. Burns, 3–14. Hoboken, NJ: John Wiley & Sons.

Lipovetsky, Gilles. 1983. *L'ère Du Vide. Essais Sur L'individualisme Contemporain*. Paris: Gallimard.

Lipovetsky, Gilles. 2007. *La Felicidad Paradójica*. Barcelona: Editorial Anagrama.

Lopez, Shane J., C. R. Snyder and Jennifer Teramoto Pedrotti. 2003. "Hope: Many definitions, many measures." In *Positive Psychological Assessment: A Handbook of Models and Measures*, edited by Shane J Lopez and C.R. Snyder, 91–106. Washington, DC: American Psychological Association.

Luthans, Fred, Carolyn. M. Youssef and Bruce J. Avolio. 2007. *Psychological Capital. Developing the Human Competitive Edge*. New York: Oxford University Press.

Lyubomirsky, Sonja, Laura King and Ed Diener. 2005. "The benefits of frequent positive affect: Does happiness lead to success?" *Psychological Bulletin* 131:803–855.

McLaughlin, Kenneth. 2010. "Psychologization and the construction of the political subject as vulnerable object." *Annual Review of Critical Psychology* 8:63–79.

Miller, Alistair. 2008. "A critique of positive psychology: Or 'the new science of happiness'." *Journal of Philosophy of Education* 42:591–608.

Miller, Geoffrey. 2012. "The smartphone psychology manifesto." *Perspectives on Psychological Science* 7(3):221–237.

Mongrain, Myriam and Tracy Anselmo-Matthews. 2012. "Do positive psychology exercises work? A replication of Seligman *et al.*" *Journal of Clinical Psychology* 68:382–389.

Pérez-Álvarez, Marino. 2012. "La psicología positiva: Magia simpática." *Papeles del Psicólogo* 33(3):183–201.

Pérez-Álvarez, Marino. 2013. "La psicología positiva y sus amigos: En evidencia." *Papeles del Psicólogo* 34(3):208–226.

Peterson, Christopher and Martin E. P. Seligman. 2004. *Character Strengths and Virtues: A Handbook and Classification*. New York: Oxford University Press.

Peterson, Christopher, Nansook Park and Martin E. P. Seligman. 2005. "Orientations to happiness and life satisfaction: The full life versus the empty life." *Journal of Happiness Studies* 6(1):25–41.

Reivich, Karen., Jane E. Gillham, Tara M. Chaplin and Martin E. P. Seligman. 2005. "From helplessness to optimism: The role of resilience in treating and preventing depression in youth". In *Handbook of Resilience in Children*, edited by Sam Goldstein and Robert B. Brooks, 223–237. New York: Kluwer Academic/Plenum Publishers.

Ryan, Richard M., Veronika Huta and Edward L. Deci. 2008. "Living well: A self-determination theory perspective on eudaimonia." *Journal of Happiness Studies* 9(1):139–170.

Ryff, Carol D. 1989. "Happiness is everything, or is it? Explorations on the meaning of psychological well-being." *Journal of Personality and Social Psychology* 57(6):1069–1081.

Schui, Gabriel and Günter Krampen. 2010. "Bibliometric analyses on the emergence and present growth of positive psychology." *Applied Psychology: Health and Well-Being* 2(1):52–64.

Seligman, Martin E. P. 2002. *Authentic Happiness: Using the New Positive Psychology to Realize Your Potential for Lasting Fulfillment*. New York: Free Press.

Seligman, Martin E. P. 2005. *Positive Psychology Center. Summary of Activities*. (www.ppc. sas.upenn.edu/ppcactivities.pdf).

Seligman, Martin E. P. 2008. "Positive health." *Applied Psychology: An International Review* 57:3–18.

Seligman, Martin E. P. 2011. *Flourish: A New Understanding of Happiness and Well-Being –and How to Achieve Them*. London: Nicholas Brealey Publishing.

Seligman, Martin E. P. and Mihaly Csikszentmihalyi. 2000. "Positive psychology. An introduction." *American Psychologist* 55:5–14.

Seligman, Martin E. P. and Mihaly Csikszentmihalyi. 2001. "'Positive psychology: An Introduction' – Reply." *American Psychologist* 56:89–90.

Simmons, J. P., L. D. Nelson and U. Simonsohn. 2011. "False-positive psychology: Undisclosed flexibility in data collection and analysis allows presenting anything as significant". *Psychological Science* 22(11):1359–1366.

Smelser, N. J. 1989. "Self-esteem and social problems: An introduction". In *The Social Importance of Self-Esteem*, edited by A.M. Mecca, N.J. Smelser and J. Vaconcellos, 1–23. Berkeley, CA: University of California Press.

Smith, Roger. 1997. *The Norton History of the Human Sciences*. New York: W.W. Norton.

Waters, Lea. 2011. "A review of school-based positive psychology interventions." *The Australian Educational and Developmental Psychologist* 28(2):75–90.

Williams, Raymond. 1977. *Marxism and Literature*. Oxford, UK: Oxford University Press.

Zupančič, Alenka. 2008. *The Odd One In*. Cambridge, MA: MIT Press.

Toward a post-normative critique of emotional authenticity
Conclusion

Eva Illouz

In a lecture he gave in Paris and New York in 1978, Roland Barthes offered an astonishing view of literature with regard to his past as the foremost proponent of the highly formalist school of post-structuralist literary criticism (Barthes 1986 [1984]; Culler 2002). Musing about Marcel Proust, and particularly about those moments where the narrator was anxiously waiting for the kiss of his mother or reflecting about the death of his grand-mother, Barthes claimed he received them as "moments of truth." And the nature of this truth lay in the fact that these moments delivered strong emotional experiences: "Suddenly literature coincides absolutely with an emotional landslide, (with) a cry" (Barthes 1986 [1984]: 287). It is a moment of truth which has nothing to do with realism, with the goal of imitating the real. Recalling Aristotle's view of tragedy and poetry, Barthes goes as far as claiming that the novel itself is an act of emotional truth, that literature cannot be an act of bad faith. *The power of the novel is* "the truth of affects, not of ideas" (Barthes 1986 [1984]: 289). For one of the greatest theoreticians of literature as a linguistic game of ellipses and omissions, this is a striking position, vaguely reminiscent of concepts Barthes would have disavowed such as Tolstoy's "sincerity as the mark of true art" in his essay *What is Art?* (Tolstoy *et al.* 1995 [1897]). Barthes, of course, did not refer to sincerity per se, but the opposition he draws between emotional landslide and bad faith points to a dichotomy between the emotionally true and the false. Emotions are bestowed not only an expressive status (to express the subjectivity of an author, a narrator, a text) but an epistemic one as well, as they establish the truth of the reading experience. Literature is opposed to the false consciousness and bad faith which obscures to ourselves who we are, where "who we are" is best captured in emotional experiences.

Let me shift to another example, this time from American popular culture. In 2005, Oprah Winfrey, the well-known TV talk show host, endorsed James Frey's autobiographical account, *A Million Little Pieces*. Oprah selected the book for her powerful book club and turned it into a bestseller. The memoir detailed his story of trauma, the time he served in prison, his story of drug addiction. It was, however, later revealed that most details (including the prison episode) were fictional and had no bearing to reality.[1] Oprah Winfrey first expressed anger at being cheated, but later modulated her opinion and cautiously re-endorsed the book:

[t]he underlying message of redemption in James Frey's memoir still resonates with me, and I know it resonates with millions of other people who have read this book. What is relevant is that he was a drug-addict who spent years in turmoil from the time he was 10 years old drinking and tormenting himself and his parents, and stepped out of that history to be the man that he is today and to take that message to save other people and allow them to save themselves ... To me, it seems to be much ado about nothing.[2]

What Oprah meant to say was that this book – however faked or invented – conveyed an emotional truth, beyond realism and truthfulness. More exactly, its true truthfulness so-to-speak resided in an emotional truth that transcends bio-graphical events.[3] According to Winfrey, that truth is more important than the factual circumstances supposed to reflect it. Oprah Winfrey expresses here a widespread opinion about the authority of feelings. Indeed, another fake memoir which became a world-wide bestseller was defended by the author using similar arguments: As reported by the *Guardian*:

Defonseca's extraordinary story was published almost 20 years ago as *Misha: A Mémoire of the Holocaust Years*. The book describes how, when she was six, the author's Jewish parents were taken from their home by the Nazis, and how she set off across Belgium, Germany, and Poland to find them on foot, living on stolen scraps of food until she was adopted by a pack of wolves. She also claimed to have shot a Nazi soldier in self-defense. The story was a huge bestseller, and was made into a film in France, but in 2008, it was found to be fabricated. The author – whose real name was found to be Monique De Wael – said that "it's not the true reality, but it is *my* reality," and "there are times when I find it difficult to differentiate between reality and *my inner world*." She is also not Jewish, it was discovered. "Yes, my name is Monique De Wael, but I have wanted to forget it since I was four years old," she admitted in 2008. "My parents were arrested and I was taken in by my grandfather, Ernest De Wael, and my uncle, Maurice De Wael. I was called 'daughter of a traitor' because my father was suspected of having talked under torture in the prison of Saint-Gilles. Ever since I can remember, I *felt* Jewish (emphasis added)."[4]

Both examples of the fake memoirs suggest clearly that emotional rather than fac-tual authenticity has become a source of authority. To subjectively *feel* Jewish is a substitute for and equivalent to the actual institutional or biological membership of a Jewish community. Feelings actually serve here as the content of biography. In that sense, objective reality becomes less relevant than the ways in which one's emotions establish the truth of one's experience. Whereas many, if not most, cul-tures would not place the truth and value of an experience in its emotionality, modern culture views emotionality as a source of truth, as Barthes, Oprah Winfrey and Defonseca – each in their own and different style – put it. Emotions become the repository of truth and life experience. Emotions here define the truth of a subject.

The crucial difference between Barthes and Winfrey–Defonseca, however, is that the latter two were converted into commodities – and even became best-sellers – while Barthes' landslide is not recyclable as a commodity. It is an intimate experience of the reader with himself, mediated by a book. But for Defonseca and Oprah Winfrey, emotions are converted into a performative ontology: experience is translated in emotional authenticity which is turned into a cultural commodity, a novel, a talk show, an autobiography. The authenticity of emotions is performed thus through commodities. This illustrates the difficulty I want to raise at the end of this book: given how pervasive the commodification of emotions has become, that is, given that emotions are converted into commodities and commodities into emotions, how are we to evaluate critically emotional truth and authenticity? Is Barthes' emotional truth superior to the one invoked by Oprah Winfrey or De Wael or to the emotional landslide people experience when consuming a horror movie, listening to sad music, or engaging in the retrieval of traumatic memories in a therapy session? These questions are crucial since as Honneth argues (2004: 467): "The creation of biographical originality has become something required of individuals themselves: more and more the presentation of an 'authentic self' is one of the demands placed upon individuals, above all in the sphere of skilled labour". As this book has argued, a considerable part of consumer culture fabricates, manages, displays, and reenacts emotions under the form of the emotional commodity, emodities, thus compelling us to tackle the question that is at the heart of a critical theory of capitalism: how are we to evaluate and criticize the ways in which emotions have been emphasized in capitalism? Is there an Archimedean standpoint from which the intensification of subjectivity entailed by the market of emotions can be evaluated? If so many of our emotions are produced in and by the commodity realm, can we still distinguish between authentic and inauthentic emotions, Barthes' emotional landslide and Defonseca's invented biography, a vacation in Club Med from an educational *Grand Tour*, music listened to in concert halls and one designed to engineer a specific affect, a movie commercially intent on producing the emotion of horror and a movie intent on awakening a viewer's consciousness? And more importantly: *how* should we distinguish between those authentic emotions – produced for example by the reading of a high brow novel – from those transient emotions produced by the market and its packaged commodities – whether it be coolness, excitement, lust, relaxation, anger management, emotional happiness, and self-improvement? In order to discuss the emotional truth advocated by Roland Barthes and Oprah Winfrey, and to understand whether there is a difference between them, we need a normative theory.

Authenticity or the new politics of emotions

Critical theory as we know it is ill-equipped to evaluate "emotional truth," because emotions are not objects to be evaluated by outside observers.[5] They inhere in the subject and can hardly be legislated from outside and from above the person experiencing them. While we know how to evaluate claims in the aesthetic or scientific realms, we know far less what such evaluation would mean in the emotional realm: should we prefer expressiveness or self-control? With the exception of a few valiant attempts to bring the normative into emotional life (Burkitt 1997; Calhoun 2001; Hochschild 1979; Honneth 2004; Nussbaum 1996, 2003; Stearns and Stearns 1985; etc.), our philosophical vocabulary has little equipped us to critique emotional experiences. However, because emodities aim to produce the authenticity of the subject, we can invoke the philosophical tradition in which "authenticity" has critically figured since Adorno's *The Jargon of Authenticity* (2013 [1964]).

An authentic self differs from other cultural definitions of self, in that it is defined by the view that selves have an ontology, a psychic core beyond social and cultural conventions. Emotions are the building blocks of that ontology, simultaneously what constitutes the self and helps express it. Until the eighteenth century, there was no concept of authenticity because there was no ontology of the self, no view of the self as having deep, innate, a-social and individual properties, which demanded techniques of authentication, techniques to discover and display that buried inner truth.[6] Rousseau (2000 [1755]) – followed by Kierkegaard and Nietzsche –posited a moral truth that inhered in the self ("l'état de nature") which society had subsequently obstructed. The meaning of authenticity shifted around the nineteenth century (Taylor 1989). It was not anymore a moral voice within conscience itself, but became an expression of truth inside the self and thus opened the way for the modern view that authenticity was an emotional affair. If it was the better and truer part of ourselves which lay beneath the buildings of civilization, authenticity became a call of shedding norms and social roles, the voice of an innate, primary nature that had been muffled. Authenticity thus served as a tool to criticize social order, to empower the individual against conventions and institutions, and can be said to have been a crucial development in the formation of a secular psychological subjectivity which started with the invention of the novel, progressed with Romanticism, and found its ultimate expression in the Freudian revolution, which affirmed for example the primacy of individual sexuality over taboos and social control. For example, the psychoanalyst Donald Winnicott (1954, 1956) distinguished between the false and the true self, making the first a kind of self that was overly socialized, conventional, and obedient to social rules.[7] The recovery of the authentic non-obedient self became the goal of therapy, the sign of mental health, to be found in unmediated, raw experiences of art, travel, or sensual pleasure. Once authenticity was made to depend on the appropriate recovery of one's family history, it entailed cultural and consumer techniques where the authentic self became at once produced and consumed by the patient/client. For example, one could produce in oneself an authentic sexuality by seeking therapeutic advice and sexologists to free one's sexuality; such freed sexuality is in turn consumed, the end product of a chain of consumption and self-production, as when a freed sexuality consumes sexual toys, pornography, and tourism. The production and consumption of authenticity has become a central structuring vector of emotional consumption and an anchor to criticize emotional commodities. Objective and subjective authenticity – authenticity which inheres in objects and authenticity which constitutes the subjectivity of the person— mutually call for each other and make it more difficult for the critic to separate social spheres.

My analysis offers a different view of the consumption process from the one that has been classically offered by Colin Campbell. Campbell (1987: 496–500) views consumption as a cyclical pattern. The consumer imagines the emotions that will be generated by consumption; but the actual consumption of material goods fails to deliver the desired amount of pleasure, and the disappointment thus leads to more consumption. This implies that Campbell assumes the subject has an authentic will, distinct from and even in conflict with, the act of consumption. In contrast, my argument here is that there is no gap between these processes, since the authenticity is produced throughout the consumption of emodities.

The axis consumer market/authenticity articulates the self and its emotions around three different temporal axes: through lost memories and trauma, the self engages in techniques of memory to recover the buried and thus authentic past. The psychotherapeutic market relies on this practice of authenticity, where the recovery of the past and its memories are a practice of authentication of the self. Practices of a recovered self – mediated by the therapeutic market – are further performatively transformed into commodities through various cultural media such as autobiographical memoirs, talk shows, or therapy sessions, and thus generate further consumer practices, emotional chains which connect to and shape the reader–consumer's self. Authenticity shaped the self through another temporal dimension which intensified emotions in the present, especially in the leisure sphere: consumer authenticities are lived as emotions and emotional exchanges and are objectified in objects, experiences, designed spaces, and atmospheres.[8] The self experiences itself in a bodily, spontaneous way, through self-consciously pursued emotions obtained in the manipulation of mood-inducing music, aesthetically designed spaces of restaurants, bars, discotheques, and their managed atmospheres, touristic locales, which all form what Walter Benjamin (1983 [1928–1929], [1934–1940]) called dream worlds of consumption. Dream consumer worlds solicit and overstimulate the body through emotions. Authenticity also became a future oriented project, mediated through self-help culture and New Age spirituality which worked at reshaping the body, the mind, and the emotional make-up of the subject. In self-help and New Age culture, authenticity was to be achieved through psychological narratives of self-discovery and self-realization projecting the self onto an improved version of itself. Given the capacity of authenticity to shape the self in these three temporal dimensions, can it still be criticized? Given that authenticity is the main and central meaningful practice of selfhood through consumption, how are we to criticize it?

The philosopher Charles Taylor argues that the avatars of authenticity in contemporary culture should be properly criticized, while its original model should be upheld. He writes:

> The picture I am offering ... is rather that of an ideal that has been degraded but that is very worthwhile in itself, and indeed, I would like to say, unrepudiable by moderns. What we need is neither root-and-branch condemnation nor uncritical praise; and not a carefully balanced trade-off. What we need is a work of retrieval, through which this ideal can help us restore our practice.
>
> (1991: 23)

As a purely private and subjectivist project, contemporary authenticity does not enable us anymore to conceive of modes of self-fulfillment that are dialogical (other-centered) and that emanate from something "more or other than human desires or aspirations." Authenticity is a valid ideal only if raised in a horizon of significance, which, according to Taylor, can only be collective. "Authenticity is not the enemy of demands that emanate from beyond the self, it supposes such demands" (Ibid.: 41). Taylor then wants to distinguish valid and invalid, self-defeating and valuable practices of authenticity. The task of the critic here is to retrieve a lost meaning; to bring to the fore a practice that belonged to a different period and rebuild its meaning in a context that has become impermeable to that meaning. Valid authenticity leans on a collective framework, the invalid (practices of) authenticity on self-centered goals. This is because, as Charles Larmore (2010: 38) suggests in reference to Herder, authenticity cannot be disconnected from membership to culture which alone provides a sense of felt conviction. Only from within the core of that conviction – which is non-reflexively embedded in language – one can make choices and engage in moral evaluations and, one would add, have emotions that connect one to a coherent culture, rather than to a self-absorbed exercise in self-expressiveness. But Taylor's position, in my opinion, leaves whole the problem of critique of modern authenticity which is highly individualized and which exists mostly through the market. Reconstruction of lost meaning as a critical strategy does not get us any further in finding a plausible strategy to avoid the Scylla of a normative critique that leaves social actors unmoved and the Charybdis of internal critique, which sticks so closely to what people desire that it cannot produce a meaningful critique. The critique of emotional authenticity presents us with a dilemma: as the meaningful horizon of subjectivity, it cannot be disposed of; yet, as the main conveyor belt of anti-political and consumer forces, it has no potential for increasing reflexive moral consciousness, for implementing intersubjective communication, and for bringing about social change, and must thus be criticized.

The problem with critical normativity

Applied to emotions and the inner life, normative critique seems to be a more difficult enterprise than ordinary cultural critique. While cultural critique can rely on normative judgment to establish "good" or "bad," emancipatory or repressive content, it has few or no tools to undertake the same operation on emotions.

Critical sociology – as its name indicates – contains normative premises which, for them to retain their force must at least partially and potentially be located outside what people do and believe in, and it is precisely the force of this "externality" that is difficult to uphold in the realm of emotions.

The first problem of critical normativity has to do with distance, harboring values or models of conduct that are so distant from lived emotional experience that it would demand an overhaul of one's emotional make-up. Distant critics undercut their own effectiveness because, when they harbor ideals and values that are too difficult to achieve, they are not heard. This can become all the more the case when these ideals are articulated by a group of specialists (academics) or political activists which develop a specialized language and values deemed to be "utopian," "impractical," or "unrealistic," too far from the normal, routine structures of the daily life of a group.

The second problem of critical normativity – holding on to moral norms in the name of which we criticize an object – is what I would call the problem of *epistemic democracy*, that is, the fact that subjects have imposed a truth about themselves that they did not know, or worse, that they did not want to hear because that truth conflicts with their self-definition. The claims of epistemic democracy take the form of: why would you, the critic, claim to know about me something which I do not recognize in me? Why would you, the critic, feel entitled to tell me what I do not know or do not wish to know about myself? And doesn't this knowledge give you a standpoint to look (probably) down on me? Epistemic democracy cannot be easily disposed of when the individual rights are incessantly affirmed both in the political and cultural spheres, thus reinforcing the individual's claims to the legitimacy of their subjectivity, whatever its contents and materials. To put things differently, the procedures to attain truth claims in the realm of emotions are mostly based on self-introspection and are thus not easily given to the objectivist modes of evaluation entailed by critique.[9]

The third objection to normative critique of emotions is methodological and has been best articulated by Bruno Latour (1999, 2004, 2007, 2012) who has argued against a normative critique of culture which, in his view, is unaware that it uses two asymmetrical scales: one which points to the illusions to which others fall prey; and another one, which provides the critic with his own grid to analyze and explain the social and which he views as facts. The critics then, according to Latour, are compelled to engage in an activity that contains a certain amount of bad faith. They use critical concepts to discuss a social reality they do not like, all the while being uncritical vis-à-vis one's favorite concepts (Latour 2004: 242–243). He calls this the Fairy and Fact position: others' beliefs are illusions, one's own are hard facts (Ibid.: 237–238). Against such asymmetrical treatment of the two positions, Latour advocates treating all practices and beliefs equally, not in the name of moral relativism, but in the name of grasping the various positions that make up a field without presuming to know in advance the historical victory of one's position over another or its moral superiority (Latour 1999: 13–15; 2007: 35–7, 165–172). For Latour, neither epistemology nor morality should grant us – sociologists and historians – the right to dispossess actors of the good reasons they have for acting and believing the way they do. The Latourian objection is then a methodological one and calls for a principle of symmetry in the analysis of the different opinions and positions taken by actors. Symmetry turns out to be opposite to the critical attitude, which chooses sides, and implicitly compares practices to what they could and should be. Because of these various objections, normative critique has evolved to become what I would call an *internalist* critique, defined as a form of critique which does not superimpose any "should" on the group it criticizes but rather emerges directly from it. Such critique is supposed to overcome the problems of a strong normative critique. Is internalist critique then better suited to emotions?

Is the critique of emotions an internalist critique?

Michael Walzer has famously drawn the contours of such critique and has spoken forcefully against what he calls the philosopher on the mountain who talks with radical detachment and so-called impartiality. For him (Walzer 2002), Marcuse and Foucault are in the same category in that none of them professes to be close to the values and preoccupations of those they criticize (they would normally be opposed because the first has strong normativity, while the other lacks it). Walzer is interested in those voices that compel us to action, and these voices have a quality of closeness which is the crucial quality of the social critic (Ibid.: xiii). The best critics, Walzer says, are those who have the courage to speak up to those they feel close to, where nearness is defined as a moral tie, a personal engagement with those one criticizes. "Their critique has the sensitivity, intimacy, and grasp of detail that are the features of confessional literature" (Ibid.: xv). How exactly is this achieved and which method is the critic to use? Walzer remains vague, and offers nothing more than a few metaphors that have to do with tone, closeness, and mirroring. Mirroring is in fact the best approximation we can get to understanding what he means. Comparing the critic's strategy to that of Hamlet's glass who raises a mirror to his mother so that she can see herself as she truly is, the critic does not offer an alternative political landscape, only a technique to make another look at him/her self without turning his/her eyes away: "Come, Come and sit down. You shall not budge. You go not till I set you up a glass. Where you may see the inmost part of you" (Shakespeare 2012 [1599–1602]: 187). Walzer claims then that by reminding us of our true values, our cherished beliefs, what kind of image we want to project to the world, and by seeing who we truly are, by looking at the reflection of ourselves in the mirror, we can be compelled so-to-speak to adopt a critical position, without being admonished by a critic who stands on an Olympian mountain (Walzer 2002: 230–235). Walzer's internal critique would suggest that in order to criticize emodities, we should use the vocabulary that is familiar to contemporaries to speak about authenticity, to be found mostly in popular concepts and the science of psychology. But as was shown in this book, psychology has itself been a conveyor belt for the commodification and intensification of emotions. It cannot be used as a vocabulary that would transcend the domain it wants to criticize.

Moreover, Walzer confuses the sociological "distance" of the critic – which he adamantly wants to avoid – and the distance or difficulty of the values advocated by the critic: surely some values are both recognizable *and* distant. Marcuse himself, one of the über patrician critics, used norms and standards that could be easily recognized, calling to separate sex from the market for example. Yet, Marcuse is thought by Walzer to be the paramount example of Olympian and patrician distance (Walzer 2002: 170–190). Critique thus may seem distant because of its tone or social location, but actually invokes known or familiar values. Critique often operates incrementally by generalizing and extending to new fields known moral vocabularies and framings (for example, movements in favor of animals rights generalize the concept of rights from humans to animals) (Benford and Snow 2000; Lowe 2006, 2008). Such critique cannot be strictly classified as internal or external to the worlds of the recipients. Furthermore, if we view critique as having practical effects, as compelling change or self-examination, I am not sure this effect is not better obtained by what Walzer calls critics "on the mountain" (Walzer 2002: xii). Certainly Foucault, Marcuse, or MacKinnon had a significant impact on the self-understandings of the actors of their time, precisely because of the novelty of their arguments, of the startling light they shed on old understandings. It is thus difficult to understand how self-understandings can be changed or at least reexamined without a lateral or vertical intellectual movement that brings a critic far from the people s/he speaks to. It is difficult to see how GLBTQ people or feminists could criticize homophobia or patriarchy by being close so-to-speak to those values. Surely there is a place for modes of thinking and critique that mark a radical departure from previous forms of thought, for critique as a way to startle rather than evoke the familiar. Finally, and perhaps most seriously, Walzer's internal, familiar critique is inadequate to the contemporary sociological situation of critique. The beginning of capitalism was accompanied by the possibility of criticizing it from outside its reach and compass, because the realm of economics was still separate from the realm of values. Yet, capitalism has steadily shaped and reshaped our emotional and moral world, co-opting critique, and making emotions the object of endless scrutiny. What are then the conditions left to the critic to criticize these emotions?

Although I have been an advocate of a Walzer-like internalist critique, the more I have researched the conjunction of capitalism and emotions, the more I have come to think that Walzer's internalist position is more adapted to small communities than to complex, modern societies. Internal critique suits communities that are tightly bound by values and norms, rather than societies whose normative structure is so fragmented that they leave whole the question of whose values one should mirror. Just how we are to choose our values among many competing ones and how far or how close we should stay to these values is left undiscussed by Walzer. The Hebrew Prophet, for example, whom Walzer (2002: 4) uses as the paradigm for his social critic – is also a member of a group – the Israelites – who held very harsh attitudes toward enemies or blasphemers. Should the critic endorse those values as well? Walzer cannot tell.

If capitalism has steadily shaped and reshaped the consumer's subjectivity from the beginning of the twentieth century, the life-world cannot be used anymore to criticize capitalism, because subjectivity and its empowerment through ethics or psychology have been the incessant focus and the object of the strategy of capitalism. The more the subject becomes empowered in its subjectivity, the more difficult it has become to find a common language, except that of emotions, psychology, and authenticity. In contemporary capitalist societies, the individual is the culmination of capital as a machine of subjectivation. As Gilles Deleuze and Felix Guattari put it, capital acts as a formidable "point of subjectivation that constitutes all human beings as subjects" (1980: 571), with the so-called creative class as the one articulating for others the parameters of their emotional subjectivity. Given that capitalism has shaped subjectivity itself, that subjectivity cannot be used in critique. Neither the externalist position nor the internalist- immanent one can be held anymore, because the native's point of view is the vector carrying forward the very system we want to criticize. As Adorno put it:

> The alternatives – either calling culture as a whole into question from outside under the general notion of ideology, or confronting it with the norms which it itself has crystallized – cannot be accepted by critical theory. To insist on the choice between immanence and transcendence is to revert to the traditional logic criticized in Hegel's polemic against Kant.
>
> (Adorno 2014 [1967]: 294)

This dilemma is historically rather than theoretically driven and compels me then to suggest that the critique of capitalism and of emotional life should be formulated within the framework of what I would call a post-normative critique.

Strategies for a post-normative critique of capitalism

As this collective monograph has made abundantly clear, emotional authenticity is a social *dispositif*, a chain of rituals and objects deployed in space through which authenticity is performed. If some spaces and atmospheres feel more conducive to certain emotions, it is a part of a semiotic, emotional, artifactual, spatial *dispositif* in which authenticity is performatively *produced*: a Club Med, a greeting card, a cool café, or a horror movie, are all about the performative production of emotional authenticity through consumer goods and consumer experiences. Objects, spaces, music act on the body, on the senses, on the embodied relationship of the subject to the world. The history of consumer culture is the history of an endlessly proliferating world of objects, which stimulate the self and the body, making them participate in dream worlds of anticipated and remembered emotional experiences (Baumgarten 2013 [1739]; Benjamin 1983 [1928–1929],

[1934–1940]). Aesthetic objects generate emotions precisely because they give a form to experiences (Simmel 1918 [1904]: 188–197).

A post-normative critique then starts from the following observation: subjectivity has moved to a radical plane of immanence in which meaningfulness is not provided by collective meanings but rather by aesthetic objects and experiences in which the senses and emotions become self-referential and act as agents of subjectivation, as departure points of subjective, emotional experiences. Using and twisting Hannah Arendt's expression in another context, emotions are located in what she called (2013 [1958]) the "in-betweenness" of human existence,[10] here between subjectivity and object, between emotions and consumer practices.

A post-normative critique is one that must avoid being dismissive of experiences, and yet find a way to enable the articulation of a gap between the "is" and the "ought." Only when we point to this gap, can we say we are in the activity of critique. A post-normative critique must then accomplish the following task: take seriously actors' self-understandings and their horizon of expectations, without yielding to the account people give of themselves, because we need to enable the formulation and articulation of norms that transcend people's self-understandings.[11] (Subjective) reasons should be integrated, as much as possible, in the analysis of (objective) causes. Moreover, and this is an important point, a post-normative critique is not a fixed normative position; rather, it changes with the very nature of that which it criticizes. If capitalism has been extraordinarily successful at incorporating its critiques and moving along its own detractors (Boltanski and Chiapello 2005), then surely, critique must do the same vis-à-vis capitalism, that is, shift its own tools and strategies. Post-normative critique, then, need not have a fixed normative position, but can instead offer a tactic and strategy shift and change with its target. Third, post-normative critique should treat sentiments and objects as if they were on an equal plane. Against the tenets of critical theory, we must abolish the distinction between subject and object. On the contrary, the epistemology put forward by this book suggests that emotions are *not* interior or psychological. In fact, emotions are expressions of social relations mediated by objects, situations, spaces, atmospheres, sensori stimuli.

Once we abolish the distinction between subject and object, we can view emotions as carrying the network of objects and persons (Latour 2012). Once this move is accomplished, that is, once we apply a symmetrical understanding of emotions and objects, we can engage in an understanding of emodities. I mean to drive a wedge between "understanding" and critique, where the historical elucidation of emodities precedes critique. Moreover, by "understanding" I do not mean the kind of hermeneutic understanding of actors' worlds which has long dominated the German historicist tradition (Beiser 2011: 346–354). Rather, I mean a kind of understanding that is present in naturalist philosophies, such as that of Spinoza.

Commenting on Spinoza, the French philosopher André Comte Sponville suggested that "On ne juge que ce qu'on ne comprend pas" ("We judge only that which we do not understand," quoted in Canto-Sperber 1996: 1441). From Spinoza's standpoint (2012 [1662]), we cannot judge the good or bad of an action anymore than we can say if rain or snow are good or bad. To proffer a moral judgment is always the result of an insufficient understanding of the chain of causality that led to the event or object we are trying to explain. Understanding the chain of causes and necessity neutralizes the moral point of view. Such attitude thus precludes the use of a critical language, understood as a normative language. This is because when we judge, we do not explain, we do not see the full range and chain of causes. And yet, to describe or re-describe the chain of causes of an event or property of subjectivity and authenticity, to trace subjectivity back to a chain of causes creates what I would call *critical effects*, because contemporary subjectivity is conceived as *sui generis*, as self-generated. For that reason, once subjectivity is viewed as one element in a long chain of causes, it loses the illusion of its self-generated autonomy, of its seeming spontaneity.

Emotional authenticity can be criticized today only by operating a Spinozian move, by describing or re-describing the chain of causes which create and shape it, what the group of authors of this book have done. In the face of the increasing powerlessness and lack of efficacy of normative critiques, the only powerful tool that is left to critique is the tracing of these experiences to the historical chain of causes that produced them. Like Spinoza's famous stone which, if thrown and if endowed with consciousness, would think it moves of its own will, intention, and desire, our emotional consciousness moves unaware of the movements that propels it in the world. This is, as Spinoza famously said, "that human freedom, which all boast that they possess, and which consists solely in the fact, that men are conscious of their own desire, but are ignorant of the causes whereby that desire has been determined" (Spinoza 2012 [1662]: 390). To speak about the determination of contemporary emotions is precisely what contemporary sociologists, philosophers, and critics can do best. The point here is not to reopen the debate about whether we are determined or free; the point is a more sociological one: it is to analyze the social world on a plane of radical immanence in which objects and human beings, emotions and consumption are made equivalent in their interconnectedness, and are historically elucidated, rather than morally evaluated. This elucidation is not far from the aim of critical theory. As Zurn put it in his book on Axel Honneth, "the basic idea of critical theory is to carry out the charge that Marx set for a new journal in 1843: 'the self-clarification (critical philosophy) of the struggles and wishes of the age'" (Zurn 2015: 4). Self-clarification is obtained through description of the chain of causes which makes us the specific subjects we have become. As with Foucault's critical method – the juxtaposition of historical frames – this strategy brings into relief the framework of evaluation itself (see Butler 1990). This position then counts on the rhetorical effect of the historical re-description of practices to produce a *critical effect* – and is not rooted in a critical *position*. Here we do not align illusions against facts, but rather allow for the historicity of subjectivity to be in full display. We do not aim to show the arbitrary character of what we take to be truth itself as much as show the ways in which certain modes of being are experienced as overwhelming and inevitable.[12] A post-normative critique of emotional authenticity then has no fixed a priori normative position (e.g., it does not decide in advance if the self should be embedded in a community or not); it wants to abolish the distinction between subject and object (and thus abolishes the view that emotional life is most full when "uncontaminated" by money or objects); it uses immanence as a tool to unsettle cultural hierarchies (seeing individuality, spirituality, emotionality as having inner logics to be deciphered, and follows the methodological scientific injunction to explain through a chain of causality why and how things are the way they are); and it implements the principle that the critical impact of a text does not reside in its intent (telling people how false their desires and consciousness are), but rather in its effects, in the ways in which it is appropriated in and by civil society. These are the guidelines to draw a new post-normative critical theory of consumption and authenticity.

Conclusion

Post-normative critique is an intellectual practice of ambivalence. In his ASA 1997 Presidential address, Neil Smelser made two important points: one is that social reality is often inherently ambivalent (containing conflicting processes); but also that our own psychological so-to-speak approach to the real is ambivalent (Smelser 1998). Smelser makes a further and interesting point in claiming that some social institutions in fact foreclose ambivalence (one example is the survey which, in asking "do you like or dislike" a certain political issue or character forecloses the ambivalence which most respondents may feel). Normative critique is often a way to foreclose ambivalence, while post-normative critique opens itself up to an ambivalence that is to be deciphered. In a provocative article, four psychologists gathered evidence that ambivalent states of mind might be in fact more accurate in their evaluation and completion of specific cognitive tasks (Rees *et al.* 2013). Un-affective states seem to be less accurate in their capacity to evaluate situations. The ambivalent mind is the one which, having become aware of the chain of causes which shape subjectivity, is able to entertain multiple perspectives which explore the effects and consequences of each path.

I do not know if this model of critique is suitable for other domains such as politics or economics. But the model of post-normative critique I have outlined here is suited to the realm of emotions and subjectivity, which are themselves ambiguous and often barely accessible to awareness. Sociology becomes critical again not when it espouses a clear ideological point of view, but when it documents the long chain of social institutions that shape subjectivity and endorse ambivalence as a style of knowledge.

In a striking metaphor, Michel Serres recounts the following story (which I am summarizing here): In the Golden Legend (this is the thirteenth-century compilation of Christian legends compiled by Jacques Voragine), Lutece was the site of a miracle:

Denis, the bishop of Lutece, was arrested by the Roman soldiers, sent to prison to be beheaded on the Montmartre Hill; but the soldiers are lazy, they do not want to go all the way up, and decide to behead him on the way. The head rolls on the pavement, and Denis stands up, picks [up] his head, and continues to go up his way [sic], all the way to the hill.

(Serres 2012: 27)

For Serres, this is a metaphor for cognition in the era of new technologies: the computer has become the head which we willingly put off and on; the cognition – which was previously internal – now becomes external – beheaded. We may say the same thing about authenticity: it has become a head we may, at will, put on and off through various consumer practices to experience not the stability of a common world shared with others, but the project of shaping an emotional self, intensely subjectivized, close to intimate others, separate from the world. Emotional authenticity mediated by the market then implodes from within the function which Arendt had assigned to objects, namely to be durable markers of human life and continuity. The durability of objects, according to Arendt, gave them the independence to withstand "the voracious needs and wants of their living makers and users" (Arendt 2013 [1958]: 137). People could "retrieve their sameness, that is, their identity, by being related to the same chair and the same table" (Ibid.: 137). Sameness is now a far more complicated project, searched and obtained through an authenticity mediated by intangible emotional commodities that ever fracture more widely our common world.

Notes

1 A Million Little Lies. (2010, July 23), The Smoking Gun. Retrieved December 18, 2015, from www.thesmokinggun.com/documents/celebrity/million-little-lies.
2 Winfrey stands behind "Pieces" author. Writer has been accused of exaggerating memoir (January 12, 2006), CNN.com Retrieved December 18, 2015, from http://edition.cnn.com/2006/SHOWBIZ/books/01/11/frey.lkl/.
3 It is interesting to note that in an interview with Larry King, Frey argues for his defense in the same tone: "the book is about drug addiction and alcoholism …The emotional truth is there." Silverman, M. S. Oprah on Frey Book: "I Believe in James" (January 12, 2006), *People*. Retrieved December 30, 2015 from: www.people.com/people/article/0,,1148131,00.html.
4 Flood, A. (May 12, 2014). Author of fake Holocaust memoir ordered to return $22.5m to publisher. *The Guardian*. Retrieved from www.theguardian.com/books/2014/may/12/author-fake-holocaust-memoir-to-return-22m.
5 As shown in the book there are ways to evaluate the production of emotional states and experiences. Here I mean to a different type of evaluation – the evaluation of "subjective," "inner," emotional feelings.
6 Recalling *Le Neveu de Rameau* in Diderot's eponymous book (Diderot 1925), we may say that for the pre-modern self, there are no stable or deep properties to be discovered. In the famous dialogue, the philosopher pays him a compliment and declares he has a delicate soul. The neveu (nephew) replies "Lui: Moi, point du tout. Que le diable m'emporte si je sais au fond ce que je suis." And he continues: "En general, j'ai l'esprit

rond comme une boule, et le caractère franc comme l'osier: jamais faux, pour peu que j'ai interêt d'être vrai; jamais vrai pour peu que j'ai interêt d'être faux. Je dis les choses comme elles me viennent, on n'y prend pas garde. J'use en plein de mon franc-parler. Je n'ai pense de ma vie ni avant que de dire, ni en disant, ni après avoir dit. Aussi je n'offense personne" (quoted in Lecourt 2013: 41). Here, the self has no clear ground, anchor, or ontology. It is forever shifting with the situation and cannot thus be the object of practices of authenticity.

7 For a brilliant analysis of Hegel's theory of "struggle for recognition" that is based on the work of Donald Winnicott and George Herbert Mead, see Honneth (1995).

8 Marketing turned authenticity into a property of products (e.g., Absolut Vodka connotes more "authentic" than other vodkas) and later of companies themselves (see Gilmore and Pine's manifesto for making brands and companies authentic (Gilmore and Pine 2007). The semiotics of authenticity are varied: it can consist in a personal story about the product ("this yogurt was invented by the Theorodakis family in the 1850s"); by attaching it to a tradition (luxury Bordeaux wine for example); by turning it into a natural product (emphasizing its natural ingredients); by emphasizing its unique craftsmanship, attached to a single name and person; by connecting it to wild, non-industrialized landscapes, by stressing its minimally industrialized production (authentic fabric, place, or food). Authenticity is not only an image attached to objects, but an economic surplus value extracted from touristic sites, renovated neighborhoods, vintage clothes, or dishes.

9 A possible solution offered by Honneth's (1995: 92) discussion on the struggle for recognition in which he claims that social change is dependent on the normative demands that are internal to the relationship of the subjects' mutual recognition.

10 "But for all its intangibility, this in-between is no less real than the world of things we visibly have in common. We call this reality the 'web' of human relationships, indicating by the metaphor its somewhat intangible quality. To be sure, this web is no less bound to the objective world of things than speech is to the existence of a living body, but the relationship is not like that of a facade or, in Marxian terminology, of an essentially superfluous superstructure affixed to the useful structure of building itself" (Arendt 2013 [1958]: 183).

11 We can view the critique that Benford and Snow (2000) and Lowe (2006, 2008) describes as one type of post-normative critique.

12 In other words, I offer to adopt the classical strategy of demystification or de-naturalization as the basis of critical thinking, but without assuming:

a) An ontology of surface vs. depth when the mechanisms are laid in the under-surface.
b) An Archimedean normative basis.

Bibliography

Adorno, Theodor W. 2013 [1964]. *The Jargon of Authenticity*. London: Routledge.
Adorno, Theodor W. 2014 [1967]. "Cultural criticism and society." In *Critical Theory: A Reader*, edited by Tallack, Douglas, 287–297. London: Routledge.
Arendt, Hannah. 2013 [1958]. *The Human Condition*. Chicago, IL: University of Chicago Press.
Barthes, Roland. 1986 [1984]. *The Rustle of Language* (trans. Richard Howard). New York: Hill and Wang.
Baumgarten, Alexander. 2013 [1739]. *Metaphysics: A Critical Translation with Kant's Elucidations, Selected Notes and Related Materials*. New York: Continuum Publishing.

Beiser, Frederick. C. 2011. *The German Historicist Tradition.* New York: Oxford University Press.

Benford, Robert D. and David A. Snow. 2000. "Framing processes and social movements: An overview and assessment." *Annual Review of Sociology* 26(1):611–639.

Benjamin, Walter. 1983. Das Passagen-Werk (1928–1929, 1934–1940) (trans. Rolf Tiedemann), 2 Vols. Frankfurt am Main, Germany: Suhrkamp.

Boltanski, Luc and Eve Chiapello. 2005. *The New Spirit of Capitalism.* London: Verso.

Burkitt, Ian. 1997. "Social relationships and emotions." *Sociology* 31(1):37–55.

Butler, Judith P. 1990. *Gender Trouble: Feminism and the Subversion of Identity.* New York: Routledge.

Calhoun, Craig. 2001. "Putting emotions in their place." In *Passionate Politics: Emotions and Social Movements,* edited by Jeff Goodwin *et al.*, 45–57. Chicago, IL: University of Chicago Press.

Campbell, Colin 1987, *The Romantic Ethic and the Spirit of Modern Consumerism.* New York: Blackwell.

Canto-Sperber, Monique. 1996. Dictionnaire d'éthique et de philosophie morale. *Paris, Presses Universitaires de France.*

Culler, Jonathan D. 2002. *Barthes: A Very Short Introduction.* New York: Oxford University Press.

Deleuze, Gilles and Félix Guattari. 1980. Mille plateaux: Capitalisme et schizophrénie II. Paris: Editions de Minuit. [Title translated in English as *A Thousand Plateaus: Capitalism and Schizophrenia*].

De Spinoza, Benedict. 2012 [1662]. *On the Improvement of the Understanding.* North Chelmsford, MA: Courier Corporation.

Diderot, Denis and Charles Asselineau. 1925 [1805]. *Le neveu de Rameau.* Paris : Payot.

Gilmore, James H. and Joseph B. Pine. 2007. *Authenticity. What Consumers Really Want.* Boston, MA: Harvard Business School Press.

Hochschild, Arlie Russell. 1979. "Emotion work, feeling rules, and social structure." *American Journal of Sociology* 85(3):551–575.

Honneth, Axel. 1995. *The Struggle for Recognition: The Moral Grammar of Social Conflicts* (trans. Joel Anderson). Cambridge, UK: Polity Press.

Honneth, Axel. 2004. "Organized self-realization: Some paradoxes of individualization." *European Journal of Social Theory* 7(4):463–478.

Larmore, Charles. 2010. *The Practices of the Self.* Chicago, IL: University of Chicago Press.

Latour, Bruno. 1999. *Pandora's Hope: An Essay on the Reality of Science Studies.* Cambridge, MA: Harvard University Press.

Latour, Bruno. 2004. "Why has critique run out of steam? From matters of fact to matters of concern." *Critical Inquiry* 30(2):225–248.

Latour, Bruno. 2007. *Reassembling the Social: An Introduction to Actor-Network-Theory.* Oxford, UK: Oxford University Press.

Lecourt, Dominique. 2013. *Diderot. Passions, sexe, raison.* Paris: Presses universitaires de France.

Latour, Bruno. 2012. *We Have Never Been Modern.* Cambridge, MA: Harvard University Press.

Lowe, Brian M. 2006. *Emerging Moral Vocabularies: The Creation and Establishment of New Forms of Moral and Ethical Meanings.* New York: The Rowman & Littlefield Publishing Group.

Lowe, Brian. 2008. "Animal rights struggles to dominate the public moral imagination through sociological warfare." *Theory In Action* 1(3):1–24.

Nussbaum, Martha Craven. 1996. "Compassion: The basic social emotion." *Social Philosophy and Policy* 13(1):27–58.

Nussbaum, Martha Craven. 2003. *Upheavals of Thought: The Intelligence of Emotions*. Cambridge, UK: Cambridge University Press.

Rees, Laura, Naomi B. Rothman, Reuven Lehavy and Jeffrey Sanchez-Burks. 2013. "The ambivalent mind can be a wise mind: Emotional ambivalence increases judgment accuracy." *Journal of Experimental Social Psychology* 49(3):360–367.

Rousseau, Jean J. 2000 [1755]. *Discourse on the Origin of Inequality* (trans. Philip Franklin). Oxford, UK: Oxford University Press.

Serres, Michel. 2012. *Petite poucette*. Paris: Le Pommier.

Shakespeare, William. 2012 [1599–1602]. "Hamlet: Prince of Denmark." *The New Cambridge Shakespeare*. Cambridge, UK: Cambridge University Press.

Simmel, Georg. 1918 [1904]. *Sechzehn Vorlesungen gehalten an der Berliner Universitat*. Munich and Leipzig, Germany: Duncker & Humbolt.

Smelser, Neil J. 1998. "The rational and the ambivalent in the social sciences: 1997 presidential address." *American Sociological Review* 63(1):1–16.

Stearns, Peter N. and Carol Z. Stearns. 1985. "Emotionology: Clarifying the history of emotions and emotional standards." *The American Historical Review* 90(4):813–836.

Taylor, Charles. 1989. *Sources of the Self: The Making of the Modern Identity*. Cambridge, MA: Harvard University Press.

Taylor, Charles. 1991. *The Malaise of Modernity*. Concord, ON: Anansi.

Tolstoy, Leo, Richard Pevear and Larissa Volokhonsky. 1995 [1897] *What is Art?* Harmondsworth, UK: Penguin.

Walzer, Michael. 2002. *The Company of Critics: Social Criticism and Political Commitment in the Twentieth Century*. New York: Basic Books.

Winnicott, D. W. 1954. "Mind and its relation to psyche-soma." *British Journal of Medical Psychology* 27(4):201–209.

Winnicott, D. W. 1956. "On transference." *The International Journal of Psychoanalysis* 37:386–388.

Zurn, Christopher. 2015. *Axel Honneth*. Cambridge, UK: Polity Press.

Index

Abbott, Andrew 38, 45, 49, 79, 96
academic 80, 84, 148, 150–1, 154–5,
    157–61, 166, 175–8, 190, 203; fields
    of positive psychology, sources of
    176–7; psychological knowledge 154–5;
    research on happiness 178
actors 5–6, 8, 11, 15, 18, 79–80, 96,
    149, 204–5, 207; dispossessing 204;
    emotional 5; modern 9; ordinary 10;
    professional 166; social 166, 202
acts 5, 13, 16, 74, 89, 105, 174–5, 185–6,
    197, 207; of choice and consumption14,
    16, 175, 201; criminal 108; emotional
    12; of emotional truth 197; linguistic
    15; prostitution-related 109; relational
    21; semiotic 13; sexual 110
adolescents 84–5, 87, 184
Adorno, Theodor W. 7, 71–3, 200, 206
advertising 12–13, 86, 88–9, 102, 113,
    127; agencies 88; campaigns 88, 133;
    hoardings 113; professions 12; sex
    services 108; techniques 88
affective capitalism, notion of 14
Agathangelou, Anna M. 106–7
agency 107, 178, 185; aesthetic-emotional
    61, 63, 70; lack of 185; sexual 106
Ahmed, Sara 5, 182
Alaluf, Yaara Benger 33–51
albums 18, 64–5, 68–70; consistent 68;
    pre-sequenced 68; rock 18, 64; single 18
ambience 45; classless 45; general 105
American International Pictures 87–8
American movie industry 79–81, 98
American psychologists 13, 20–1, 51,
    59–60, 62, 84, 149, 151, 154–5, 157
analysts 126, 152–3, 167
Anderson, Ben 103, 105, 161
anger management 164, 190, 199

anxiety 40, 43–4, 65–6, 148, 151, 155–6,
    178, 181, 184, 191; and depression
    156, 178, 181; neurosis 151; social 20;
    soothing 64
Arab residents 111
Arendt, Hannah 207, 210
art 36, 61, 66, 71, 136, 187, 197, 200; and
    classic culture 36; consumers 71; high
    71; and nature 61; sacred 73
Arvidsson, Adam 107, 112, 114
assumptions 9–10, 33, 97, 104, 181, 183,
    188; anthropological 165; core neoliberal
    182; foundational 178; neoliberal
    ideological 191; positive psychology's 179
atmospheres 15, 18–19, 45, 51, 91, 102–4,
    114, 201, 206–7; emotional 6, 63, 65–6;
    grim 82; inclusive 45; magical 111;
    managed 201; romantic 6, 15; seductive
    102; sexual 19, 111; and spaces 206;
    urban 102–4, 106, 115
Audience Research Institute 86, 88
audiences 67, 72–3, 79–83, 85–7, 89–98,
    147, 161; adolescent 88; contemporary
    93; emotional 86, 95; female 95; mass
    95; popular 178; target 83, 89–90, 95;
    teenage 96–7; traditional 96
authenticity 6–9, 13, 15, 21–2, 123–4,
    167–8, 185–8, 199–202, 206, 208–10;
    in commercial sentiment 123–42; and
    commodification 22; ethnography of 7,
    124, 126; of gestures 142; in greeting
    card communication 124; notion of
    185, 188; post-normative critique of
    emotional 197, 209; practices of 13,
    201–2; subjective 51, 201

babysitter services 46
background music 67–8, 72, 91